Performing American Identity in Anti-Mormon Melodrama

Studies in American Popular History and Culture

JEROME NADELHAFT, *General Editor*

Women and Comedy in Solo Performance
Phyllis Diller, Lily Tomlin, and Roseanne
Suzanne Lavin

The Literature of Immigration and Racial Formation
Becoming White, Becoming Other, Becoming American in the Late Progressive Era
Linda Joyce Brown

Popular Culture and the Enduring Myth of Chicago, 1871–1968
Lisa Krissoff Boehm

America's Fight over Water
The Environmental and Political Effects of Large-Scale Water Systems
Kevin Wehr

Daughters of Eve
Pregnant Brides and Unwed Mothers in Seventeenth-Century Massachusetts
Else L. Hambleton

Narrative, Political Unconscious, and Racial Violence in Wilmington, North Carolina
Leslie H. Hossfeld

Validating Bachelorhood
Audience, Patriarchy, and Charles Brockden Brown's Editorship of the *Monthly Magazine and American Review*
Scott Slawinski

Children and the Criminal Law in Connecticut, 1635–1855
Changing Perceptions of Childhood
Nancy Hathaway Steenburg

Books and Libraries in American Society during World War II
Weapons in the War of Ideas
Patti Clayton Becker

Mistresses of the Transient Hearth
American Army Officers' Wives and Material Culture, 1840–1880
Robin Dell Campbell

The Farm Press, Reform, and Rural Change, 1895–1920
John J. Fry

State of 'The Union'
Marriage and Free Love in the Late 1800s
Sandra Ellen Schroer

"My Pen and My Soul Have Ever Gone Together"
Thomas Paine and the American Revolution
Vikki J. Vickers

Agents of Wrath, Sowers of Discord
Authority and Dissent in Puritan Massachusetts, 1630-1655
Timothy L. Wood

The Quiet Revolutionaries
How the Grey Nuns Changed the Social Welfare Paradigm of Lewiston, Maine
Susan P. Hudson

Cleaning Up
The Transformation of Domestic Service in Twentieth Century New York City
Alana Erickson Coble

Feminist Revolution in Literacy
Women's Bookstores in the United States
Junko R. Onosaka

Great Depression and the Middle Class
Experts, Collegiate Youth and Business Ideology, 1929–1941
Mary C. McComb

Labor and Laborers of the Loom
Mechanization and Handloom Weavers, 1780–1840
Gail Fowler Mohanty

"The First of Causes to Our Sex"
The Female Moral Reform Movement in the Antebellum Northeast, 1834-1848
Daniel S. Wright

US Textile Production in Historical Perspective
A Case Study from Massachusetts
Susan M. Ouellette

Women Workers on Strike
Narratives of Southern Women Unionists
Roxanne Newton

Hollywood and Anticommunism
HUAC and the Evolution of the Red Menace, 1935–1950
John Joseph Gladchuk

Negotiating Motherhood in Nineteenth-Century American Literature
Mary McCartin Wearn

The Gay Liberation Youth Movement in New York
"An Army of Lovers Cannot Fail"
Stephan L. Cohen

Gender and the American Temperance Movement of the Nineteenth Century
Holly Berkley Fletcher

The Struggle For Free Speech in the United States, 1872–1915
Edward Bliss Foote, Edward Bond Foote, and Anti-Comstock Operations
Janice Ruth Wood

The Marketing of Edgar Allan Poe
Jonathan H. Hartmann

Language, Gender, and Citizenship in American Literature, 1789–1919
Amy Dunham Strand

Antebellum Slave Narratives
Cultural and Political Expressions of Africa
Jermaine O. Archer

Fictions of Female Education in the Nineteenth Century
Jaime Osterman Alves

John Brown and the Era of Literary Confrontation
Michael Stoneham

Performing American Identity in Anti-Mormon Melodrama
Megan Sanborn Jones

Performing American Identity in Anti-Mormon Melodrama

Megan Sanborn Jones

Routledge
Taylor & Francis Group
New York   London

First published 2009
by Routledge
605 Third Avenue, New York, NY 10017
4 Park Square, Milton Park, Abingdon, Oxon OX14 4RN

Routledge is an imprint of the Taylor & Francis Group, an informa business

First issued in paperback 2013

© 2009 Megan Sanborn Jones

Typeset in Sabon by IBT Global.

All rights reserved. No part of this book may be reprinted or reproduced or utilised in any form or by any electronic, mechanical, or other means, now known or hereafter invented, including photocopying and recording, or in any information storage or retrieval system, without permission in writing from the publishers.

Trademark Notice: Product or corporate names may be trademarks or registered trademarks, and are used only for identification and explanation without intent to infringe.

Library of Congress Cataloging in Publication Data

Jones, Megan Sanborn.
  Performing American identity in anti-Mormon melodrama / by Megan Sanborn Jones.
    p. cm.—(Studies in American popular history and culture)
  Includes bibliographical references and index.
  1. Mormons in literature. 2. Melodrama, American—History and criticism.
  3. American drama—19th century—History and criticism. 4 Theater and society—United States—History—19th century. I. Title.
  PS338.M65J66 2009
  812'.052709382893—dc22
                                                         2008055412

ISBN13: 978-0-415-80059-4 (hbk)
ISBN13: 978-0-415-84987-6 (pbk)

For my children.

Contents

List of Figures   xi
Acknowledgments   xiii

   Introduction: Outside/Inside America   1

1   The Christian Melodramatic Mode   23

2   Rapists: The Sexual Fantasy of Polygamy   48

3   Murderers: The Necessity of Honorable Violence   83

4   Turks: Appropriating Ethnicity   117

   Conclusion: The Paradox of Identity   152

Notes   161
Bibliography   191
Index   201

Figures

1.1	"Camp Meeting."	44
2.1	"The Mormon Problem Solved."	65
2.2	"Representative Women in Zion."	76
3.1	"Custer's Last Charge. Brevet Major General George A. Custer, Lieutenant Colonel 7th U.S. Cavalry. Killed in Battle with the Sioux, June 25th 1876."	98
3.2	McKee Rankin as Sandy in *The Danites*.	104
4.1	Bayard Taylor in "A Morning in Damascus."	126
4.2	"A Desperate Attempt to Solve the Mormon Question."	141
4.3	The courtship of Herbert and Boadicea.	143

Acknowledgments

I was first introduced to anti-Mormon melodrama a decade ago and what started out as a passing curiosity in this body of work has turned into a much longer relationship. While my scholarly interest in the subject has waxed and waned over the past ten years, what has been consistent is the gracious support of a number of individuals and institutions. I gratefully acknowledge the staff at Brigham Young University's Interlibrary Loan office and the L. Tom Perry Special Collections Library. They have been invaluable in searching out single dusty copies of these plays and other hard-to-find material.

In the dissertation incarnation of this project, I was mentored by my outstanding committee at the University of Minnesota Twin-Cities: Michal Kobialka, Sonja Kuftinec, and Gail Graham Yates. They were followed by generous colleagues who volunteered their valuable time to read or discuss versions of this manuscript. I am especially grateful to Amy Peterson Jensen, Wade Hollingshaus, Scott Magelssen, Darl Larsen, Alan Sikes, and Heather Nathans for their insight and support. The Theatre and Media Arts Department, under the direction of Chair Rodger Sorensen, and the College of Fine Arts and Communications of Brigham Young University supported me financially with grants, release time, and research assistant funding. Editors Benjamin Holtzman and Jennifer Morrow at Routledge were flexible, encouraging, and available to answer all my questions about moving through the publication process. Additionally, anonymous reviewers of this manuscript strengthened the final work as I struggled to incorporate their exacting comments.

The research assistants I have worked with over the years have gone above and beyond in the thankless job of finding sources, organizing bibliographies, transcribing scripts, and editing. More importantly, they provided a listening board, thoughtful advice, and much needed moral support. I thank each of them—LeeAnne Hill Adams, Shelley Graham, Brittany Fitzgerald, and Deleah Emery-Waters. I also must thank the 2008 TMA 202 students who proofread the final manuscript. Special thanks goes to Marel Stock, who spent two years working with me on this project. Her detailed assistance strengthened my work. Her friendship strengthened me.

Finally, I wish to thank my family for their loving support. My mother, Dr. E. Sue Sanborn has always served as an example to me of a woman who thoughtfully balanced her challenging academic career and motherhood. I still want to be just like her. My father, James Sanborn, has a strong listening ear and is a great advocate of hard work. I appreciate him for listening to me, and then telling me to go and get things done. My sister, Ashley Bruggeman, has counseled me, laughed at me, and made me laugh as I've moved through this long project. I treasure our relationship more that she will ever know. Her husband Alan has been willing to read my work and discuss it with me in ways that are always compelling. My precious son Cohen is the greatest joy in my life and our time together away from this project has been the best time I've spent. My deepest love and appreciation go to my husband, Glen Jones, without whose unfailing support, critical insight, intellectual conversation, and superior parenting skills, this book would not have been possible.

Introduction
Outside/Inside America

In February of 1881, a new play opened at Booth's Theatre in New York.[1] Attributed to a Chicago journalist named James B. Runnion, the play was entitled *One Hundred Wives*, and it was heralded as "an American play, because it deals with a subject wholly and essentially American. The subject is Mormonism—a flagrant evil which is allowed to thrive, weed-like, in our free land."[2] The review continues on to praise the production for its "many novel features of dramatic strength," and its "spacious picturesque scenery and . . . series of striking pictures." Most importantly, the reviewer noted that Mr. Runnion's work is "entertaining and illustrates truthfully in some degree a life which is for the most part utterly beyond the knowledge and comprehension of our people."[3]

This *New York Times* review points to a number of issues at play in anti-Mormon melodrama. First, the subject is considered by the reviewer to be "wholly American," or, as a reviewer of the play in the Chicago press *The Daily Inter Ocean* puts it, "the story told is designed to depict horrors of Mormonism for the edification of the American people."[4] One of the primary themes that runs through reviews of anti-Mormon melodrama and in the scripts of the plays themselves is the idea that revealing the "horrors of Mormonism" is an American enterprise. Another issue is revealed by the reviewer's recognition of the dramatic skill of the production. Anti-Mormon melodramas were primarily scripts intended for, and receiving, fully-mounted productions on stage. The impact of the performance of American identity is made literal in the staging of Mormons and Americans in these plays. Finally, the review points to the purpose of the play—sharing with the audience unknown truths about Mormon life. In differentiating between the Mormon villains on stage and "our people" in the audience, the reviewer is making clear the distinction between Mormons (them) and Americans (us).

This review is a typical critical response to the dozens of anti-Mormon melodramas published and produced in the late nineteenth and early twentieth centuries. Many were hits on Broadway. Others found popularity touring across the country and abroad. Still others were closet dramas—written in a dramatic form, but never performed on stage. All are plays that have faded into obscurity during the twentieth century. What they have in common is their use of Mormon characters as evil villains who opposed American heroes and heroines. In these melodramas, Mormons were portrayed as rapists, murderers, and Turks—all characters anathema to mainstream American culture.

This book analyzes nineteenth-century anti-Mormon melodramas to expose how their representation of Mormon deviance was a foil against which American virtues and values were performed. Investigating how melodramatic Mormon villainy conflicted with normative behavior reveals how identity construction forms in parallel with, and in contrast to, difference in society. The performances of various nineteenth-century American fears, and the socially acceptable resolution of these fears in anti-Mormon melodramas created a space for audiences to imagine a unified American identity.

This study is based on the relationship between Mormons and Americans, or the self and the Other as articulated in recent scholarship on alterity, identity, and representation. This focuses a critical lens on the construction of the Other and its function in the creation and use of hegemonic discourse. The groundbreaking work of Foucault, Certeau, Bhabha, and Levinas suggests a starting point for the study of difference.[5] Foucault suggests that the forceful exclusion/exorcism of the Other is an act of identity formation of the self—rather than viewing history as a process of recuperation and human self-constitution. He identifies the end of the nineteenth century as the time when this identity formation led to "the search for a total history, in which all the differences of a society might be reduced to a single form, to the organization of a world-view, to the establishment of a system of values, to a coherent type of civilization."[6]

Foucault's position here is in opposition, mainly, to Hegel's reflexive alterity in which plurality and difference are moments in a movement toward harmony. Foucault instead traces history in terms of exclusion and estrangement—the subordination of otherness by the hegemony of the self. His exploration of discursive identity articulations has had repercussions as scholars in a number of fields have expressed racial, gendered, or political otherness in terms of a powerful self.

In the introduction to *Nation/Narration* (1990), Bhabha complicates Foucualt's evaluation in proposing that the complex relationship between the self and the other cannot be read exclusively in terms of binarial (and therefore adversarial) relationships:

> The "locality," of national culture is neither unified nor unitary in relation to itself, nor must it be seen simply as "other" in relation to what is outside or beyond it. The boundary is Janus-faced and the problem of outside/inside must always itself be a process of hybridity, incorporating new 'people' in relation to the body politic, generating other sites of meaning and, inevitably, in the political process, producing unmanned sites of political antagonism and unpredictable forces for political representation.[7]

His insights suggest a way to analyze the representations of groups such as Mormons who were marginalized in nineteenth-century America as complex sites of political engagement. Mormons were a new people insofar as their beliefs and practices set them outside the mainstream Protestant Christian traditions that formed a significant aspect of American identity following the Great Awakenings of the mid eighteenth and early nineteenth centuries.[8]

As Bhabha suggests, however, this border of belief was less a fixed boundary and more two sides of the same coin as Mormons were simultaneously outside and inside American culture. While the process of hybridity by which Mormons were incorporated into the American body of politics did not occur until the twentieth century, in the period of anti-Mormon melodramas, Mormons in America generated "unmanned sites of political antagonism and unpredictable forces for political representation."

Mormons created a site of difference largely through the practice of polygamy. Of all the doctrines or practices that placed Mormons outside American identity, polygamy was by far the most politically antagonistic. Concerns about plural marriage in mainstream America were exacerbated by the aggressive missionary efforts of the Church that attracted converts from both (predominantly) the United States and Europe.[9] The fear of a growing Mormon kingdom founded on polygamy helped to create the anti-Mormon rhetoric so evident in the late nineteenth century. Mormons were therefore a key group for generating other sites of meaning that impacted how America imagined itself during this period—dealing with Mormons required America to retrench certain political positions, advance some new ones, and refigure others.

Recognizing the negotiations necessary to the formulation of identity comes in no small part from my own position both inside and outside my work. As a practicing member of the Church of Jesus Christ of Latter-day Saints, I come to this project with an institutional knowledge of the history, doctrine, and practices of the Church as well as a belief in its principles. As a scholar and historian, however, I am keenly aware of the processes of the writing of history, the procedures of exclusion that dictate how knowledge is put to work, and the discursive and material power of institutional authority. I cannot help but read Mormon historical texts through these theoretical frames that complicate and enrich both my scholarship and my religious practice.

I examine the representation of Mormons on the melodramatic stage in a way that recognizes the complex networks of interaction between Mormon and American identity as imagined in popular culture. One of the unique aspects of anti-Mormon representation is that the image of Mormons in popular culture, with very few exceptions, was uniform across mediums and throughout the century. While various issues (plural marriage, suffrage, statehood) may have come to the fore at different times, depending on specific political or historical events, the way that these issues were articulated linguistically and visually remained relatively consistent.

Gary L. Bunker and Davis Bitton treat this issue in their important collection of anti-Mormon cartoons, caricatures, and illustrations entitled *The Mormon Graphic Image, 1834–1914* (1983). While they divide their collection of images into three periods (and then each of these three periods into three chronological sub-periods), these divisions are marked less by a shift in representation than by the variances in output of anti-Mormon images.[10] As Bunker and Bitton explain, early images came almost exclusively from illustrated books and presented the image of Joseph Smith as a fraudulent prophet. Once the popular medium for graphic images moved to periodicals, "Brigham Young became a focal point, with his rotund figure, bearded face, and independent manner inviting caricature."[11] This caricature was extended to treat the predominant topic of anti-Mormon images—that of polygamy and its connected issues. As Bitton and Bunker conclude:

> ... [T]he simple fact is that most of the illustrations treating the Mormons were not low-key or objective; they were cartoons and caricatures with an obvious point of view. And that point of view was, with almost monotonous regularity, negative ... [V]iewers of this material came away with the impression that Mormon males were all bearded ogres, that the only marriage pattern in Mormondom was polygamy, or that the women were without exception disheartened and depressed.[12]

If the Mormon popular image was consistent, what did change was how America responded to the perceived threats. As a result, I am moving outside a linear chronology to treat three particular sites of anxiety that recur in anti-Mormon melodrama—gender, violence, and race—in order to trace the various tactics by which the anxieties were alleviated by the action in the plays. Rather than treating representational shifts across time, I generalize the issue to provide a snapshot of the era, then deeply examine the different threads connected to it. The drawback of this methodology is to flatten out some of the historical specificity of the period. The benefit is to focus attention on how the performance of identity, on and off the stage, responds not only to historical, but fictional forces.

Terryl L. Givens deals with the particulars of representing Mormons in fiction in his work *The Viper on the Hearth: Mormons, Myths, and the Construction of Heresy* (1997). Givens views the early Mormon religion as outside/inside America: "clearly alien to and incompatible with" the fundamental religious and cultural values of America, but observes that its "origins and composition were inextricably bound up with American institutions, ideals, and gene pools."[13] He suggests that the problematic status of Mormons as a radical group that did not blatantly manifest difference complicated the way in which it was represented:

> On examining the *uses* to which [fictional] representations of Mormonism have been put, it becomes clear that America's ongoing process

of self-definition has been facilitated by the appropriation of images of a handy, ready-made Other. The Mormon Villain, it turns out, is integrally related to an evolving American self-definition.[14]

It is this self-definition, or as I suggest, *performance* of American identity that is the object of my study.

It is important to note that designating one group as "marginalized" and another as "dominant," even to critique the hegemony or explore the process of hybridity, reaffirms the very power positions that the examination hopes to deconstruct. In the case of Mormonism in nineteenth-century America, studies—from Harold Bloom's seminal examination of the role religion plays in American culture, *The American Religion* (1992) to Paul Reeve's spatial history of Southern Paiutes, Mormons, and miners, *Making Space on the Western Frontier* (2006)—have firmly established the Church of Jesus Christ of Latter-day Saints as an integral part of the history of the United States rather than a marginalized group contributing from the outside. This work does not presume to question the acceptance of Mormon contributions to the development of the American West, to the religious landscape of the country, or to its cultural development.

Instead, the juxtaposition of Mormons and Americans in this study is based on the vision of Mormons articulated in the late nineteenth century. The perception of Mormons in America didn't come exclusively or even predominantly from the Mormons themselves, but more so from America's confrontation with Mormonism. An overwhelmingly negative representation of Mormons pervaded American popular culture from the religion's inception in 1830 into the early twentieth century wherein Mormon and American were considered mutually exclusive identities. Anti-Mormon rhetoric was found in newspapers, novels, political cartoons, political speeches, magazines, music, and plays.

ANTI-MORMON RHETORIC

Following standards applied in religious and American studies, the term "anti-Mormon" is used throughout this work as a means to describe a wide range of practices—from political to legal to playwriting—that responded to the Church of Jesus Christ of Latter-day Saints with prejudice and invective.[15] The term anti-Mormon first appeared in 1841 in the title of an almanac dedicated to "showing the treasonable tendency and the wicked imposture of that great delusion, advocated by a sect, lately risen up, in the United States, calling themselves Mormons, or Latter Day Saints."[16] Anti-Mormon political parties were established throughout the century to defend the country from the Mormon threat.[17] The height of anti-Mormon expression was during the years when the Mormon practice of polygamy was common public knowledge (1850–1890).

While today, there is wide debate about the continued use of the term anti-Mormon by Mormon apologists to describe individuals or groups that criticize the Church of Jesus Christ of Latter-day Saints, in the late nineteenth century, the term was used by the critics themselves to describe their position. The use of the term by political, religious, and social groups suggests that the anti-Mormons saw their position in direct opposition to the Mormons. The variety of media in which anti-Mormon rhetoric appeared reveals the widespread popularity of the opinion. The binary of Mormon/American established by anti-Mormon rhetoric in the nineteenth century clearly does not speak to the complex lived reality of Mormons and anti-Mormons. Instead, it reveals an idealized vision of both, with the Mormons represented as an extreme evil. Opposing them were upstanding and righteous American heroes and heroines.

Melodramas that featured these villains and heroes were exclusively staged in major urban areas: New York City, St. Louis, Philadelphia, Portland, San Francisco, and while records point to sold-out houses, the audiences still would not have been large enough to shape national opinions about Mormon villainy. The style in which Mormons were drawn in these plays, however, agrees with other representations in wider circulation at the time. The novel was perhaps the most popular medium for creating and circulating anti-Mormon sentiment. The first full-length novel about Mormons was John Russell's *The Mormoness; or the Trials of Mary Maverick*, published in 1853. Another fifty were published by the end of the century. These novels took a number of shapes, from fictional memoirs to pseudo-journalistic exposés to action-adventure stories to satires.

The popularity of these works was supported both by economic developments in publishing (the new use of wood pulp instead of rags to make paper, the construction of the mass printing press, and the application of the fast newspaper cylinder presses to book publishing, which brought prices down from two dollars to as low as 7 cents per volume) and a drastic rise in literacy rates. According to 1840 census data, there was a 91% literacy rate for the Caucasian adult population in the United States.[18] Recent studies have shown that reading was a major pastime not only in America's cities, but also in remote rural areas as well.[19]

Popular music was another venue for promoting the image of the villainous Mormon. The early nineteenth century was a coming of age for American music, especially American popular songs. By the end of the Civil War, popular music, available through sheet music and song sheets (one page lyric sheets without the music), was an integral part of American middle-class culture. Even away from the urban centers where the music was created, the songs could be purchased and integrated into daily life. Songs came from a variety of venues: autonomous works, songs from plays, operettas, operas, and burlesques. Music that was sold on sheets indicates what appealed to society, and reflects some of the opinions and tastes of the nation. Anti-Mormon songs ranged from frontier topics like "The Mormon

Cowboy" to racial parodies like "The Mormon Coon," where an ex-slave picks up on the habits of the Mormons out West and marries as many women as will have him.[20]

The prevalence of Mormon characterizations in popular music was recorded in local and national magazines as well. To take one example, *Nik Nax,* an entertainment publication of the early nineteenth century, used jokes, riddles, comic verse, and satirical illustrations to make news, rather than report it. In the July 1858 issue, a song sheet for "The Mormon Love Song" was published. The lyrics point to a popular vision of Mormons, and emphasize the variety of means by which this image was spread through the nation:

> Say, Susan wilt though come with me
>   In sweet community to live?
> Of heart, and hand, and home, to thee
>   A sixteenth part I freely give . . .
> I promise thee a life of ease
>   And for thyself I'll let thee choose
> Such duties as thy fancy please;
>   Say Susan, canst thou still refuse?
> Sephronia cooks and sweeps the floors,
>   And Hepzibah makes up the bed,
> Jemima answers all the doors
>   And Prudence combs the children's heads . . .
> Into thy hands such tasks as take
>   A dignity, will I consign;
> I'll let thee black my boots, or make
>   The sock and shirt department thine.
> I'll give thee whatso'er thou wilt—
>   So it be but a sixteenth part;
> It would be the deepest depth of guilt
>   To slight the rest who share my heart.
> Then wilt though not thy fraction yield
> To make up my domestic bliss?
>   Say yes—and let our joy be sealed
>   With just the sixteenth of a kiss.[21]

Magazine reports, chapters from novel exposés, editorial letters, and other writing could be disseminated through these popular journals to outlying communities. Even more important to these periodicals was the introduction of political cartoons and illustrations that made up a major aspect of the publications. Bunker and Bitton argue that "there had been other important vehicles of expression before—books, pamphlets, broadsides, almanacs, separately published prints—but none of these had as much power to shape attitudes among large numbers of people as did the illustrated periodical."[22] By the mid-1860s many of these illustrated journals such as *Harper's Weekly, The Wasp, Vanity Fair,* and *Puck* reached circulations surpassing one hundred thousand. Every one of them featured anti-Mormon items.

While Mormons were represented in popular media as outside American culture, part of the fears about them as a group emerged from the ways in which they were also very much inside American culture as well. Some Protestant Christians of the period may have accused Mormonism of being a heretical cult, but Mormons perceived themselves as being inheritors of the sacred land of America. They saw one of their primary callings to be civically engaged, to uphold the Constitution, and to preserve the American way of life. When called upon, Mormons served in the army, most notably in the Mormon Battalion of the Mexican American War (1846–1848).[23] Mormons ran for public office, and served locally and nationally as elected officials. Even in the nineteenth century, maintaining a material separation between Mormons and Americans was difficult as Mormons were so evidently involved in national civic duty.

Additionally, Mormons *looked* like Americans. Most members of the Church were from the northeast of the United States and early international converts were from Canada, England, Scandinavia and Wales. There was nothing remarkable in fashion, form, or face to set Mormons apart from Americans. So in many ways Mormons were very much inside America. What set them outside was their religious doctrine and how that doctrine was enacted in daily practice. In particular, the Mormon vision of the sacred position of America and their vision of the Mormon role in maintaining this position placed them outside the borders of American Christian thought of the time.

A PECULIAR PEOPLE

Wrestling with their outside/inside status in America was a source of both concern and pride for Mormons. These competing sentiments are summed up in the early Mormon use of the phrase "a peculiar people" to describe themselves. This phrase comes from passages in the Old Testament where the Lord sets the children of Israel apart and dedicates them to himself and "above all other nations that are upon the earth."[24] In requisitioning this phrase for themselves, Mormons both drew a connection to a chosen people in a promised land, and reaffirmed their belief that the Lord had called them "above all other nations."

From the Church's inception, Mormons cultivated their reputation as a peculiar people, which in turn created a number of sources of great anxiety for Christian America. First, the Mormon Church presented itself as an entirely new religion rather than a reevaluation of normative Christianity. Mainstream Protestant churches (Methodist, Presbyterian, Baptist,

Episcopalians, and Congregationalists) conflated Mormon teachings with the worst type of un-American rhetoric. One of the main concerns was with the Mormon belief that Joseph Smith was a prophet of God who was called by revelation to reestablish Christ's gospel on the earth. In his autobiographical history, Smith records that in his visitation with Jesus Christ and God the Father, Christ told Smith to join none of the churches, as the true church of Jesus Christ had been lost following the death of the original apostles. The extension of belief in this vision is that Joseph Smith became God's only approved messenger on earth and his teachings come directly from God in ways unfamiliar to Protestant churches. The perception of Mormonism as not Christian was exacerbated by Smith's claim to have been additionally visited by the angel Moroni who instructed Smith and led him to a set of records engraved on golden plates that Smith subsequently translated as *The Book of Mormon*.[25]

Even in the period of the Second Great Awakening that celebrated extraordinary physical manifestations of the divine in everyday life, a visit from angels, Jesus Christ, and God the Father, and a set of golden plates that contained new scripture was remarkable, and ill-received.

More to the point, Smith's claims set up an identifiable space of difference between Mormons and normative Christians through the active rejection of already established religions and aggressive proselytizing.[26] As with their papist fears, Christian Americans expressed concerns that the rapidly growing number of Mormons were loyal to Joseph Smith and his religious organization, and not to the President and the government of the United States.

The majority of those with whom Smith shared his vision considered him to be lying, possessed, or mentally ill, and blasphemous in any case. His assertion of these events, and his followers' belief in their truthfulness, underlined for Christian America the fact that in rejecting the type of Christianity upon which America was founded, Mormons were in fact rejecting America itself. The notion of a kingdom of God that functioned within America as it was then constituted seemed counter-intuitive to the American public. Instead, this doctrine was envisioned as the rhetoric of secessionism; a Mormon kingdom would grow up as a threat to the well being of the nation.

Early Mormons set themselves outside America when they formed communities based on membership rather than citizenship. These served as moral centers against the deviancy and unrighteousness of the corrupted nation. Joseph Smith established the Church of Jesus Christ of Latter-day Saints in Fayette, New York in April 1830.[27] The next year, he and all his followers settled in Kirtland, Ohio where they built a temple and gathered an increasing number of members. Escalating violence against Church members prompted a move in 1838 to Far West, Missouri. The Mormons' stay there lasted less than a year. On 27 October 1838, Governor Boggs issued an "Extermination Order," which led to the Haun's Mill Massacre in which 17 Mormons were killed, and 15 severely wounded. In his executive order Boggs declared, "The Mormons must be treated as enemies, and must be exterminated or driven from the state, if necessary, for the public good."[28] The Mormons left almost immediately for Illinois following the violence at Haun's Mill.

In Illinois they purchased swampland to develop Nauvoo, a city that at its peak was the largest city in the state outside of Chicago. However, increasing hostility from their county neighbors, the murders of the founding prophet Joseph Smith and his brother Hyrum, and violent raids on settlements outlying Nauvoo prompted the abandonment of the city in favor of a safe haven outside the United States. The pattern established here is not only a geographical movement, but a theoretical one as well, as it demonstrates the complex relationship between normative culture and transgressors to it—a geography of alterity. In each place that the Mormons settled, their neighbors perceived them as outsiders. This was aggravated by the insularity of the Mormon community: they isolated themselves geographically, economically, religiously, and educationally.

While Mormons externally participated in national government—paying taxes, becoming involved with local politics, and setting up businesses—the thrust of their civic engagement was to work within the government to support their religious practices and beliefs. They frequently would not sell land or water rights to non-Mormons by passing laws that required county surveyors to issue a title of possession that was countersigned by Church leaders. They wouldn't shop at non-Mormon stores, but instead, banded together to set prices, establish guidelines for quality assurance, and police the supply chain.[29] The legal system in the early Utah territory was manned entirely by Church bishops, who were elected unanimously, and "dispensed justice by inspiration."[30] Mormons followed the dictates of Joseph Smith then Brigham Young and subsequent leaders as prophets, called by God to lead them in righteousness. They put these beliefs into practice with a number of visibly distinct practices that conflicted with American culture and law—a code of health that forbade the drinking of alcohol or the use of tobacco, the building of temples, and most noticeably, the practice of polygamy. This difference was conceived by the Protestant majority as un-American and was materialized in violence and expulsion.

Salt Lake City was a physical reminder of this geographical outside/inside position. To outsiders in the early days of the Church, Utah was a walled city run by a theocracy of lechery from which there was no escape. Part of this perception came from the geographic realities of the Salt Lake Valley. Surrounded either by mountains, desert, or water, Salt Lake City was isolated by enormous tracts of unsettled frontier; in 1847, it was 1000 miles from Salt Lake City to any other population center.[31] The dual position of Brigham Young as both Latter-day Saint prophet and Salt Lake Territory Governor also reinforced the perception. Although he only served one term, the image of Young as a theocrat remained in place in both history books and cultural imagination.

Introduction 11

In contrast, the Mormons who gathered to Utah felt it was a safe haven, a territory outside the United States where they would be left to worship in peace. In 1846, William Clayton, secretary to Brigham Young and a member of the first pioneer company, wrote the hymn "Come, Come Ye Saints," which served as an anthem to early pioneers. It remains perhaps the most beloved piece of music in the Mormon faith. The third verse of the hymn records Mormon feelings about the Utah valley:

> We'll find the place which God for us prepared,
> Far away in the West,
> Where none shall come to hurt or make afraid;
> There the Saints will be blessed.
> We'll make the air with music ring,
> Shout praises to our God and King;
> Above the rest these words we'll tell—
> All is well! All is well![32]

In 1847 when the Saints arrived in the Salt Lake Valley, they had traveled outside the borders of America, into Indian Territory, and finally into Mexico. Quickly setting up a system of government under the auspices of the Church, settlers constructed homes, damned rivers, planted crops, and laid out streets.

Despite their efforts to establish a "kingdom of God" away from governmental structures, Mormons found themselves, within a year of the exodus, back in United States territory. Brigham Young immediately applied for statehood as the state of Deseret, but was denied the request. Instead, the Federal legislature organized Utah as a United States Territory in 1850, with Brigham Young as the governor.[33] The years that followed saw increasing conflict between Mormon and American perceptions of Utah—non-Mormons saw the growing population in the territory as a threat to America, while Mormons strengthened themselves economically, militarily, and religiously in order to stave off what they perceived as coming persecutions.

Nelson Winch Green, in the preface to his "tell-all," *Fifteen Years Among the Mormons* (1860), responded to the conflict with a call to "hang all of the [Mormon] leaders of any note."[34] For Green, this was the necessary outcome of the unavoidable approaching war between "the people of the United States, and the Saints in Utah."[35] His clear differentiation between Americans and Mormons is both geographical and ethical. He continued:

> This Government, ranking among the first Christian powers of the earth, owes something to civilization and the world as touching the solution of this Mormon question. The assumptions and errors of these "latter-day Saints," are too monstrous and radical to pass with a mere rebuke. They should be crushed in the bud.[36]

Americans are civilized and Christian. Logically then, Mormons are both savage and unchristian, or as Green put it, "have repudiated the common instincts of humanity."[37] Exposés such as this one lent authority to the growing separation between American and Mormon, Christian and Saint.

These tensions boiled over in 1857, when President Buchanan sent a large military force to quell the "Mormon rebellion," and established a non-Mormon governor of Utah Territory. While this war was resolved without bloodshed, conflicts between the United States government (in Washington D.C.) and the Church government (in Salt Lake City) continued throughout the period of the Civil War, through the joining of the Pacific and Continental Railroads (1869), through the years of anti-polygamy legislation and the Church's Manifesto officially abandoning the practice, until 1896, when Utah was made a state.[38]

It is unsurprising that most anti-Mormon melodramas are set either in Salt Lake City or in the Utah desert. The position of Utah in cultural imagination, both today and in the past, is a complex example of the way in which Mormons were both inside and outside America. The Mormon vision of America was that of a country established by God to serve as the land promised for the emergence of the restored gospel of Jesus Christ. America, for Mormons, was a facilitating agent for the establishment of the Church of Jesus Christ of Latter-day Saints, and for its growth across the nation. As such, Mormons perceived themselves as able to function autonomously within the United States. There was no need for integration with normative America, as the sacred calling of the United States was to serve as the birthplace and support of the Church of Christ in modern times.

SACRED AMERICA

The mainstream vision of America was that of a country established by Christians devoted to the worship of God. The laws built into the country to support religious freedom were less a legalization of any worship practices, and more a recognition of the heritage of the Protestant majority. Any religion outside normative Protestantism encountered governmental restrictions on voting rights, worship practices, holiday observances, and tax exemptions. Many also encountered inequality in opportunities for education, for public service, and for land-ownership. Others were targets of violence. It seems clear that early America interpreted freedom of worship almost exclusively to mean a freedom from international interference of Protestant Christian worship.

Politically, American religion was most evident in the reification of what Ben Franklin called "Publick Religion"—the notion that a citizen's respect for the United States of America was not just patriotism, or love of country, but was a religious reverence for the nation. According to this belief, America has a special place in God's plan and therefore its founding leaders, documents, and holidays have a sacred meaning. The idea of Public or Civil Religion arose at the end of the eighteenth century, is built into the Constitution, and came into widespread practice during the nineteenth century. The Pledge of Allegiance, and its dogma of "one nation under God," became a standard part of patriotic celebration. Various national holidays gained a religious tone—Thanksgiving was confirmed a national day of prayer and repentance while other holidays, most notably the Fourth of July, began to collapse patriotic and religious icons. George Washington appears in nineteenth-century artwork as a saint in military dress with a halo, resting in heavenly clouds of glory. Patriotic songs were penned by religious writers for inclusion in church hymnals.[39]

Perhaps the most influential political evidence of America as a nation touched by God is the Doctrine of Manifest Destiny—an idea that had one of the longest-reaching material effects of the century. The early 1800s in America saw tremendous growth not only in population, with increased immigration, but also in foreign demand for goods. International investment in American enterprises and advances in industrialization led to an explosive prosperity. The new economy provided space for extraordinary material and political gain; people of all classes scrambled to acquire wealth. As the country expanded toward the West Coast, Americans embraced the opportunity to gain lands, riches, and most importantly, gold. In 1845 an eastern editor originated the now-standard term for the God-approved right to expansion: "Our Manifest Destiny is to overspread the continent allotted by Providence for the free development of our yearly multiplying millions."[40]

While the inherent moral superiority that underlies the principle may be suspect for its blatant oversight of the irreparable damage caused by the settling of the continent, the problems of the policy didn't stop an estimated 350,000 people from trekking across the plains to settle in California, Oregon, or Utah between 1841 and 1867.[41] While some may have been moved (literally) by a sense of cultural entitlement, most probably made the journey as a result of the almost mythic cultural draw of the West—a land where anyone from any class or creed could make a home and prosper.

Richard Slotkin suggests that the frontier was a real geography "defined less by maps and surveys than by myths and illusion, projective fantasies, wild anticipations, and extravagant expectations."[42] Cultural imagination about the frontier, however, was not a narrative unconnected to the material realities of the Industrial Age. It was a myth that served as a foundational ideology that impacted public policy from Custer's Last Stand to the Vietnam War. For Slotkin, "myth therefore performs its cultural function by generalizing particular and contingent experiences into the bases of universal rules of understanding and conduct; and it does this by transforming secular history into a body of sacred and sanctifying legends."[43]

As Slotkin articulates, underlying both the myth and reality of the West was the notion that God himself had created the land of wondrous beauty to be tamed, settled, and made fit for his use. This vision of sacred America is a theme that runs from writers of the time through the major first historian/theorists of the post-frontier, Frederick Jackson Turner and Theodore Roosevelt, to the contemporary work of western historiographers. Herman Melville, for example, connects America directly to a sense of holy purpose and privilege:

> God has predestined, mankind expects, great things from our race; and great things we feel in our souls. The rest of the nations must soon be in our rear. We are the pioneers of the world; the advance-guard, sent on through the wilderness of untried things, to break a new path in the New World that is ours.[44]

Rhetoric such as this in every aspect of American society drew clear parallels between God's intervention in life and the responsibility Americans had to live up to his expectations.

Mormons, however, appropriated America's sacred position for themselves in an interpretation of scripture (both old and newly revealed) that assigned the sacred nature of America exclusively to the Mormons. This vision of America came into conflict with the white Protestant majority of the nation. Built into doctrines preached by Latter-day Saints are a series of beliefs that reaffirm the divine purpose of America as the birthplace of the restored gospel of Jesus Christ. Mormons believed (and still believe) that America was "discovered" both in ancient times and in the modern era by men led by divine inspiration.[45]

The Book of Mormon makes clear the inspired hand of God in bringing people to America. Not one, but several peoples in *The Book of Mormon* are brought to this continent, which is given to them as a promised land if they would keep God's commandments.[46] For Mormons, this promise remains true, and much of the attitude of the early Church on any number of issues can be traced to this doctrine. Conflicts with the United States government merely rekindled in the Saints a desire to obey the commandments of God concerning economic practices, mission calls, military duty, or the institution of polygamy. In doing so, they saw themselves as *more* faithfully American than those who opposed them since they clearly understood the national repercussions of disobeying God's commands.

Later discoveries of America are also held to be divinely inspired. *The Book of Mormon* prophesies of a man who would be influenced by God to go across the ocean "even unto... the promised land."[47] An early twentieth-century Mormon leader, James E. Talmage underlined the sacred nature of Columbus' voyage:

> Think you that all this was due to human effort unaided and uninspired?... In every age and in every land God has raised up men to carry on his purposes, and like the master of men He is, He uses even

the selfish desire of mankind, their passions and their prejudices, their antipathies, their loves and their hates by overruling for the general good. Queen Isabella wanted brighter diamonds for her ears, more illustrious pearls for her neck, richer spices for her table, rarer perfumes for her boudoir: but the hand of the Lord was in what she did![48]

The indigenous people of the Americas, Columbus, and subsequent explorers are all viewed as divinely inspired harbingers of Christ's restored gospel. In the late nineteenth century, Brigham Young and the Mormons felt a more particular inspiration that led to the settlement of the Salt Lake Valley.

The Mormon exodus could easily have taken the pioneers to more environmentally hospitable lands—California, Oregon, Washington. Instead, Brigham Young staunchly insisted upon the valley he had seen in a prophetic vision. He later wrote in his journal, that upon arriving in the valley: "The spirit of light rested upon us and hovered over the valley, and I felt that there the Saints would find protection and safety."[49] In each of these cases—ancient and modern—Mormons perceived journeys to (or across) America as God-directed. For Mormons, America is the land chosen by God and established by his hand to bring about his purposes.

PRODUCTION AND PERFORMANCE

This book traces the performance of American identity through anti-Mormon melodramas written in the period between 1850–1890. The first known anti-Mormon melodrama, *The Mormon Prophet* by William H. Rhodes, was published in 1845. It was a closet drama that, according to early theatre history texts, was "never acted but sometimes was read to appreciative audiences."[50] It did not, however, treat the main subjects of anti-Mormon melodrama that emerged following the 1850 public announcement that the members of the Mormon Church were practicing polygamy. Polygamy and its perceived attendant ills—violence (particularly the 1857 Mountain Meadows massacre) and hints of Turkish erotic exoticism—remained the primary topic for melodramas throughout the century. I have found records of two dozen different anti-Mormon melodramas that played on stage during this period. Twelve of them were published and are still extant. The others were all performed, and left production histories in newspaper reviews, advertisements, production photos, and performance notices. In no way do I suggest that the plays I treat in this work represent all of the anti-Mormon melodramas that were written or played in theatres across America. My research here serves as a starting point for the collection and analysis of these plays.

This study ends in 1890, but not because this date marks the last recorded performance. That doesn't occur until the *Polygamy* by O'Higgins, Harvey Jerrold and Harriet Ford played in New York at the Playhouse Theatre from

December 1914 to March 1915. As one review states, however, this play treats polygamy differently than the plays that came before in that *Polygamy*, set in the present day of 1914, illustrates polygamy *after* the official abandonment of the practice. The authors were so concerned that they not be seen as attacking the Mormons that they added a pre-curtain speech to the melodrama to be read by one of the actresses appearing in the production, Miss Mary Shaw. She stated, "The authors would have me tell you merely that they are trying to show that polygamy is an attempt to get more out of life than there is in it."[51] This treatment of polygamy as metaphorical rather than historical is underlined by a *New York Times* announcement for the show that explained, "the piece takes its title from a question propounded in the first of its four acts, 'Are all men natural polygamists?'"[52]

Rather than a specifically Mormon threat, this play broadens the topic of polygamy to one of what another announcement calls "a new play of marriage in America."[53] Here, Mormondom is not in opposition to America, but polygamy is actually a way of discussing American marriage generally through the lens of the curious habits of modern-day Mormons. The key to this shift in tone comes in the previously mentioned setting—the play takes place in 1914 after the official abandonment of polygamy. On 25 September 1890, Wilfred Woodruff, the President and Prophet of the Church of Jesus Christ of Latter-day Saints, issued an official statement that the Church should cease the practice of polygamy. The following October, Church members formally accepted the manifesto as doctrine.[54] While there continued to be rumors of polygamy, dramatic representations of Mormons seemed to fade from public interest after 1890—there are only records of a half-dozen anti-Mormon melodramas staged between 1890 and 1914. The acceptance of Utah as a State in 1896 effectively ended the trend for anti-Mormon melodrama, except for a very few new plays like *Polygamy*. To focus on the most prolific period of anti-Mormon melodrama, then, this study is limited from 1850–1890.

Polygamy and the violence and exoticism that accompany it also point to how gender, violence, and race are issues central to the American character. In the late nineteenth century, public discourse focused on defining and delimiting how these concerns function in a society working to create a unified national identity. How anti-Mormon melodramas wrestle with these issues suggests that the desire for a cohesive American identity was nearly impossible to fulfill. Examining the relationship between Mormons as subordinated characters and their dominant American scene partners reveals the ways in which these works functioned to perform an idealized American identity.

Mormons were made strange to America in late nineteenth-century popular culture through a variety of means; images, impressions, anxieties, and fears were made visible in fiction, journalism, on stage, and in the political arena. The standard representation had a material impact not only on the social and legal treatment of Mormons, but also on the way in which the nation configured itself. By focusing on melodramas, I am drawing attention to the way American identity was *performed*. Playwriting has a very different relationship with the audience than writing for print alone. As one review of the play *The Mormons* (1858) suggests, the merit of drama rests not only in the artistic and aesthetic appeal of the work, but also in the response of the audience:

> Judged by the usual canons of criticism, the "Mormons" would not stand very high as a specimen of dramatic art, but it has the merit of suiting the audience it was written for, and it interests, excites, and amuses in spite of its incongruities and shortcomings. The different scenes daguerreotype as nearly as possible what is known of life in Utah, and the absurdities as well as the wickedness of the Mormon faith and practice *are brought home vividly to the audience*. This makes it one of the most successful of the "contemporaneous drama," as this description of play has been well designated.[55]

Here, the play is not perceived as good writing, but it is a good performance because of the impact that it had upon the audiences attending. Even more interesting, the reviewer suggests that the play "daguerreotypes," or photographs, "life in Utah." The invocation of a frozen picture of truth and reality lends an air of documentary reporting that exceeds a textual analysis of the melodrama as literature alone. It is in the actual performance that this play moves from a work with "incongruities and shortcomings" to "one of the most successful of the 'contemporaneous drama'" on stage in New York at the time.

In examining theatre as performance, one is faced with the contradiction of being grounded in text in order to discuss a live event. The only way to "view" plays of the past is through the written records that serve as evidence of their existence. And yet, vital to the study of performance is to foreground the work beyond the written documents, even if it is the study of a performance that cannot be seen or perhaps was never seen at all. As mentioned earlier, I have only found twelve anti-Mormon melodrama scripts of the two dozen plays recorded. So there is a division between plays with scripts and plays with a documented performance history. On one end are celebrated productions such as *The Danites,* which has both been published in a few collections and which has an extensive production history that is well-documented in newspaper reviews, photographs and playbills as well as theatre history scholarship.[56] On the other end of the spectrum is the production for which there are two small notices in *The New York Herald* on 24 March, 1858. They both announce that the Bowery theatre will present a "new drama," entitled variously *Utah; or the Devil Among the Mormons* or simply *The Devil Among the Mormons.*[57] With no author, script, cast list, reviews, or production evidence like programs or photos, this play can only be considered for examination insofar as the title suggests it uses Mormons as villains.

Most of the anti-Mormon melodramas in the study fall somewhere in the middle—plays that have scripts and some performance history that flesh out the performative space. Others, however, reside outside/inside the performative space. A number of the plays with extant scripts have no record of production or were never intended for stage. Others have extensive production records, but the scripts themselves have been lost. In treating all of these anti-Mormon melodramas as performance, I echo the concern articulated by Andrew Sofer in *The Stage Life of Props* (2003): "I am keenly aware of the pitfalls of such an approach. When writing about a particular piece of stage business, it is sometimes hard to draw the line between reasonable supposition and armchair fantasy."[58] Using the methodology of production analysis helps draw and maintain this line in my study.

In their work on Restoration theatre, Judith Milhous and Robert D. Hume define production analysis as text interpretation "specifically aimed at understanding it as a performance vehicle."[59] Sofer suggests this method is a way of reconstructing a stage event "using such cues as verbal and actual stage directions, visual records of historical performance, and (where available) eyewitness accounts."[60] Production analysis in this sense is not bounded by what actually happened in a particular moment of stage, which is defined by Milhous and Hume as performance analysis, but by the multiple possibilities for performance as suggested by the vestigial archive. I will treat the eight scripts I use extensively in this work following this model of analysis.

Four of these eight plays have performance histories in addition to the scripts that allow me to slip between production and performance analysis: *The Mormons; or, Life at Salt Lake City* (1858), *Desert Deserted; or, The Last Days of Brigham Young* (1858), *The Danites in the Sierras* (1877), and *Fonda; or, The Trapper's Dream* (1880). Two of the plays have no performance record, but were clearly meant for the stage. *Brigham Young; or, The Prophet's Last Love* (1869) and *Zion* (1886) were published as acting editions complete with costume descriptions, prop lists, and/or stage directions that abbreviate stage space (as in "Exit, c." to indicate an exit center stage.) Finally two of the scripts, *The Prophet* (1878), and *Evelyn Gray; or, History of Our Western Turks* (1890) were closet dramas never intended for stage.

I treat all of these plays in the same way—as productions ripe with performative potential. In so doing, I consider the actions as embodied and live for an audience. In the face of an archive full of gaps and inconsistencies, I rely on evidence drawn from places where the archive is more complete. I make assumptions, for example, about how an actress may have performed a role in *Brigham Young* (for which there are no records of a live performance) based on reviews of actresses playing similar roles in other anti-Mormon melodramas. I also make assumptions based on my own intuition as a director, actor, and scholar.[61]

This is not the first study to examine American identity as performed in melodrama. In Jeffrey Mason's *Melodrama and the Myth of America*, he examines "how America performed 'America' during a portion of the nineteenth century—how its people enacted their collective self-concept, or their sense of cultural identity."[62] He uses five plays from 1829–1889 to focus his study around the direct intersection between melodramatic representation and specific historical events. He concludes that being an American in the nineteenth century, whether on or off the stage was a process of establishing a position in the discourse of America as an idea or myth.[63] Mason puts it this way: "The myth defines The American in terms of his difference from those who are not The American; the outsiders provide the contrast whereby his essence may be clearly confirmed, and the signs of Otherness rebound off of one another in an endless free-play of race, gender, power, and even geography."[64] His study serves as a methodological foundation for my work insofar as he treats performance rather than text—suggesting that melodrama articulates shared values of all participants: author, actors, and audience.

However, he maintains a focus on being American as a socio-political identity and does not explore the impact of religion on American culture in the nineteenth century or on religious groups such as Mormons in American frontier history. This perspective of melodrama as an articulation of a particular religious worldview is, in fact, almost entirely missing from all recent studies of American melodrama. Anti-Mormon melodramas are generally treated only insofar as they are considered a subset of "frontier" melodrama. This scholarly gap exists in large part because the field has moved from expansive histories of the genre as in the work of Quinn or Rahill,[65] to detailed and focused historiographies of melodrama that contextualize melodramatic performance in terms of space (Bank), economics (McConachie), and reform (Frick).[66]

Mason briefly mentions the play *The Danites in the Sierras* as another example of "California mining drama" in his chapter on Bartley Campbell's *My Partner* (1879) and the West.[67] Gary A. Richardson expands on this reference to consider how *The Danites* exemplifies frontier melodrama's romantic and spiritual vision of nature. For Richardson, *The Danites* also provides other signposts typical of the genre: violence as normative and the technique of maintaining conventional eastern morality but dressing it up for the frontier.[68]

For Richardson, however, the focus of frontier melodrama, including *The Danites* is economic. He argues that with very few exceptions, western migration was a function of the gold rush. The very setting of frontier melodrama is dependant on the audience's perceptions of work and wealth connected to the West.[69] Violence is also glossed as a function of economics: "Given the amount of money either seen or referred to in these works, it is not surprising that they explore the proliferation and consequences of violent and ruthless greed."[70] Richardson's analysis here treats *The Danites* as interchangeable with other frontier melodramas like Bartley Campbell's *My Partner* or Augustin Daly's *Horizon*. In many ways, he is correct. The use of the Mormon villain, which Richardson suggests is an example of a group marginalized on the frontier, is functionally no different than the English villain in *My Partner* or the Mexican one in *Girl of the Golden West*.

I would argue, however, that the Mormon villain is a particularly complex site that requires analysis beyond identifying Mormons as a marginalized group. Mormons, unlike the English and Mexicans, were either actually American or could pass for one; fears about their assimilation into culture complicated their representation. Additionally, representations of Mormon villains would evoke in audiences less an economic connection than a religious one. No matter the similarity between how Mormon villains and other villains behaved, the reason for the villainy of Mormons connects directly back to religious doctrine and practice. Roger A. Hall foregrounds this point in his impressive work on American frontier melodrama.

Hall first references anti-Mormon melodrama in his expositional history of early frontier melodramas in the 1850s. He identifies the three anti-Mormon plays that were performed within two months of each other in 1858 in New York: *The Mormons; or Life at Salt Lake City* at Burton's Theatre, *Life of the Mormons at Salt Lake* at the National Theatre, and *Deseret Deserted; or, The Last Days of Brigham Young* at Wallack's Theatre. Here, Hall suggests: "To a predominantly white, Christian audience, the plight of the Mormons provided ideal melodramatic material. Polygamy threatened the moral order with its implications of unbridled sex, and stories of Mormon violence perfectly satisfied melodrama's need for rapacious, conspiratorial villains."[71] His identification of the audience as white and Christian presumes an opposition in the figures of the Mormons on stage, and if Mormons were the ideal melodramatic villain, it was because of the threat it posed to a Christian culture.

Hall makes this same connection in his history of McKee Rankin, Joaquin Miller and *The Danites*. He identifies that the play is based on a "gruesome story" of the wife and children of a man who participated in the mob responsible for the murder of Joseph Smith. The story relates how one by one, the family is slain or disappears, all allegedly victims of Mormon assassins, the Danites. Just one month after the opening of the play Orrin Porter Rockwell, a suspected Danite, was indicted for murders (the Aiken massacre) committed in 1858. These two incidents appear on advertising for the production and as Hall argues, "blended together various border names and incidents to provide an exciting mixture with a patina of authenticity."[72] The use of current events about Mormons and folk stories to create public interest in *The Danites* reveals again how anti-Mormon melodramas manipulated the Mormon threat for their own ends.

Unlike Hall's work on frontier melodrama generally, I am not attempting to put forward an exhaustive collection of anti-Mormon representations, due in equal parts to my critical method, the limited extant play texts, and the vast number of other sources that intersect the topic. Nor do I trace a pattern of evolution in these plays from their first appearance to their culmination. Instead I have carefully selected a limited number of texts that will illustrate my point through extended analysis rather than numerous examples. Each of the following chapters therefore has a specific focus, but many of the ideas and institutions run through all of them. Protestant Christianity, to take one example, is featured in Chapter One's discussion of melodrama, then emerges again in Chapters Three and Five as a structure of social authority that mediated the relationship between the identity and performance of gender and ethnicity.

The style in which American religious sentiment was enacted intersects with another dominant mode of performance in the nineteenth century—melodrama. Understanding the ways in which these two representational practices evidence similar styles, structures, messages, and meanings comprises the work presented in Chapter One. Particularly, I focus on the ways in which religious rhetoric of the time is shaped in a distinctly melodramatic style, just as religious practice borrowed melodramatic structure and staging techniques. Both religion and melodrama wrestled with three major aspects of American life in the late nineteenth century: the process of Christian conversion, the importance of social reform, and the rise of middle class culture. Religion and melodrama also intersected in areas of national concern—in anti-Mormon melodrama and in churches across America. A major, if not the major concern following the Civil War was polygamy.

That Mormons should practice a liberal sexual experiment was not entirely unusual in the reform-minded nineteenth century. That they should promote a society based on unchecked sexuality, enslave women in bondage, or give them the right to vote was frightening in the aftermath of the Civil War. Social anarchy, slavery, and women's rights, were national concerns about Mormons; rather than perform these concerns, however, anti-Mormon melodramas remained focused on the horrors of polygamy and repeatedly staged scenes from their ideas about those horrors—the jealousy, madness, suicide, physical abuse, lechery, rape, and power. The specific performance of gender is my subject in Chapter Three. The nature of the stage performance foregrounds the literal use of the voice and body to rehearse and reproduce valuable characteristics of American identity. Anti-Mormon melodramas provided audiences with a close look at the shocking yet strangely attractive phenomenon of polygamy. However, while the staged representations were complicated, the conclusion of the plays customarily reinforced traditional roles for men and women and the ultimate primacy of the monogamous family.

Criminality is another identity performance that was central to anti-Mormon melodrama. In Chapter Four, I assess how theatrical depictions of Mormon murders affirmed the notion of honorable violence as a respectable characteristic of American identity. As the villains, Mormon murderers were conceived as criminal to every possible code of honor; they broke federal laws and community rules, and displayed a lack of basic human ethics. The way in which American heroes opposed Mormon aggression suggested a model of behavior in which appropriate violence was not just acceptable, but a necessary aspect of American identity.

The invention of a new race of Mormon Turks, the subject of Chapter Five, illuminates a final aspect of American identity. In the mid to late nineteenth century, economic and literary trade with Asia and U.S. foreign policy helped contribute to a public awareness of and interest in the East. This led to a discourse in which the representation of Oriental culture served to establish an exotic foreign Other against which America could define itself. If the East was indolent, ornamental, sensual, and dark, the West was hardworking, practical, morally conservative, and white. Mormons did not fit into these neat categories as they were perceived as indolent and sensual in character but they were clearly white in appearance. To resolve this seeming contradiction, Mormons were drawn figuratively, and sometimes literally, as Turks. By creating an exotic place and race for Mormons, Americans identified a shape and color of America that responded to nativist concerns of the time.

On December 15 1881, Ann Eliza Young, a famously divorced polygamous wife of Brigham Young, attended a Pittsburg production of *One Hundred Wives*. When a reporter asked her what she thought of it, she replied, "I think it will be one of the most valuable agents in the suppression of polygamy that we have yet known . . . At the period covered by the play—1856–1857—none of the incidents in this drama would have been impossible or unusual. The sensational parts of it are less thrilling than events of history."[73] Her response reveals the complexity of reading history from the margins. Much of the history of Mormon Americans, especially as they were represented on stage in the late nineteenth century is discontinuous. Their history also intersects with other individuals and groups on the fringes of American history—criminals, religious revivalists, suffragists, melodramatists, Native Americans, and utopian visionaries. Tracing the emergences of these marginalized histories and identifying moments where they merge, overlap, and collide is my core methodology.

My focus on the background provides an opportunity to both engage with history, and put mainstream American into sharp relief. Identity is performed in anti-Mormon melodramas as Mormon villains—rapists, murderers, and Turks—posed threats to the nation that were explored and then resolved in a way that upheld an enduring vision of nineteenth century America. Ann Eliza Young recognizes the tension between the popularly envisioned categories of Mormon and American in her interview. She simultaneously connects herself to the outside while aligning herself with the inside. Speaking as an authority for Mormon events in 1856–1857 (events which would have occurred when she was 12 years old) places her firmly as a member of the very group she is distancing herself from. Her comments, however, not only critique, but also advocate the "suppression" of polygamy and Mormonism. For Young, the power of performance is a "most valuable agent" for shaping public opinion. Rather than attempting to discover American identity by looking at it directly, then, this work takes a cue from Ann Eliza Young by looking at the performance of American identity in anti-Mormon melodrama.

1 The Christian Melodramatic Mode

> Dat is right, Lizy, trust in the Lord—he is our best friend—our only comforter.
>
> —Uncle Tom in *Uncle Tom's Cabin*

Owen Davis, a playwright at the turn of the nineteenth century, provided a tongue-in-cheek structural breakdown of melodrama that suggests why it has been critically disdained:

ACT I.—Start the trouble.
ACT II.—Here things look bad. The lady, having left home, is quite at the mercy of the Villain.
ACT III.—The lady is saved by the help of the Stage Carpenter. (The big scenic and mechanical effects were always in Act III.)
ACT IV.—The lovers are united and the villains are punished.[1]

The argument, no matter how it is wrapped, invariably reduces itself to what appears to be a critical disbelief that poorly (for the most part) written plays which elevated extreme sensationalism and sentimentality were the dominant dramatic form on two separate continents for nearly a century. As a result, early critics swing between harsh condemnation of the genre—and the "uneducated masses" who attended it—and a condescending attempt to recover the importance of the genre, despite its "obvious" lack of literary validity.[2]

Probably the first survey of melodrama was in a dissertation written by William S. Dye in 1919. Dye focused on melodrama in England in the early nineteenth century and his goal was to "supply some information about an almost unknown group of plays and playwrights."[3] Little changed in the next fifty years, with scholars such as Montrose J. Moses, Maurice Wilson, and Michael Booth each presenting his definition of melodrama, and defending the genre as important with examples drawn from a number of different plays. While the focus for each of these authors is different, the project remains the same: to bring to light an understudied, yet important period of theatre history by defining the genre and justifying its existence.[4]

The resulting perception of melodrama remained unchanged for years. Frank Rahill offered the following description of melodrama. Widely quoted by other scholars, it is a useful summary of the way in which melodrama was and is commonly viewed:

> Melodrama is a form of dramatic composition in prose partaking of the nature of tragedy, comedy, pantomime, and spectacle, and intended for a popular audience. Primarily concerned with situation and plot, it calls upon mimed action extensively and employs a more or less fixed compliment of stock characters, the most important of which are suffering heroine or hero, a persecuting villain, and a benevolent comic. It is conventionally oral and humanitarian in point of view and sentimental and optimistic in temper, concluding its fable happily with virtue rewarded after many trials and vice punished. Characteristically it offers elaborate scenic accessories and miscellaneous divertissements and introduces music freely, typically to underscore dramatic effect.[5]

While this critically reductive definition ignores much that does not fit into its delimitations, Rahill's observations are not unhelpful.

Contemporary conceptions of melodrama have expanded beyond Rahill to treat melodrama in its larger historical and literary contexts. The work of David Grimsted and Peter Brooks mark this shift in scholarship. For example, in his extensive look at American theatre 1800–1850, Grimsted suggests that melodrama provides a space to study cultural manifestations of early nineteenth-century America that were so pervasive to the society that they are nearly invisible to analysis. Sites of transgression are easier, he believes, to identify, but cannot exist without establishing the primary sacrosanct ideologies that dictate the form and content of melodrama. Grimsted moves past the survey model to delve into the specifics of American melodrama 1800–1850 and how the popularity of the form provides a unique document by which to examine American national identity.[6]

More recently, focus has shifted to examining the specific and detailed position of melodrama in larger historical, national, and cultural formations. Michael Hays and Anastasia Nikolopoulou suggest in their introduction to the critical anthology *Melodrama: The Cultural Emergence of a Genre* (1999) that "the generic mutability of melodrama is a sign that it responds more to historical than to aesthetic demands, no doubt because it occupied a space that, unlike tragedy and comedy, had no canonical history or status to limit it."[7] The tension articulated here is between examining melodrama as genre, beholden to specific aesthetic demands, but also as a mode of expression that functions within a specific historical moment.

Elaine Hadley addresses this tension by introducing what she calls the "melodramatic mode." She sees the genre as maintaining "familial narratives of dispersal and reunion, its emphatically visual renderings of bodily torture and criminal conduct, its atmospheric menace and providential plotting, its expressions of highly charged emotion, and its tendency to personify absolutes like "good and evil" but not restricted to the stage. Instead, for Hadley, the melodramatic mode is comprised of these features, which echo Rahill's early definition of melodrama, while simultaneously serving as a "polemical response to the social, economic, and epistemological changes" of early nineteenth-century market society in England.[8]

This articulation of a melodramatic mode resolves, in some way, the tension between genre and historical artifact and foregrounds the relationship between the two—melodramatic dramaturgical features are inseparably connected to melodrama's function in society.

Taking *Uncle Tom's Cabin* by George Aiken (1852) and *The Prophet* by Bayard Taylor (1874) as case studies reveals the ways in which the melodramatic genre intersected with the spiritual articulations of the Second Great Awakening in what might be considered the Christian melodramatic mode. These two plays represent a range in theatrical practice—one was a vastly popular stage production and the other a closet dramatic poem. They were written years apart, but were both written during what Bruce A. McConachie calls "business class theatre for the respectable."[9] Both plays also present strong visual images that responded to the American imagination. Jo-Ann Morgan suggests that the power of popular imagery is not a product *of* the consumer, but a product *for* the consumer. As a result, the product is created to fulfill the expectations of the patron wherein "tastemakers protect cultural hegemony."[10] As plays with very clear moral agendas, *Uncle Tom's Cabin* and *The Prophet* presented images that conformed to social issues already in circulation. Most importantly, both plays evidence the melodramatic poetic justice, moral polarity, and spectacle that also appeared in religious performance.

Elaborating on the religious attitude of the nation builds on an observation already familiar in sociology and religious studies. Robert H. Abzug points out that recent trends in these fields concentrate on finding political or economic conditions to explain the connections between social change and religion. He argues, however:

> We can only understand reformers if we try to comprehend the sacred significance they bestowed upon these worldly arenas. For even as some of today's scholars glean mostly 'secular' significance from religion, the antebellum reformer saw mainly transcendent meanings in politics, society, and the economy.[11]

Examining the junctures of religion during the Second Great Awakening and melodrama on the nineteenth-century stage reveals the performative nature of religious expression and the Christian rhetoric of melodramatic performance. It becomes clear that plays like *Uncle Tom's Cabin* and religious revivalism are melodramatic modes responding to the dominant discourse of the Second Great Awakening.

UNCLE TOM'S CABIN AND THE SECOND GREAT AWAKENING

For over thirty years, Reverend Ludovicus Weld (1766–1844) was the minister of the Hampton, Connecticut Congregational Church. A strict orthodox, Weld led both his parishioners and his family in the traditions of earlier

Calvinists. He preached basic Congregationalist traditions: individualism (each congregation was headed by Christ alone, and was not mediated by any earthly organization), education (Harvard, Yale, Williams, Amherst, Oberlin, and other universities were founded by Congregationalists), and democracy (each member of a congregation had equal voice to decide its own form of worship). In 1821, he was selected by the Connecticut State Legislature to deliver the annual election-day sermon, which he entitled *The Kingdom of Grace Merits Universal Patronage.*

This sermon was a part of Connecticut's election-day events. Those selected for the honor were expected to speak to the events current to the election and also to the more universal responsibilities of the people as Christian citizens. Preached on election day, then widely published, the Election Day Sermon served as a reminder that the nation was built on Christian principles and provided regular reassertions of the common belief that a nation well-instructed in biblical politics would be preserved from the tyranny and corruption of nations that ignored God's laws.

In his 1821 sermon, Weld stated that: "[The earth] was designed as a theatre on which to display sovereign mercy in redeeming and preparing a people for the Lord."[12] The metaphor suggested here, the earth as a theatre upon which humans play divinely appointed parts, resonated with American society in the nineteenth century on a number of levels. Weld's dramatic vision was meant to prompt citizens to engage in their God-ordained rights to self-government, but the sermon's collapse of performance and piety also becomes an engaging way of looking at the religious worldview that dominated early nineteenth-century American thought and behavior. Abzug describes the impact of American religions on society as the logical extension of America's belief in this "cosmic theater" of God articulated by Weld.[13]

In this theatrical metaphor, human life on earth is a play written by God whose cast is all humankind and divine figures. The paradise of Eden is the first act and humankind's current state is the second. Only God the Director knows how long the play will last, how and when the third act will be ushered in, and how the finale will be concluded. The Bible serves as prompter's notes, and earthly church organizations are stage managers who try to keep the actors on schedule and playing the correct parts. Abzug concludes that for most Christian Americans at the time, "the cosmic drama lent a sacred framework to existence."[14] The subject matter of Weld's lecture, and its delivery as part of a civic tradition, point to the way in which religion pervaded nineteenth-century American society. It suggests how theatre as a generic form held such power in popular culture to be the most appropriate metaphor to describe God's plan on earth.

Beginning a century earlier, America went through a series of religious reforms, or awakenings, that culminated in the greatest explosion of heterodoxies in American history.[15] The 30-year period between 1830–1860 is commonly called the Second Great Awakening—a self-named revival movement whose message of social reform converted the nation. Early religious enthusiasm in upstate New York and backcountry New England developed simultaneously with camp meeting preaching in Kentucky, Tennessee, and the Carolinas.[16] By 1850, over 25% of the American population belonged to a church, a disproportionate increase from 7% only 50 years earlier.[17] The success of the revival in the reform spirit of New England, the development of new populist religions, and the demonstrations of Southern camp meetings led to efforts to spread religion to the frontier.

The revival message, the process by which it was preached throughout America, and the obstacles it encountered illuminate a number of issues in American culture that were in transformation in the nineteenth century. The Second Great Awakening, however, was not the only arena where these concerns were being explored. Melodrama and the religious revival of the second half of the nineteenth century are intimately engaged; both religious and stage performances evidence the same style, structure, concerns, and solutions. Religious practice borrowed melodramatic structure and staging techniques, and religious rhetoric of the time is shaped in a distinctly melodramatic style. Examining one of the most celebrated works of this period reveals this Christian melodramatic mode.

The publication of Harriet Beecher Stowe's work *Uncle Tom's Cabin* in 1852 was a literary phenomenon. Its immense success and the lack of copyright laws led to numerous versions of the play, which toured widely for decades. Biographer Forrest Wilson notes, "From the autumn of 1852 until 1931, at least, *Uncle Tom's Cabin* was never 'off the boards' in America." Within months of the publication of the novel, stage productions were mounted—at least nine different versions played in theatres before the Civil War; the version by George Aiken, who initially wrote the play in 1852, has gained a reputation as the definitive stage version.[18]

Thomas Gossett, in his work on *Uncle Tom's Cabin* and American culture, suggests that "Perhaps as many as fifty people would eventually see *Uncle Tom's Cabin*, the play, for every one person who would read the novel."[19] However, as Jeffrey Mason effectively argues, it is impossible to trace the order of the experience for audiences; "one could not see the play without reference, direct or by reputation, to the novel, and vice versa, so of the discourse in which Aiken's play was embedded, the dominant text was the play's immensely popular source."[20] The circulation between page and stage is one that is dominated by not only the necessary plot reductions and changes to make the novel a viable theatre piece, but also the changes in form from novel to melodrama.[21]

The move from a sentimental novel to a reform melodrama was made easier by the heightened emotion that ran through both forms. Sarah Meer argues that moral drama of the 1850s capitalized on the tight control melodrama had on audience reaction by using "stark morality and sensational effects" with the same goal that the sentimental novel manipulated emotion—for didactic purposes. As a result, "The melodramatic patterns of virtue and villainy were used to dramatize the issues championed by benevolent movements, and spectatorial pleasure was tempered with moral evangelism, enabling a pious and decorous enjoyment of the dramatic."[22] Here, Meer articulates the deeply entwined threads of religion, emotion, and drama that Stowe records as the conception of her work.

Stowe was the daughter of one of the most powerful voices of religious awakening, Lyman Beecher, a Congregational Minister. Raised in a strict religious environment, she taught at the Western Female Institute, which her sister founded, until her 1834 marriage to widower Calvin Stowe, a Biblical Literature professor at Lane Seminary in Cincinnati. In her 1878 introduction to the book, Stowe describes the writing process in the third person: "From that time the story can less be said to have been composed by her than imposed upon her. Scenes, incidents, conversations rushed upon her with a vividness and importunity that would not be denied. The book insisted upon getting itself into being, and would take no denial."[23] She makes it clear that her artistic expression was an extension of her religious beliefs.

Daniel Gerould, in his introduction to George Aiken's melodramatic adaptation, suggests that Stowe's claim that God dictated her work was remarkable: "No ordinary [author] would acknowledge as co-author the Almighty!"[24] Yet, if Stowe is to be believed, her novel was not a melodrama, or even a work a fiction, but was instead a divine revelation. The "melodramatic" world of the play was, according to Stowe, not an overt construction of a popular sentiment, but a reflection of a particularly religious worldview. John Frick underlines this point of view when he suggests that:

> [M]oral reform was the foundation upon which social reform rested and the majority of the early social reformers were theoretically trained religions leaders. Hence, evolving from common roots in American religion, for many years social and moral reforms were, for all practical purposes, virtually indistinguishable. In this context, such revered nineteenth-century long-running box office hits as *Uncle Tom's Cabin* . . . were thus both moral *and* social treatises.[25]

In the conclusion of her book, Stowe explains that she was moved to write after her encounters with fugitive slaves in Ohio. She recounts that when she heard religious Northerners debating whether it was their duty to return slaves to their home states, she thought, "These men and Christians cannot know what slavery is; if they did, such a question could never be open for discussion. And from this arose a desire to exhibit it in a living dramatic reality."[26] The transition of the story from page to stage emphasized "dramatic reality" and provided an even more realistic vehicle for the narrative through innovative theatrical spectacle.

The translation from page to stage, however, was impacted by restrictions in the generic form of melodrama. Mason argues that:

Stowe traced the quest for human value within the destructive oppression of slavery, while Aiken followed the stylized mumming of simplified characters within the neat limits of melodrama . . . Melodrama itself is a means to incarnate and expiate its audience's fear; "evil" is the name of those fears, and the villain is its agent. The villain must die to lay fear to rest, and virtue must triumph to affirm the world view that melodrama's audience cherishes and to restore the moral order.[27]

While many contemporary scholars tease out the exceptions to this rule, not only in *Uncle Tom's Cabin,* but also in the wide range of melodramas that played throughout the century, most invariably return to the dominance of this form and its three key elements: poetic justice, moral polarity, and spectacle.

POETIC JUSTICE AND REFORM

One of the major doctrinal messages of the Second Great Awakening was the social function of religion, and melodramas of the nineteenth century frequently promoted reform. These plays and the revival movement that inspired them were significant vehicles for the message of religious action in daily practice, action that was guaranteed rewards both on stage and in heaven. The Christian melodramatic mode is defined by this poetic justice—both religion and melodrama required personal action in the face of external forces that dictated what can be done. Rosemarie Bank argues that:

> [P]oetic justice is the cardinal ethical tenet of melodrama, indeed that poetic justice is a structural necessity in melodrama (that is, melodrama dos not exist as a form without it.) Since poetic justice is a statement about the world as it ought to be, the action of melodrama may actually reward virtue and punish vice, or simply establish the premise that this is the way things ought to be in the world.[28]

Poetic justice is a social phenomenon, one that confirms an idealized vision of society. This same vision of the possibilities of how things ought to be in the world was fundamental to a Christian worldview. Clear and eternal rewards and punishments were a daily part of American life during the Second Great Awakening.

Leaders of the revival like Charles Grandison Finney, Lyman Beecher, and Theodore Weld promoted a code of personal conduct marked by self-restraint and modesty. They established institutions, churches, schools, missions, to implement the code, and organized aggressive proselytizing programs to disseminate it.[29] Revival leaders provided their congregants with a firm belief that "their way of life was God's way for all men."[30] As a result, it was a Christian's duty to alter society to fit God's prescribed code of conduct.

The great reform movements of mid to late nineteenth-century New England were intimately bound up with the message of the revival. Suffrage, temperance, and especially abolition became not just social concerns, but religious ones. These same concerns were topics for popular melodramas of the day.

Mark Twain, in his collected writings from 1868–1871, *Contributions to the Galaxy,* suggested the impact of drama in teaching religious reform: "It is almost fair and just to aver (although it is profanity) that nine-tenths of all the kindness and forbearance and Christian charity and generosity in the hearts of the American people today, got there by being filtered down from their fountain-head, the gospel of Christ, through dramas and tragedies and comedies on the stage . . . ."[31] Joining novels, stories, home journals, and newspapers, theatre became a site for promoting social reform through poetic justice as stories of warning (in which the lack of reform leads to disaster) and reward (in which reform guarantees a happy ending).

City mystery dramas, like those featuring Mose the Bowry B'hoy, dealt with the growing violence of the big city. Thomas de Walden's *The Upper Ten and Lower Twenty* (1854), was one of the most popular of this genre and followed the downfall of a betrayed husband to alcoholism and debauchery in some of New York's most notorious neighborhoods. Domestic melodrama was an even more popular trend that reinforced correct female behavior, the primacy of the American family, and the absolute necessity of pastoral female morality as the anchor of that family. Temperance plays evidence their clear reform agenda, with titles like *Ruined by Drink; In Four Acts, Marry No Man If He Drinks,* and *The Fatal Glass; or, The Curse of Drink.*[32]

Rosemarie Bank foregrounds the specificity of each of these forms and reminds that "a play can extol the very democratic virtues it subverts, urge conformity to social values it both lauds and undermines, and appeal to the diverse membership historians have classified as the antebellum middle class." As a result, melodrama is "not a fixed position—a political, social, or even moral testament—but a way of acting and a legitimation of performing outside as well as inside the playhouses."[33] Bank's focus here on acting and performance broadly construed, as well as the complex and inconsistent moral messages of melodrama suggests the primacy of personal action both in the melodramatic form and in nineteenth-century daily life.

Preachers of the Second Great Awakening taught that mankind had already been forgiven by grace and could achieve forgiveness by reaching out to God. Led by the prolific and dominant voice of Charles Finney, denominations participating in the revival of the Second Great Awakening reminded believers that because of God's grace, humankind owed primary allegiance to him. National harmony was achieved then, not due to an acknowledgement of governmental control, but to obeisance to a higher code of moral beliefs and ethical practices.

As a result, a Christian's civic duty was absorbed by two consequential functions of revivalism that impacted reform movements of the period. The first is a conservative demand to identify and maintain what is good in society through institutional and legal restraints. The second is the frequently radical imperative to correct, abolish, or reform those aspects of society that are contrary to God's will.[34] This theology not only promoted, but required individual action—a revival principle that also figures into the action-driven plots of melodrama.

Bayard Taylor, journalist, author and poet, wrote his play *The Prophet* in 1874 as a dramatic poem about the development of a new American religion. In his writings, he is unclear as to which religion he is illustrating, but proposed that the play was "designed only to represent phases of spiritual development and their external results, which are hardly possible in any other country than ours," which suggests that he is writing about an exclusively American religion.[35] If David Starr was a young prophet in America, it seems reasonable to assume that Taylor was at least aware of the life of Joseph Smith who, like the fictional Starr, received visions to establish a new church, quickly gained followers, built a temple, introduced the doctrine of polygamy, and then was martyred in defense of his faith.[36] Additionally, contemporary reviews of the works all draw a Mormon connection. A reviewer in *The Boston Daily Advertiser* points out that "the insidents [sic] of the poem are suggestive in a general way of facts in the history of the rise of the Mormon sect"[37] while the reviewer in *The Daily Inter Ocean* (Chicago) is more pointed:

> "*The Prophet* is a dramatic poem, of the rise and early history of Mormonism ... The disguise of the leading characters is—as was intended—very transparent. David Starr is Joe Smith, though a much more sincere and noble man; Nimrod Kraft is Brigham Young, a singular compound of intelligence, resolution, cunning, and a sort of religious enthusiasm which sometimes passes for religion, but is a very different thing."[38]

Whether Taylor intended or not, *The Prophet* was taken by readers and reviewers as an anti-Mormon play.

The Prophet follows the rise and fall of prophet David Starr, who is visited by angels who instruct him to organize a new religion. Starr's marriage to his childhood sweetheart Rhoda is complicated by a subsequent revelation to establish the practice of polygamy and to take another wife. The play is uniquely written in iambic pentameter verse and was published as a "poem" rather than a script for performance. It is also unusual in its portrayal of the prophet, Starr, as a truly visionary man, misunderstood by non-believers and led astray in later years by an evil advisor, Nimrod Kraft. The play ends with Starr's assassination, but not before he renounces polygamy. Kraft, however, vows to uphold all of the prophet's revelations and as the curtain closes, steals all of the sect's wealth and escapes from the mob to reestablish the church in a far-away land.

The journey of Starr resonates with the lives of several early reformers of the Second Great Awakening: Joseph Smith certainly, but also Charles

Finney, Henry Miller, Sarah and Angelina Grimké, John Humphrey Noyes, and Mother Ann Lee. Each of these reformers took responsibility for correcting the misconceptions they perceived in Christianity and set about to re-envision religion through their actions. Livia, Starr's second wife in *The Prophet* is overt in her articulation of the importance of this personal responsibility:

> I live at last! 'Twas more than love inspired
> This counter-plot, though love like mine were more
> Than cause and needful spur. I love and move,
> Bid others live and play the parts I set,
> Concentrate petty force to one end
> Which grandly must succeed, or grandly fail,—
> But, either way, I act![39]

Livia might as well have been speaking to the reform spirit of the nineteenth century that required believers to "act!"

Melodrama is generally perceived as driven by this notion of correct moral action, the conflict between righteous desires and sinful complications. Just as nineteenth-century Christianity taught that mankind's fate has already been determined by Christ's sacrifice that allowed grace to save to the world, so was the fate of the melodramatic hero predetermined by the structure. In melodrama good triumphs as evil is overcome; it is this poetic justice that is one of the marks of the melodramatic genre. In the late nineteenth century, Christianity taught the similar message that every human can partake of God's grace if they but withstand temptations to make use of the foregone conclusion—righteousness leads to heaven.

On the melodramatic stage, religious sentiment was perhaps even more visible in the climax and resolution. On stage, realistic dangers to the heroes and heroines were invariably resolved by miraculous feats of rescue and intervention. Both the effects themselves and the resolutions that the effects were contrived to achieve pointed to the miraculous events of everyday life and the continual presence of a higher power in the trials and the rewards of individual action. The clear character delineations of good and evil supported this vision as the good, who were God-fearing and humble, found salvation through extraordinary means. The evil, who might temporarily triumph through a misuse of power or position, were always overcome in the end by a providential punishment.

In *The Prophet*, the poetic justice of the ending seems entirely missing—David Starr, the melodramatic hero, is killed by the Army. The villain of the piece, Nimrod Kraft, escapes capture at the end of the play and vows that "Zion lives and shall be strong, through me!"[40] Looking at this ending through the lens of eternal rewards and punishments, however, reveals that poetic justice does in fact prevail. Starr's greatest guilt is his ability to be swayed into immoral action by stronger characters, but he goes to his death a changed man. Once he realizes that his people plan on defending him against the army, he decides to give his own life up instead. His decision comes in a conversation with his wife Rhoda. In remembering moments from their life together, Starr recounts two different episodes where they witnessed natural wonders—the beauty of the sky, the power of a storm—and that in these miracles, he saw and spoke to God.

These moments of divine intervention contextualize his decision to become a martyr for his people. He reassures Rhoda: "Fret not for me: my body must be as dead/Before my soul is verily alive."[41] His death at the end of the play, rather than being read as a punishment, is in fact his salvation and a higher reward. Rhoda, as the heroine is also rewarded. While her husband is no longer with her physically, his decision to abandon attachment to his second wife allows Rhoda to exult that "He is all mine at last!"[42]

The escape of Nimrod Kraft is more complex as there is not even a hint of punishment for his sins (manipulation of Starr, support of polygamy as a means for rampant immorality, murder, theft) during the action of the play. As reviews of the play recognize, however, Kraft is but a thinly veiled Brigham Young. Published just three years before Young's death, the play assumes a recognition of the long and eventful life of Kraft/Young in Salt Lake City. Kraft prophesies of this future that, to the audience, was a past and present reality:

> We will submit, in all external forms,
> Even to the Gentiles; then in secret pass
> The river, bearing our most precious goods
> Beyond their reach: our spies have gone abroad,
> And found another Eshcol in the West.
> Within our hands lies all we builded [sic] here,
> And they, upheld by faith, shall build again![43]

Kraft cannot be punished in this *The Prophet* because his villainy extended beyond the world of the play into extended representation in other media and into real life. His actions in the play serve as a background to the already-excepted popular image of Brigham Young as a villain.

The centrality of individual action to both melodramas and Christian reform points to a paradox of agency: while a believer is free to choose good from evil in daily practice, several new religions illuminated a connection to the divine in which believers were literally compelled to righteousness. Many leaders of new churches perceived their callings as prophets to be the result of an outside vision that required action and allowed for no choice but obedience.[44] In melodrama external force is always bounded by the world of the play—natural disaster, the machinations of the villain, or misplaced evidence. The melodramatic form is therefore action-centered and compels moral choice on the part of its characters. The Christian melodramatic mode suggests the compunction of moral choice on and off the stage as new church leaders of the Second Great Awakening received a religious call that could not be avoided or changed.

The Shakers, for example, were led by Quaker "Mother Ann" Lee, the female second coming of Christ, whose visions prompted her to lead her followers from England to New York, where they established communities based on New Testament principles and celibacy. John Humphrey Noyes's spiritual witness of personal sinlessness prompted his establishment of the Oneida Perfectionists, while James and Ellen White received visions that helped to guide their establishment of the Seventh Day Adventists.

In his autobiographical history, Joseph Smith states clearly that the miraculous event that prompted his establishment of the Church of Jesus Christ of Latter-day Saints was an outside superhuman intrusion on life:

> I had actually seen a light, and in the midst of that light I saw two Personages, and they did in reality speak to me; and though I was hated and persecuted for saying that I had seen a vision, yet it was true; and while they were persecuting me, reviling me, and speaking all manner of evil against me falsely for so saying, I was led to say in my heart: Why persecute me for telling the truth? I have actually seen a vision; and who am I that I can withstand God, or why does the world think to make me deny what I have actually seen? For I had seen a vision; I knew it, and I knew that God knew it, and I could not deny it, neither dared I do it.[45]

Smith's entire life and eventual death were melodramatic rather than tragic if his calling is read as a miraculous event that intervened in his life.

While Smith's experiences suggest a melodramatic vision of God's interaction with humankind, the doctrine of his Church is still absolutely grounded in personal responsibility for choosing right and avoiding evil. The emphasis on salvation through grace in Christ after all a person can do is similar across almost all of the heterodoxies of the Second Great Awakening. Here, once again, Christian life is part of the melodramatic mode. Characters in plays can be defined by how they act in the face of conflict and disruption. Tragedy and comedy are similar: whether characters accept the terrible society despite itself (tragedy) or accept terrible society because it is silly not to (comedy), society is always, in the end, accepted as it is. Melodrama, on the other hand, is unique in that the very structure requires the hero to either change society or be radically changed within that society. The function of change is central to the reform message of nineteenth century heterodoxies and the necessary action that leads a melodramatic character to poetic justice.

In the late nineteenth century, American urban reforms were centered on two areas. The first issue was health, which led to reevaluations of social medical practice and individual diets and the national spread of the temperance message. It also impacted religious organization with the establishment of churches such as Christian Scientist, and with the emergence of divine healing as a central feature of worship. The second issue was equality—racial (abolitionism), economic (labor reforms), and gender (suffrage). Abzug argues that "radical reformers sought to make American society holy by broadening and sacralizing the meaning of equality, by making sacred the details of everyday life, and by reimagining the basic structure of society on earth and spiritual being after death."[46] Early churches are melodramatic as they were led by visionaries who either drastically changed society or who were drastically changed themselves as they reimagined American society.

While many reformers looked outward for change, others looked inward with the establishment of radical communities that attempted to fundamentally alter American public and private systems. Some, such as the Shakers and the Mormons, established socialist governments where all goods were held in common by the group. Others, such as the Seventh Day Adventists, lobbied against Sabbatarian laws that established Sunday as America's day of rest. The Shakers, with their doctrines of celibacy, and the Oneida Perfectionists, with their concept of complex marriage, attempted to reform marriage practices.[47]

Charles Finney is perhaps the most well-known revivalist of the age. He preached a doctrine of sanctification that consisted of subordinating every aspect of life to God. A Presbyterian lawyer, Finney one day experienced a radical conversion he would later call the "baptism of the Holy Ghost" that prompted his entrance into the ministry. Never formally trained as a preacher, Finney began conducting revivals in upstate New York. His message was simple: a Christian will have "not a mere *desire* to do good but a willing good, a benevolence that controls his conduct, that is active, blessed, godlike."[48] His establishments of "New Measures" were intended to promote this controlling benevolence. They included an "anxious bench" where believers could sit and publicly announce their sin, and "excitements," or reactions to an outpouring of the Holy Spirit that led to fainting, weeping, and other uncontrollable physical manifestations. For Finney, the goal of faith was universal reformation.

The work of reformers that were inspired by the revival message of the Second Great Awakening necessarily encountered obstacles to their messages. The radical feminists and abolitionists Sarah and Angelina Grimké, for example, were disfellowshipped from their Quaker community and publicly denounced from Congregationalist pulpits for their message of equality for women and slaves. Angelina made it clear, however, that their message was not socially motivated, but was part of their testimonies of Christ: "Whatever is morally right for a man to do, it is morally right for a woman to do. I recognize no rights but *human* rights—I know nothing of men's rights and women's rights; for in Christ Jesus, there is neither male nor female."[49] Reform was a religious calling that required individual change. The melodramatic mode requires external forces in the world of the play that push characters to change.

In his work on formula stories as literature, John G. Cawelti suggests that formulaic genres, such as those in melodramas, are predominant in culture because of a "network of assumptions" that balances the needs and values audiences seek in literature with a work's impact on them and their culture. Formulas, then, can be analyzed for the ways in which they "become collective cultural products" by the extent to which "they successfully articulate a pattern of fantasy that is at least acceptable to if not preferred by the cultural groups who enjoy them."[50] In other words, nineteenth-century audiences enjoyed melodrama because they knew exactly what it was they would get of the experience—action that compelled moral choice that was rewarded materially and spiritually.

This analysis of melodrama might suggest a detachment of audience engagement, since they already knew what would happen. Cawelti, however, points out that the success of the formula is based on the variations within the expectation. With staged melodrama, for example, plots that slavishly meet genre standards and bring nothing new to the form are uninteresting because the audience has no need to realign their thinking to account for the alterations. Plots that radically alter the pattern and either reverse or ignore the expectations are unfulfilling because the audience cannot trust what is being presented. It is only those works that creatively reinterpret the journey to the expected end that allow audiences to both engage in the work, and feel rewarded for their efforts. The complex use of poetic justice in *The Prophet* is one example of a radical reinterpretation of the form that still upholds the expectations of the genre.

One of the reasons that melodrama remained so popular for so long is the way in which its structure allows for the genre to be manipulated. In every play, audiences could expect the world would be presented as it should be, and the effects would be spectacular. In the same way, audiences knew what to expect from their Christian lives: an eternal reward with spectacular effects for the good, and a spectacularly dark (and hot) punishment for the evil. The life journey of a believer and the exciting plot twists and turns in melodrama, however, were unexpected.

The Christian melodramatic mode reveals how society in the late nineteenth century paid close attention to varieties of daily life, but were less concerned with the outcome, which was dictated by their personal actions. The reform movements that grew out of religious sentiment promoted personal action that articulated the same actions on stage as characters dealt with external forces through great heroics. In both life and on stage, these actions were rewarded or punished according to poetic justice. Moral polarity, the strict division of good and evil in character that leads to poetic justice, is also a central aspects to the structure of both melodrama and religious conversion.

MORAL POLARITY AND CONVERSION

Revivalists gained converts in a variety of ways: some joined new churches after much study and conversation while others were struck by the Holy Spirit in an instantaneously life-changing experience. In both cases, however, conversion was a highly individual event where God spoke directly to a sincere believer in a clear pattern of recognition, confirmation, and action. This process of conversion resonates with melodramas, and while the theatrical terms to describe the process are different, the intent is the same. In melodrama, moral polarity is the function of neatly dividing characters into virtuous or wicked types. The character type then has a material repercussion in the world of the play through poetic justice, the system of fixed rewards or punishments. The doctrines of revival churches preached an identical worldview of righteousness, wickedness, rewards, and punishments. The structure of the Christian melodramatic mode is based on the development of this pattern and by the dramaturgical elements of moral polarity and poetic justice.

On the subject of moral polarity, Mason argues, "The ideal model is so clearly and firmly drawn that it virtually mandates an opposite, a dark, alternative model known as 'evil' and defined as whatever diverges from virtue."[51] Even McConachie, whose work traces the specific shift of melodramatic formations across time, maintains his analysis in the framework of traditional melodramatic conventions. In fairy-tale melodramas of the early nineteenth century, for example, McConachie suggests that "melodramatic villainy is close indeed to 'neoplatonic evil' that seeks to tear down paternalistic utopia." He reframes moral polarity in his discussion of later nineteenth-century reform melodramas: "The villains of these melodramas act out of irrational passion and urge immediate gratification on their victims; in effect, they embody the opposite attribute of the man of principle."[52] The reason for the villainy may have shifted with the sea of socio-economic changes across the century, but the villain remains and serves as the absolute foil to the hero and the good.

Early converts during the Second Great Awakening were culled from a number of specific locations across the country. The busiest of these was the "Burned-Over District" of upstate New York, a series of small villages who were visited frequently and with much fervor by traveling preachers. Finney gave the name to the district after it proved a target for revivalists who flooded in to preach to the growing working class communities that sprang up during the construction of the Erie Canal. A number of innovative religions were founded by lay-people from the Burned-Over District, including Mormonism, the Millerites, and the Fox sisters of Hydesville, New York who conducted the first table-rapping séances that grew into the Spiritualism movement.

The converts to all of these movements went through a process that convinced them to change their lives to follow the new message of the gospel. For example, early readers of the Book of Mormon were invited to gain their own spiritual witness of the work. The end of the book records this promise:

> Behold, I would exhort you that when ye shall read these things . . . ponder it in your hearts. And when ye shall receive these things, I would exhort you that ye would ask God, the Eternal Father, in the

name of Christ, if these things are not true; and if ye shall ask with a sincere heart, with real intent, having faith in Christ, *he will manifest the truth* of it unto you, by *the power of the Holy Ghost.*[53]

This passage suggests that reading and studying the Book of Mormon will bring recognition of the truth, which will then be confirmed by supernatural means. This expectation of manifestations by a higher power marked conversion to many revival churches. Finally, inherent in confirmation is the requirement to act upon it through formally declaring oneself a member of the religion through baptism or other initiatory rites.

One of the most common signposts of melodrama is a very obvious dramaturgical structure: exposition, inciting moment, rising action, climax and resolution. The exposition sets the stage, introduces the audience to the major players in the piece, and provides any necessary background information. The inciting moment is the introduction of the conflict around which the plot evolves. Rising action is the series of encounters that further the conflict and heighten the dramatic stakes. These are resolved in the end in a climax, which in melodrama frequently called for an act of violence. Finally, the play is resolved and the loose ends are tied up. This dramaturgical structure is not unique to melodrama; Greek tragedy, well-made plays, and even some works of Shakespeare follow this model.[54]

It also mirrors a similar pattern documented by Second Great Awakening Christians—the pattern of conversion. During this time of spirituality that evidenced itself in very public ways, conversion was a community experience. Believers gained their initial conviction of sinfulness after hearing the word preached to a congregation. This word, in addition to the religious information gathered by believers through their own Bible study, provided an exposition to conversion. After being prompted by the Holy Spirit, a believer would be overcome—an inciting incident that set the process of conversion into action. This was followed by a long period of inner conflict and resolution, which made up the body of the conversion experience, and climaxed in a sense of spiritual release, or what the Presbyterians called "comfort."

Once converted, a believer's life became dictated by rules of morality and justice that helped guide Christians towards their final resolution at the Day of Judgment—to be selected for eternal bliss in heaven or endless torment in hell. The linked concepts of moral polarity and poetic justice are melodramatic representations of the Christian concepts being preached at the time—humans were literally torn between God and Satan and the way in which they responded to this pull would affect their eternal reward of heaven or hell. Therefore, the melodramatic characters that were drawn as either wholly good or evil are not so much "overdrawn" as they are representative of the idealized human state.

Jeffrey Mason makes this case in his analysis of *Uncle Tom's Cabin*, where he suggests that the extended tableaux that end each act were:

allegorical images to accentuate the message that action and dialogue have conveyed . . . This does not mean that the play lacked subtlety or that the audience was unduly dense; it means, rather that the form placed ideas and their delineation in the foreground, rather than attempting to imply them in a more delicate fashion according to the values that naturalistic or realistic representation assumes.[55]

In *The Prophet*, Starr's death reveals a similar foregrounding of ideas as his last words reaffirm the social norm of monogamy and fidelity. With his dying breath, Starr asks first for forgiveness then fixes the central message of the play:

> Lord, Lord, be merciful! no time is left!
> I see no more—but yes! One blessed face:
> 'T is yours!—you're with me, Rhoda!—*you*, my
> love!

Then, the stage directions recount, "he turns towards RHODA as he speaks, and falls upon her breast, with his arms hanging over her shoulders . . . Clasping DAVID to her breast, she sinks slowly down at the foot of the altar."[56] The combined language and stage picture makes the moral idea and its delineation clear: monogamy is right and polygamy is wrong. The final tableau of Rhoda, cradling her husband in her arms in front of a religious alter evokes the sanctity of the *pieta*, which in turn emphasizes physically the already-drawn discursive parallels between Starr and Jesus Christ.

Historical records of the period discussed new religions in a similar way—emphasizing the binary between good and evil. Believers and detractors alike framed their records of the origins of the churches, their doctrine, and their growth throughout the century, in terms of this melodramatic binary. Leaders of established religions saw the splinter groups as either misled (as opposed to divinely guided) or in the extreme, non-Christian. For example, in 1894 the Quaker publication "Friends Review" ran an essay competition. The published preface to Joel Bean's entry essay clarified that the point of the competition was to answer the question "Why am I a Friend?" in a way that showed how Quakerism differentiates itself from all other religions in history. Bean responded that Quakerism is different because it is the "highest ground reached by Protestantism in the direction of spiritual Christianity," and he won first place.[57] The Mormons, Campbellites, Stoneites, Shakers, and Adventists, to name a few, all perceived themselves as faithful Christians who had seen the light of Christ's true gospel against the dark hegemonic powers of established religions who had been led astray. There seemed to be no room in religious historical records for religions that were not either heroes or villains.

The same is true in melodrama—moral polarity dictates characters that unfailingly fit into stock categories of hero, heroine, villain, or comic sidekick. To take *Uncle Tom's Cabin* as an example, Uncle Tom is the hero of the piece, and both little Eva and Eliza are the heroines. Both Tom and Eva are rewarded for their goodness in the spectacular final scene of the play where they are taken up to heaven. The Aiken version describes the scene:

> *Gorgeous clouds, tinted with sunlight. Eva, robed in white, is discovered on the back of a milk-white dove, with expanded wings, as if just soaring upward. Her hands are extended in a benediction of St. Clare and Uncle Tom who are kneeling and gazing up to her. Expressive music. Slow curtain. END.*[58]

Simon Legree is the villain of the piece, entirely evil, who is punished in the end when he is arrested by officers of the law for murder and killed while trying to escape them, an end which is significantly heightened from the novel wherein Legree simply disappears towards the end of the narrative.

Intersecting this playwriting imperative of heroes and villains with religious discourse of the period suggests that another way of envisioning polarized characters is as religious allegories. The revival preachers that dominated American Christian life made great use of stories to teach their messages. In his discussion of religious teaching styles, Grant Wacker illustrates how brief topical stories about audience members, vernacular retellings of Biblical events, and allegorical stories functioned as some of the major means of spiritual instruction.[59] In this light, the allegorical characters in melodrama can be viewed as representations of the larger religious concepts of good and evil.

To audiences familiar with allegory as a teaching style, melodramatic moral polarity was a comprehensible trope and its meaning was perceptible on a number of levels. Characters functioned both as ideal humans in the world of the play, and as personified virtues and vices representative of the morals of the Second Great Awakening. Melodramatic characters echo the concepts preached in the revival call for humanity's obedience to strict commandments and the vision of obedience's eternal reward. Moral polarity justified an audience's assumption that righteousness and obedience to a strict sense of Christian ethics would in fact bring material rewards by a God whose hand was clear in every aspect of human life. This was especially true for the growing number of religious converts from the immigrant and lower classes.

SPECTACLE AND POPULISM

What is remarkable about the religious innovators of the Second Great Awakening, and the majority of their converts, is their uniformly working-class background. The gospel taught by Finney and other revival preachers blended popular religion with what Davies identified as the rise in working-class audiences at melodramas. The audiences of the Christian melodramatic mode reveal a national trend towards social populism that was articulated in the spectacle used by churches and on stage.

Religion and art both reflected a larger class struggle of the century that was initiated with the election of Andrew Jackson in 1828. Jackson inaugurated a shift in politics and social development in America that remained until the end of the century, as he became the first president *not* to come from a wealthy and well-known colonial family. Jackson's rise from poor small-town boy to soldier to land speculator to President was celebrated at his raucous inaugural party that was open to the public. His unpolished public persona set a tone of free access and enterprise that typified the attitude of the age.

The policies of Jackson's tenure, connected with the rapid-expansion policy of Manifest Destiny, created an almost mythic expression of individualism. He established policies for rotation of terms in government and supported initiatives for national roadways to connect the nation. Most radically, he publicly spoke out in favor of returning the government to the common people.[60] The attitudes established by Jackson remained a force throughout the rest of the century and his polity suggested ways to unite large working class communities. Theatre audiences expanded not just to include, but celebrate the common people, while religious revivalism targeted converts among the poor.

Nathan Hatch suggests that religion underwent a significant shift away from being an established upper class institution to becoming a popular event:

> At the very time that British clergy were confounded by their own gentility in trying to influence working-class culture, America exalted religious leaders short on social graces, family connections, and literary education. These religious activists pitched their messages to the unschooled and unsophisticated.[61]

The mid century witnessed a surge of these common folk as pastors, preachers, or even founders of religions. Many of these preachers supported their own validity with doctrinal connections between humility, and poverty. "Communion," for example, promoted egalitarianism; Finney preached the actual possibility of perfect sanctification on earth that erased the need for an intermediary between a believer and God.

Hatch suggests that several of these sects (including Mormons, Baptists, and black churches) were in fact founded on theologies that offered poor people a compelling vision of "individual self-respect and collective self-confidence."[62] Joseph Smith, for example, was a fourteen-year-old boy with little education from a poor family when he reported the vision upon which he founded The Church of Jesus Christ of Latter-day Saints.[63] The rhetoric he records as God's word in the *Doctrine and Covenants* particularly favors not just the poor in spirit, but the materially poor as well:

Wherefore, I call upon the weak things of the world, those who are unlearned and despised, to thrash the nations by the power of my Spirit ... And their arm shall be my arm, and I will be their shield ... I will let fall the sword in their behalf, and by the fire of mine indignation will I preserve them. And the poor and the meek shall have the gospel preached unto them, and they shall be looking forth for the time of my coming, for it is nigh at hand.[64]

In this scripture, God blesses the poor and unlearned to be shielded and preserved. Other religious leaders preached similar rewards for the middle and lower working classes.

Mid nineteenth-century America saw a transfer in visibility from the rule of the upper-class, by virtue of their education and means, towards the growing middle and working classes. Populations shifted from rural America to urban centers. This growing class contributed to a rising anti-intellectual atmosphere that valued common sense over book learning. To accommodate the entertainments of these new concentrations of working class audiences newer and much larger theatres were built that charged lower ticket prices. Catering to the new urban audiences led to new theatre venues and new topics for plays. A split eventually occurred between popular and elitist forms that divided along class lines and the theatres that targeted them.

Some theatres, such as the Park Theatre in New York, were known for their high-fashion audiences, and they presented a corresponding repertoire of shows by acclaimed literary writers from America and Europe. Other theatres, like New York's Bowery, were known as centers of popular entertainment. Theatre professionals from producers to playwrights accommodated for the growing middle and lower class audiences by catering to a wide variety of tastes. An evening at the Bowery might feature jugglers, trained animals, freak performers, and short vaudeville acts in addition to a melodrama.

Audiences of melodrama found the theatre, like popular religion, to be an arena for validation of their lives and concerns. Since most theatres ran plays for only a few performances, it was easy to alter content and theme rapidly throughout a season in response to the audiences' reactions—both live at performances and in the reviews and editorials that accompanied them. As a result, by the late nineteenth century the predominance of middle-class concerns led to plays that emphasized sensation. Topics dealt with issues of respectability (self-control, principled behavior, virtuous affection) and disrespectability (prostitutes, drunks, riots, and risqué spectacles) on stage.

By the time of its second publication in 1880, *The Prophet* was a clear example of the type of theatre that playgoers of moderate means found to be instructive in upper-class respectability and an entertaining release from daily stresses. The portrayal of the title prophet David Starr as a hard-working farmer searching for religious meaning in life provided audiences with a tragic example of respectability gone astray. Starr mistakenly trusts evil companions, misreads miracles, and mistakes love for revelation, but in the end sacrifices his own life to save his followers. The dramatic tale of religious wonders, violence, and illicit romance provided readers with a release from mundane pressures as it presented a world sensational to middle-class America. With the death of David Starr, however, norms of respectability are upheld and Starr's final recognition of his wife as the "one blessed face" underscores how melodramatic plays eased what Bruce McConachie calls "the definition of respectability for men, broadened the notion of virtue for women, and empowered audiences to play their new social roles."[65]

An interesting complication to the class issues at play in religious society and on stage is the frequent use of heightened language. Despite the lower to middle class audiences of both religious revival and theatrical performance, the language of these events was generally not contemporary vernacular. In the theatre, dialogue was replete with metaphors, superlatives, exclamations, and aphorisms. In revival practice, a similar use of language was used to evoke the process of conversion and was used in the testimonies that were born of the experience. Practitioners perceived this speech, or "Canaan's Tongue," as an aspect of performing true belief.

For early revivalists, conversion transcended language barriers, sharing spiritual experiences whether with non-English speaking immigrants, deaf congregants, or English-speaking Americans, was not about language comprehension, but about feeling the spirit of the words. Speaking of this phenomenon, an early convert suggested that, "conversion and the work of grace in the soul appears . . . a strange work, and the language of Canaan as foreign as if it was Hottentot or Chinese."[66]

Both the spoken language of the Second Great Awakening and the dialogue of the stage relied on the heightened language that articulated for audiences in its very style the importance of the message. At the same time, religious practice and melodramatic staging strategically used body language to make an emotional point that transcended even verbal enunciation. Much revival worship was physical, with shaking, writhing, leaping, and falling serving as outward signs of inner spiritual movement. This was a language of the spirit that required no translation and served to erase boundaries between immigrant classes and economic classes, and between preacher and believer.

Melodramatic staging relied in great part on the use of tableaux to show the audiences the most important dramatic moments in the piece. Actors would hold particularly emotional scenes without speaking, while the lighting and the music of the piece would communicate to audiences the importance of the scene. These scenes allowed any audience member, regardless of language skills, to grasp the meaning of the moment. It also served to highlight, through theatrical choices, the clear moral world of the play.

Another unique aspect of melodramatic staging was its reliance on spectacle: the use of machinery, live animals, and special effects heightened the

Fig. 1.1 "Camp Meeting" drawn on stone by Hugh Bridport for Kennedy and Lucas Lithography (1829). Note the exaggerated physical gestures of the congregants: running with arms overhead, leaping into the air, fainting. Courtesy of the Library of Congress, Prints and Photographs Division, LC-USZC4–4554.

drama of the work. While it is clear that the reliance on spectacle often served as a substitute for other dramatic elements (nuanced characterization or fine dialogue), the spectacle is also a reflection of religious sentiment. The revival imagination took a particularly spectacular tone on the topic of the Second Coming. Ellen G. White, the founder of the Seventh Day Adventists and a former Millerite, for example, spoke of the period as one in which "something great and decisive is about to take place ... the world is on the verge of a stupendous crisis."[67]

White also drew a connection between sentimentality and action as she suggested that a true believer will show faith not only in words, but in feelings that can be read most clearly through behavior. "It is no trifling thing to say by attitude and sentiment, even though that sentiment is not expressed in words, 'My Lord delayeth his coming.'"[68] The religious world was one in which actions in fact spoke louder than words as Adventist beliefs required external proof of internal conviction.

Considering the religious spirit of "stupendous crisis" provides an alternate way of viewing spectacular effects: not as replacements for real sentiment, but a physical demonstration of that sentiment. Revival worship was especially notable for its demonstrations of wondrous spiritual occurrences.

Finney, in one of his first revival services in the Burned-Over district, was so overcome by the Spirit that he was seized with an uncontrollable laughter of "holy joy." As he preached to the villagers who had gathered, conversions began to occur, accompanied by groaning, bellowing, and falling. In later revivals this sentiment would overwhelm entire audiences: "the congregation began to fall from their seats; and they fell in every direction, and cried for mercy."[69]

Congregants attending the dedication of the Mormon temple at Kirtland, Ohio record such a variety of spiritual manifestations that the event is sometimes referred to by Church members as the Second Pentecost. Eliza R. Snow, an early Mormon leader recorded:

> There we had the gift of prophecy—the gift of tongues—visions and marvelous dreams were related—the singing of heavenly choirs was heard, and wonderful manifestations of the Elders were witnessed. The sick were healed—the deaf made to hear—the blind to see and the lame to walk, in very many instances.[70]

The histrionic, physically exaggerated displays of spiritual awakening also marked melodramatic acting, which was based in romantic narrative painting and passionate gestural movements.

From the late eighteenth century until the early twentieth century, science and art intersected in their interest in documenting and dissecting human emotions. Early illustrators recorded human expression artistically, while later works such as Darwin's *Expression of Emotions* (1872) was illustrated with photographs. The resulting efforts led narrative artists to standardize emotional states through these records of expression. William Hogarth, painting in the late eighteenth century, is perhaps best known for his manipulation of standardized expression to tell vibrant stories of London life. This style of narrative painting maintained popularity into the nineteenth century and served as inspiration for theatre playwrights. Hogarth's "Industry and Idleness" (1747) was made into two separate melodramas a century after the series was painted; "The Bottle" (1847) by George Cruikshank, Charles Dickens' illustrator for *Oliver Twist*, was dramatized in eight different melodramas.

The implication of this transfer of style to melodramatic acting is two-fold. First, illustrators were not the only ones using scientific studies of human expression as the basis for reproduction. Actor training also made use of a standardized emotional palette. François Delsarte, for example, working in France during the 1850s, created an entire school of acting based on a series of codified facial and body gestures. Melodramatic actors in Europe and the United States were trained in a similar manner—emotional states were revealed through specific facial expressions and bodily gestures that were standardized and handed down within the company.

The movement and expression of the actors came from both the operatic and balletic traditions, with the emphasis on beauty and control in form. Gestures were expansive and deliberate. Dion Boucicault, the premiere author of continental melodramas, taught:

> When you look at a person you do not turn your eye, but you turn your whole head. If you want to point, do *that* (with the arm straight out from the shoulder)—the action must go from the shoulder . . . Another thing is, do not let your gesture be too short . . . You do not know how long you can rest upon a good one. It tires you, but it will not tire the spectator.[71]

The result is a highly physical state of emotion that can be read across language and class barriers. The extraordinary reliance on physical articulation of expression echoes the similar demonstrations of emotion found in revival worship.

Even in a closet drama like *The Prophet,* stage directions point to this melodramatic performance style. In one of his first public sermons, Starr recounts his first vision with such power that a part of the rock on which he is standing *"crashes down with a great noise and reverberation. Cries of terror, and much confusion among the people"* ensue. Starr, "who has remained standing upon the rock, pale and rapt," then builds his sermon to a frenzy:

> Therefore, I take it from His open hand,
> Who made yon stones to fall. I hurl on you
> His arrows, and the shining of his spear:
> I bid believe not me, but what, renewed,
> In me is manifest. . . .[72]

This powerful call to faith is finally punctuated by thunder and lightning. The directed facial expressions of Starr and the heightened language of his sermon all suggest a melodramatic mode of acting.

The message of the Second Great Awakening was widely disseminated across the entire country by the end of the nineteenth century. Any study of institutions, whether political, educational, or cultural, ought to take into consideration the way in which this religious belief infiltrated every aspect of society. The change in religious practice encouraged Americans of every class or creed to find their own salvation through God's grace and with the help of an increasingly middle to lower class, uneducated American clergy. At the same time, the shift in theatre audiences and play topics across the century also reflected the growing power of populism. The mutual impact of religious practice and melodrama is also revealed in the way that justice functioned on stage and in the lives of Christians.

Reviewing the way in which melodrama has generally been studied by intersecting points of genre, structure, and audience with the religious sentiment of the Second Great Awakening reveals a fascinating overlap between the theatrical and religious performance in the nineteenth century. It suggests that religious expression during the time was highly performative, and that melodrama was infused with a Christian sentiment. This is the worldview suggested by Ludovicus Weld's cosmic theatre: the Christian melodramatic mode.

2 Rapists
The Sexual Fantasy of Polygamy

> Why Alice, you are quite a good girl; you are a saint by nature; I love you; your Lord and Prophet loves you . . . I will call the angels of heaven, and charge them with the especial care of your saintly and queenly body. And they shall give you unto me, that I may sanctify, by my holy touch, both your body and soul to the Lord in heaven.
>
> —Brigham Young in *Brigham Young*

> Pornography . . . is a genre devoted to fantasy, and its fantasies traverse a range of motifs beyond the strictly sexual . . . [it] is appropriated as a form of speech and deployed around subjects and issues that are the most 'unspeakable', the most buried, but also the most politically and culturally significant.
>
> —Laura Kipnis, *Bound and Gagged*

Perhaps the most remarkable feature of early Mormonism was the practice of polygamy, and in popular culture it remains one of the major defining points of being Mormon. While plural marriages have neither been practiced nor sanctioned in the Mormon Church for over a century, America is still fascinated by this marriage practice. Books such as John Krakauer's 2004 bestseller *Under the Banner of Heaven* or television shows like HBO's *Big Love!* keep the vision of Mormon polygamy in circulation, as do relatively frequent comic references to polygamy in movies and sitcoms.[1] In contemporary representations, this specter of polygamy serves as a reminder of a Mormon past, an awareness of the transgressive sexual mores still associated with the Mormon Church, and a recognition of how much popular views on Mormon sexual politics have changed.

Today, the Mormon Church is a bastion of conservative morality—professing a strict morality that calls for chastity before and complete fidelity after marriage. It is the juxtaposition of this hyper-conservative image with references to modern-day polygamy (a deviant sexual practice) that creates tension and humor. There was no such juxtaposition in the representation of the Mormon institution of plural marriage that was constructed on the melodramatic stage. Instead, anti-Mormon melodramas were cautionary tales of a real threat to America.

Polygamy was the central focus of anti-Mormon rhetoric on and off the stage in late nineteenth-century America. Political platforms were built on a promise to eradicate the practice from the country, the woman's rights movement engaged in an uneasy relationship with Mormon polygamist suffragettes, and popular images of Mormons (in novels, magazines, and political cartoons in newspapers) illustrated the practice with detail. On stage, polygamy was the most frequently performed Mormon vice and its representations ranged from the comic to the horrific. Other issues of violence, secession, and ethnic impurity that were aspects of Mormon villainy sprang from this primary and fundamental aspect of early Mormon doctrine.

Melodramatic polygamy was both titillating and repugnant, a combination that made it a particularly gripping topic on the American stage. These plays capitalized on the societal fears about sex and gender by suggesting that those involved in polygamy transgressed natural and appropriate behaviors for men and women. In anti-Mormon melodramas, challenges to the emerging ideas about womanhood and manhood in America occurred in three overlapping sites that corresponded to off-stage concerns about Mormon power. The first concern was that Brigham Young, the epitomic polygamist, was creating a society entirely based on unchecked sexual desire. This vision was complicated by a new uneasiness in terms of American manhood, where the shifting economy suggested that masculinity could be achieved through conspicuous consumption.

The second fear was that evil Mormon men were imprisoning women as sex slaves. As evidenced in popular culture and politics, slavery was the most violently contested issue of the century, with violence culminating in the Civil War. Mormons seemed to be continuing the legacy of slavery, but even worse, perpetrating it on white women. A third anxiety was, ironically, the fear that Mormon women had too many rights, as proven to the rest of the country by Mormon advocacy of women's rights. After abolition, suffrage was perhaps the most bitter social war in nineteenth-century America, and Mormon women were at the forefront of the battle.

Rather than address the socio-political issues of consumer culture, slavery, and suffrage directly, anti-Mormon melodramas dealt with these issues in a way that was far more compelling on stage—the strange sexual practices of polygamy. The plays showed the negative consequences of men and women acting outside of strictly conceived gender roles in order to contain fears about the growing power of the Mormons in Utah. They staged polygamy as not just deviant, but destructive to American society, and at the same time, pleased audiences with a sexual fantasy about its practice. The tension between pleasure and disgust of polygamy was resolved in these plays with the reaffirmation of the patriarchal family structure as a core of American identity.

The cycle of transgression and containment described as the outcome of anti-Mormon melodrama seems to suggest a return to now-reconsidered analyses of gender in the nineteenth century. The notion that nineteenth-century literature always, in the end, reestablishes gendered norms suggests a monolithic understanding of gender that was accepted by the majority of the country. The metaphor for this understanding of gender is commonly called "separate spheres," and while it has been used to discuss a wide variety of historical moments, it is usually associated with the nineteenth century in America. It suggests a binarial model of male/female, public/private, active/passive models and dominated nineteenth century feminist studies until the 1980s.[2]

Indeed, it is this assumption on which the pioneering work of Barbara Welter on the nineteenth century cult of true womanhood is based.[3] Welter argues that true womanhood revolved around four principal virtues: piety, purity, submissiveness, and domesticity. Piety, a woman's innate spirituality, was a gift given to women to help reform the more worldly men in their lives. Purity was a requisite for any true woman; popular fiction and melodramas of the period assured women that the loss of innocence could only lead to madness and death. Submissiveness was a necessary quality to maintain the order of the universe. Daughters, sisters, and wives were expected to not only obey, but be entirely dependant on men. In this way, the happiness of both the men and the women was assured. Domesticity, supported by scripture and celebrated by women's magazines, underlined that the place for women was in the home. While these attributes were in greatest circulation among middle to upper class urban white women, Welter suggests it was such a pervasive ideal—disseminated in hundreds of women's magazines, sensational novels, gift books, and religious sermons and tracts in the nineteenth century—that it dominated nearly every level of American life.[4]

For example, discoveries in biology and in the new discipline of phrenology, the study of the conformation of the skull to determine personality traits, proved that women and men were in fact essentially different. Lorenzo Fowler, one of phrenology's strongest advocates, taught that brains were proportioned differently in men and women and the difference was due to the behavioral traits that belonged exclusively to one sex or the other. In his 1842 pamphlet entitled "The Principles of Phrenology and Physiology Applied to Man's Social Relations," he stressed that women had more piety, benevolence, meticulousness, "secretiveness," and a greater love for children. Men, on the other hand, had larger brains to account for their dominance in sexual longing, violent tendencies, firmness, logic, and "causality."[5]

The biological assumptions of studies such as these led to a definition of the distinct attributes of men and women. The characteristics are in evidence not only in scientific writings of the time, but can also be read in popular literature such as anti-Mormon melodramas. In *Brigham Young; or, The Prophet's Last Love* (1869) by Henry J. McKinley, the aspects of separate spheres as outlined by Welter can be read in the courtship between Harry and Alice. This romantic comedy centers on a love triangle between

Harry, a clerk to Young, beautiful Alice, and the fictional Brigham Young himself, who hopes to make Alice his next wife. Problems ensue when Amelia, the titular "prophet's last love," discovers that Young is considering yet another bride. In the play, Amelia and Harry are helped by five of Young's other wives to save Alice and cure Young of his wandering eye for good. A second love triangle—between Young's daughter Lotty, her non-Mormon lover, Frank, and a French music teacher—provides much of the comedy in the show. In the end, all of the true lovers are united and Brigham Young vows to only love Amelia for the rest of his life.[6]

The primary distinction made between Harry and Alice is one of responsibility—Harry is responsible for the public economics of courtship, while Alice is responsible for their private emotional life. Throughout the play, Harry advises Frank on how to be a good lover; his advice is always material. In the second scene of the play he tells Frank, " . . . attend to business and increase your fortune, as fortune is the one thing pure in the eyes of wife and world."[7] Later he again encourages, "Economize life by temperance, and save your wits to make money."[8] Even Harry's language of love uses the metaphor of economy; Harry assures Frank that he is confident in Alice's love: " . . . I know where I have banked my love, on your report I should withdraw my heart's account; but she is solvent in her love for me . . ."[9]

Alice, on the other hand, like other worthy women, centers her relationship in private emotion. She explains to Lotty that Harry, "can give me a faithful heart, rich in love, which to the true woman is wealth and happiness for life."[10] She is a true woman in large measure because she is a virgin. Harry recognizes that this as a requisite when he tells Frank that he, too should love a virgin: "Emulate her purity. Let her purity make you pure."[11] Here, the true woman becomes the spiritual leader who can inspire her husband towards purity through her example. Based on this primary characteristic of a true woman, Harry is able to advise Alice how to overcome undesirable offers of plural marriage. She is to "resist them with becoming grace; not speak against their faith or institutions. Avoid to give offense." Her beauty comes from this submission and Harry loves her "for all that is good and virtuous."[12]

Alice ultimately submits not to Harry or Brigham Young, but to her father, who as the primary male figure in her life, maintains her honor. While she privately has voiced that she abhors Young and is unwilling to marry him, the public rejection of her suit comes from her father, who tells Young that "in the obedience of her heart for relief she asked her father's protection," which he was then honor-bound to provide.[13] Her purity, piety, and submission grant her a reprieve from Young's marriage suit and he recognizes her with a blessing: "Alice, give me your hand; you are a true woman . . . I would not injure you, and must forgive you, and will ask the Lord to be with you."[14] She is therefore free to marry Harry, who will provide for her and will provide her with the children she needs to fulfill her ultimate destiny.

Scholarship in the last two decades, however, reconsiders the dominance of the separate spheres metaphor through a contestation of the public/private divide, by linguistic challenges to the terms sex, gender, or even woman, or by recoveries of alternate histories that do not fit into the separate spheres model. As Linda K. Kerber points out, even "the language of separate spheres was vulnerable to sloppy use . . . When they used the metaphor of separate spheres, historians referred, often interchangeably, to an ideology *imposed on* women, a culture *created by* women, a set of boundaries *expected to be observed* by women."[15] The notion that there were pervasive gender norms that were established through men and women's magazines, over the pulpit, in novels, on stage, or by the medical establishment does not disappear, however. What the shift in women's studies suggests instead is that "separate spheres" is not the *only* way to look at the nineteenth century.

This examination of the anti-Mormon melodramas *The Mormons*, *Zion*, and *Brigham Young* as social documents draws on the work of recent directions in women's studies, particularly the notions of domesticity as articulated by Amy Kaplan. Kaplan argues that deconstructing the traditional binaries of the separate spheres still leaves in place the assumed binary of domestic/foreign. Maintaining this binary reconceptualizes the male/female divide by uniting men and women as national allies against the alien other. Kaplan then deconstructs the domestic/foreign binary by suggesting that domesticity is not a static state, but a process. She states:

> Domesticity in this sense is related to the imperial project of civilizing, and the conditions of domesticity often become markers that distinguish civilization from savagery. Through the process of domestication, the home contains with itself those wild or foreign elements that must be tamed; domesticity not only monitors the borders between the civilized and the savage, but also regulates traces of the savage within itself.[16]

In anti-Mormon melodrama, the Mormon Other, both male and female, serves the double function of the foreign savage in need of civilizing and the savage within America itself. Mormons may have been American in citizenship, but they were also desperately *not* American in their character, as evidenced by their sexual practices.

Additionally, this analysis reconsiders the binaries associated with the separate spheres by placing them in the context of the melodramatic mode. As was discussed in the previous chapter, the fundamental melodramatic elements of poetic justice, moral polarity, and spectacle allow for great flexibility in the presentation of transgression, inversion, and dissensus. In this way, melodrama functions as what Michel Foucualt calls a "heterotopia of deviation," or a counter-site that is "capable of juxtaposing in a single real place several spaces, several sites that are in themselves incompatible." Heterotopic space allows for the simultaneous representation, contestation, and inversion of cultural norms.[17] Key to this reading of anti-Mormon melodrama, however, is how the subversion of norms is ultimately reinscribed by the representation of the same—views that echo the ideas from the scholarship of the separate spheres. In other words, while it treats a complex range of behaviors and characters that do not fit into the metaphor of the separate spheres, melodrama, by its very nature, requires staging of the world as it ought to be.

I. PRIESTS OF CANT AND LUST

> Poor woman! You also are condemned to see yourself degraded, trampled on and despised. Your husband must do as the rest, or be treated as an outcast. You are doomed to a life of horror; and there stands one of the priests who immolate their victims on the altars of Cant and Lust!
> —Eagle Eye to Mrs. Woodville in *The Mormons*

In nineteenth-century popular culture Mormonism was seen as a cult established by lustful men in order have unchecked illicit sexual liaisons with as many women as they wanted. In *Brigham Young* the character of Amelia underlines this point: "Your church, religion, creed, or what you please to call it, is a shame, begot of shame, in shame maintained."[18] The Mormon institution was neither "church, religion" nor "creed," but was in very simple terms the practice of polygamy. The Mormon rapist was typified by the character of Brigham Young, who appears in many of the melodramas and personifies all that was villainous about Mormon men. In particular, these melodramas show Young using his charismatic authority—Cant—as a religious leader to lure men into lives of moral depravity. The rampant sexuality of Mormon men—Lust—left unchecked was perceived as a road to social ruin.

The exaggerated conflation of religion and violently enforced polygamy evidenced in anti-Mormon melodramas created a lurid dramatization of plural marriage that confirmed the justifiable fears of the practice. At the same time, the sensationalized enactment of polygamy on stage made for exciting entertainment. As these plays became more popular, the characterization of helpless women, evil rapists, and passionate heroes became more explicit. The result was the dramatization of polygamy as pornography in order to juxtapose appropriate gender behavior for American men.

Each night it was performed, *The Mormons* closed Act II with a thrilling tableau. Imprisoned in a darkened room full of symbols and smoke at the Endowment House in Salt Lake City, Mr. and Mrs. Woodville are surrounded by a group of licentious men dressed in dark robes. Eagle Eye, the hero of the melodrama, has been disguised as a Mormon Elder, and at the last minute throws off his robe to rescue the Woodvilles. As the music swells, the curtain "*slowly falls*," and Woodville evinces hope and fear as Mrs. Woodville "*sinks to her knees*."[19] Mrs. Woodville, falling to her knees night after night, performed a visceral yet mundane action that evokes an image of American womanhood. Her protecting husband and rescuing hero surround her. The three of them are frozen in a picture of defense against the Mormon priests who threaten their very lives.

Here, the repetitive actions of the actors established a ritual that encoded appropriate gendered behavior for both men and women. The Mormon villains stand outside the center, literally and metaphorically, as men whose secret oaths disrupt social propriety. For audiences watching this tableau, Mrs. Woodville's actions reaffirmed idealized visions of a woman defensive of her family and purity. Physically, her behavior underlines the physical delicacy that was an exaggerated aspect of female dress and comportment. Elizabeth Reitz Mullinex details how nineteenth-century fashions "were symbols of one's social, mental, emotional, and professional status and signified the social role performed by the wearer."[20] For Mullinex, women's clothing was a direct reflection of the tenets of true womanhood, particularly submissiveness:

> [F]emale dress was designed to force women into a physically subservient position by inhibiting female movement; whalebone corsets, tight-lacing practices, bustles, heavy petticoats, and impractical shoes physically handicapped women and often invited serious illness ... Indeed, some women went so far as to have their two lower ribs removed to facilitate tight stays and their little toes amputated so that they might fit into tiny, more delicate shoes.[21]

Mullinex argues that these were not masochistic trends, but ways of reinforcing true obedience. Mrs. Woodville challenges this fashion constriction, however, by her very act of kneeling down, which would have required a sweeping away of skirts and the flexibility of upper body to make the movement possible.

Ideologically, her relief at the rescue from the clutches of Mormonism where her husband was seduced by promises of power, wealth, and many wives illustrates one of the principles of appropriate sexuality in the nineteenth century. The villainy represented by the Mormon Elders in this scene added to the sexual fantasy that surrounded polygamy and defined it for America as an entirely unacceptable threat to the very fabric of society. The horrors depicted in the scene were made possible by the actual practice of polygamy as it was presented by Mormons and anti-Mormons alike.

Mormon Polygamy

The origin of the doctrine of polygamy is generally traced to a revelation received by Joseph Smith on 12 July 1843. In the presence of several other

Church leaders, he recorded a commandment "relating to the new and everlasting covenant, including the eternity of the marriage covenant, as also plurality of wives."[22] This record remains the foundation document both explaining the reasons for, the rules guiding, and the rewards for obedience to polygamy. Although a copy of it was distributed among high-ranking Church officials, the revelation was not published widely until after the 1852 public announcement of the practice.[23] Orson Pratt, a late convert to the principle of plural marriage (at one point early in his membership, he was excommunicated for his open denouncement of polygamy), was selected as the primary speaker at the 1852 General Conference in Salt Lake City. He, and all the speakers after him, proclaimed the practice of polygamy as a holy and God-given practice and promoted it as a higher form of marriage.

In her sociological study of polygamy in Utah, Kathryn Daynes points out that marriage in America was a unique blend of practices from Episcopalian, Protestant, and Roman Catholic traditions.[24] The multiplicity of marriage practices in the nineteenth century led the United States to establish a common law legal structure based on the early Roman model in which "the consent of the couple, not . . . compliance with a specific form or ceremony" was the legal basis for marriage.[25] Mormon polygamy under the common law of the United States was a more reasonable practice than it seems at first glance—anyone in the USA could be legally married without witnesses, records, or even civil or religious authority sanctioning the union.

In addition, it is clear from early marriages performed in the Church that Joseph Smith felt that marriage was an ordinance necessary for salvation. As such, it needed to be performed by one with authority directly from God to join couples according to his will. As early as 1835, Smith encouraged Mormon couples to be married by Mormon leaders rather than by leaders of other religions, or by civil authorities. He himself performed marriages despite Ohio's refusal to recognize Mormon elders as ministers. Smith stated at one such wedding, "The Lord God of Israel has given me authority to unite the people in the holy bonds of matrimony. And from this time forth I shall use that privilege and marry whomsoever I see fit."[26]

Smith was not alone in this practice, especially in the West. Itinerant preachers authorized themselves to marry in the face of both local and national laws. Nor were Mormons alone in practicing alternate marriage styles. The Strangites, originally associated with the Mormon Church, then later led by James Strang, established polygamous communities in Voree, Wisconsin and on Big Beaver Island in Lake Michigan. There were a number of utopian groups—the New England Shakers, and the Rappites (or Harmony Society) of New Harmony, Indiana—who preached communal living and celibacy. Other communities preached free love: Josiah Warren's colony, Modern Times, was founded on the principle that love relations were based on free choice for both men and women while the Oneida

Perfectionists in New York practiced the doctrine of "complex marriage" from 1848–1879.[27] The Nashoba Colony of Frances Wright was conceived as a safe place where racial and gendered segregation could be overcome through open sexual practice.[28]

In Mormon theology, salvation is an unconditional consequence of Christ's atonement, and its reward of resurrection will come to all. The degree of glory rewarded to the resurrected in the next life, however, is dependent on receiving saving ordinances, and obeying the covenants associated with the ordinances while in this life. The highest degree of glory, or the celestial kingdom, is seen as a continuation of the family unit throughout eternity. As Pratt stated in the 1852 address, "celestial marriage," had not been established to "gratify the carnal lusts and feelings of man" but instead was a method by which to provide *all* righteous individuals the opportunity to have "a numerous and faithful posterity to be raised up and taught in the principles of righteousness and truth."[29] For Mormons, marriage is not only seen as a divine institution, but as the central and only means of exaltation.

Polygamy apologists have constructed a number of different reasons why God would command his faithful to practice a marriage style that was anathema to his earlier commandments, to western culture, and to the very people from whom he required participation. In their seminal history of the Church of Jesus Christ of Latter-day Saints, Leonard J. Arrington and Davis Bitton suggest that these justifications may point to some of the concerns that prompted Joseph Smith to seek a revelation on polygamy in the first place. Practically, there might have been a concern for the need to provide for all the single and widowed women who were attracted to the Church. Theologically, in a Church conceived as a restoration of all things, the restoration of an Old Testament practice would be a necessary step. Records suggest that the practice of polygamy might have even been prompted by a missionary zeal that recognized that much of the world practiced polygamy, that one of the strongest ways to build an institution is through intermarriage between new converts and established members, and that growth in the Church was dependant as much on birthrates as conversion rates.[30]

Whatever the reason, the reaction to the public announcement of polygamy prompted concerns from both within and without the Mormon community that ranged from privately voiced struggles to highly publicized condemnations of the practice. In his famous 1859 interview with Horace Greeley, a preeminent journalist of the nineteenth century, Brigham Young answered Greeley's query about whether women approved of polygamy with the following: "They could not be more averse to it than I was when it was first revealed to us as the Divine Will. I think they generally accept it, as I do, as the will of God."[31] His response is possibly the most reasonable justification for the practice that explains its continuation for decades despite revulsion for the practice—regardless of personal feelings, Mormons felt polygamy was the "will of God."

The rest of the country, however, echoed Greeley's assessment of the practice. While he maintained that Brigham Young had "no air of sanctimony or fanaticism," he observed: "that the degradation (or, if you please, the restriction) of Woman to the single office of child-bearing and its accessories, is an inevitable consequence of the system here paramount." He worried that Mormon women "will soon be confined to the harem," but "joyfully trust[s] that the genius of the Nineteenth Century tends to a solution of the problem of Women's sphere and destiny radically different from this."[32]

This public vision of the abused Mormon woman was marked by the wide circulation of "tell-all" novels. Titles of some biographical novels published in this period document this trend: *Fifteen Years Among the Mormons: Being the Narrative of Mrs. Mary Ettie V. Smith, Late of Great Salt Lake City: Sister of One of the Mormon High Priests, She Having Been Personally Acquainted with Most of the Mormon Leaders, and Long in the confidence of the "Prophet," Brigham Young* (1858) by Nelson Winch Green, and *Exposé of Polygamy in Utah: A Lady's Life Among the Mormons: a Record of Personal Experience as One of the Wives of a Mormon Elder During A Period of More Than Twenty Years* (1872) by Mrs. Thomas B. H. Stenhouse were two of the most well-known. Former polygamous wives also had some public visibility. Most celebrated was Ann Eliza Young, who divorced Brigham Young in 1875 and spent the rest of her life publishing memoirs and presenting her experiences on the American lecture circuit. These memoirs echoed Greeley's concerns about the rights and privileges of women in Utah, but expanded on his observations with sensational details of abuse by focusing villainy on Mormon rapists.

The Truth About Polygamy

One of the great difficulties in discussing nineteenth-century polygamy is the blurry line between fact and fiction in nineteenth-century literature and the vastly conflicting records that exist—defending and defaming plural marriage. In her personal journal, Sarah Melissa Holman Johnson, the fifth wife of Benjamin F. Johnson described her "sentiments in relation to plural marriage":

> In it I find happiness, joy, peace, love and beauty . . . Six wives of us . . . have raised our families under the same roof, having separate rooms. Children of six mothers . . . most of them grown to young manhood and womanhood, are devotedly fond of each other as brothers and sisters, all of them intelligent and full of the spirit of the Gospel. We can have a dance, singing choir, theater, or any social entertainment independent of any outside our own family![33]

This record stands in direct contrast to anti-Mormon records of the same practice. In the play *Zion*, written by Dr. B. W. Hollenbeck at roughly the same time at Johnson's journal, the character Dora paints a very different picture of polygamy: "Life here is one perpetual nightmare; the sacred ties of home and family are unknown; the cheerful group around the fireside is impossible; filial love and respect are not thought of; lust with its attendant evils reigns supreme."[34]

It is impossible to know what Mormon polygamists *thought* about the practice. The records that remain were all written with the knowledge that they would be read by a wider audience. Public works of propaganda (pamphlets, sermons, political rallies) catered to the contemporary reading audience. Private writing about polygamy (correspondence of Church officials, journals, letters) might have had a more candid writing style, but were still understood to be for public consumption. Mormon doctrine suggests that humankind will be judged in heaven by the records they keep on earth; today Church curriculum emphasizes that members keep personal journals for future generations. Therefore, the conditions and experiences of polygamy as recorded by those practicing it were written with eternal judgment in mind. Since practicing polygamists believed their records would serve as a witness of their faithfulness for future generations and at the Lord's judgment, it is unsurprising that the vast majority of the writing is supportive of plural marriage.

Popular representations, on the other hand, were written overtly for a public audience who purchased the representation, and authors catered to their tastes. In the nineteenth century, Senators cited lurid novels to show the evil of polygamy and journalists faced with the fairly tame reality of Salt Lake City life constructed satirical justifications for the practice. Terryl L. Givens makes the case that in the nineteenth century, fiction and non-fiction did not function as fixed categories. Instead, purportedly "true" accounts of the horrors of Mormon life that crossed boundaries between journalism and sensationalized stories were cited as authoritative reports of actual events of polygamy. The fluidity of the categories of fact and fiction lent a documentary air to the most sensational melodramas, erased alternative accounts of polygamy, and reaffirmed public opinion of the dark representation.[35] The dominant version of Mormon history written by popular novelists and reporters was marked by an extreme sensationalism that emphasized bloody deeds and violent sex. This sensationalism was an integral part of staged melodramas.

The author of the ironically titled melodrama *Zion* was Dr. B. W. Hollenbeck, a successful doctor and moderately well-known playwright who specialized in melodramas with insane and hysterical women. While there are no extant performance reviews of the play, it was published as an acting edition with detailed prop, costume, and casting notes. The play begins in a prologue where Mrs. Day, convinced of the truthfulness of the religious message of the Mormons, leaves her husband and young child to follow an Elder Marwood to Utah. Her husband, in despair, requires his young daughter Dora to swear an oath to avenge her mother through Marwood's death. Eight years later, Dora sets aside her own love, Durand, to fulfill the oath, thinking that her father was massacred by the Mormons. She attempts to trap Marwood, but is herself imprisoned in Salt Lake City. Her long-lost mother, now nearly insane from abuse, helps her to escape where they are surprisingly reunited with Mr. Day. Together the family brings down those who destroyed their lives and the play closes on the triumphant tableau of the defeat of the Mormons.

The play is set in a society where women are locked in houses and fed only bread and water until they are near starvation. Marwood, speaking about his treatment of women to his henchman Gorham says: "I used the lash with unsparing hand—I made her a servant to my family, and caused her to do the most menial drudgery, but I could not exorcise the devil within her. You know she made several attempts to escape, I then placed her in your care and she was returned to me a maniac, and I trust will always remain so."[36] One polygamous wife spends most of the piece drifting through the streets of Salt Lake City, shrieking dark prophecies and attempting suicide. If Zion is really as *Zion* suggests, this wife would not be alone in her mad wanderings. Salt Lake City might be more like the anarchy portrayed in the stage directions in the melodrama *Evelyn Gray; or, A History of Our Western Turks*: "A wagon with the dead body of a woman is driven rapidly by. Danites, on horseback follow shouting and shooting off pistols. People hurriedly and tremblingly disperse."[37]

This view of Salt Lake City is irreconcilable with journalistic reports that it was clean, quiet, well organized, and beautifully maintained. Sir Richard Burton, for example, in his 1861 publication *The City of the Saints and Across the Rocky Mountains to California* describes that in the Salt Lake Valley "the sublime and the beautiful were in present contrast" and that he "though uninfluenced by religious fervor" could not "gaze upon the scene without emotion."[38] Yet, the descriptions of lawlessness and horror in novels, serials, and plays were so well-documented that President Buchanan was convinced that Salt Lake was a legitimate threat to the well-being of the United States. He authorized the dispatch of 2,500 Federal Troops to quell the violence and establish a non-Mormon governor of the territory.[39]

It seems safe to assume that melodramatic depictions of polygamy were also received with this same unquestioning belief. Examples from reviews of anti-Mormon melodramas illustrate this point. For example, *The Mormons; or, Life in Salt Lake City* by Thomas Dunn English opened at Burton's Theatre in New York City on 16 March 1858. The playbill for the production described it as:

> A practical view of the actual and exciting doings of the Mormons in their own homes—The Policy of their Rulers, their connection with the Indians, Hostility to the Federal Government—the workings of their peculiar domestic institutions—Sufferings of the numerous

wives and children—Public ceremonies and private habits and manners, with an interesting story of American emigrants, and the assassination by the Danites.[40]

The production played until 2 May 1858, when it moved across the country for an even longer run at Maguire's Opera House in San Francisco. Considered by some early historians to be one of the cleverest examples of comedy from the period, *The Mormons* was reviewed at the time as remarkable for its many "startling 'points' and curious *tableaux*." Its review in the *Evening Bulletin* continues, "Although in many respects Mormon life is absurdly caricatured, yet some of the incidents are historically correct."[41]

What the review does not make clear is which parts of this "practical view of the actual doings of Mormons" were caricatured and which were historically correct.[42] Instead, artistic license and documentary presentation were intermingled. As a result, regardless of the official Church stance on the place of polygamy in its complex theology, for American society, Mormonism *was* polygamy and polygamy was a hypocritical excuse for unchecked lust that leads to enslavement and murder. The concern that polygamy was a institution meant to fulfill the lusts of deviant men was contradicted by actual reports of polygamous men, who described the practice as difficult both to accept and to practice. Brigham Young, for example, insisted throughout his life that polygamy was not something he would have sought after, and that he practiced it only because it was a commandment of God. He records in the *Journal of Discourses* that when he was first asked by Joseph Smith to take a plural wife, that it "was the first time in my life that I had desired the grave."[43] This apologist's view of polygamy, however, does not erase either the abuses done in the name of righteous polygamy or the representation of that abuse, real and imagined, in popular fiction.

Mormon Men

George Burnap in his lectures on *The Sphere and Duties of Woman* (1854) suggests that a wife "is in a measure dependent. She asks for wisdom, constancy, firmness, perseverance." Her husband must therefore be strong enough physically, mentally, and emotionally to provide the guidance a wife needs. The lecture continued, "woman despises in man every thing like herself except a tender heart. It is enough that she is effeminate and weak; she does not want another like herself."[44]

From a look at the gendered rhetoric of the late nineteenth century through the lens of the separate spheres, it becomes clear that in order for society to function, the delicate balance between male and female power had to be strictly observed. Men, by nature, would be caught up in the public world—education, career, male sport, sexual drive—while women's gentle influence from the private home would keep these tendencies in check. It was a woman's responsibility to maintain her virtue at all costs, despite the natural assault that came from the more sensual man. The Reverend Jonathan F. Stearns preached that this chastity was in fact the source of female power and warned: "Let her lay aside delicacy, and her influence over our sex is gone."[45] Women were also responsible for creating a home that was so welcoming that husbands would prefer to be there, and for reforming men through their more spiritual natures.

In anti-Mormon melodramas, however, heroes are men who are active husbands and fathers in the domestic sphere (or yearn to be so) in a way that the Mormon villain is not. Here Kaplan's theory of "imperial domesticity" provides insight into how American men and women share a unified domesticity in monogamous relationships that is set apart by the foreign sexuality of the Mormon man. Imperial domesticity is the notion that while a woman's sphere was in her home, the organization and establishment of that home can and should be extended outward to domesticate the foreign.[46] Catherine and Harriet Beecher Stowe exemplify this rhetoric in their work *The American Woman's Home* (1869), which advocated "putting into practice domesticity's expansive potential to Christianize and Americanize immigrants both in Northeastern cities and across the country." However, Kaplan traces the concerns about the "internal savagery that appears to threaten the physical health of the mother." She argues that in nineteenth-century writing, focus was placed on "the pervasive invalidism that makes American women physically and emotionally unequal to their global responsibilities."[47] Another internal savagery that threatens both the physical health of women and the nation are men who keep women from fulfilling their duties to their homes, their families, and the world.

In anti-Mormon melodrama, Mormon men only want wives in order to justify uncontrolled passion. Bishop Lee in *Evelyn Gray* makes this clear when he decides to "marry" an already engaged Evelyn: "By the Almighty God, I never saw a sweeter girl in all my life. The sign of her just melt's ones' sense like wax. I must have her in spite of bridegroom and all hell. I am sick of all my old rips anyhow. Lord, I'd give my best farm for a kiss from her now."[48] Elder Marwood suggests the same in the prologue to *Zion*: "[Mrs. Day] is a magnificent woman, and I cannot afford to lose her. I am running a great risk to obtain her; but the prize is worth it."[49]

This construction of the Mormon villain and his desire for multiple sexual partners is a contradiction to domesticity that impacts both the women who are raped and the men who lose their wives to a foreign invader. Mr. Day is one such man who is forced out of the domestic sphere by the spiritual seduction of his wife by Elder Marwood. Concerned that his wife might be heeding the lies of Marwood, Day reflects that "This is the first cloud to cast a shadow upon our way; heretofore love and confidence have reigned supreme."[50] The positive tranquility of this description—a home of love, confidence, and sunshine—is shattered as Day chooses to leave home with his daughter on a quest for vengeance. The contrast between the loving husband and father of the prologue and the violent mountain man Day becomes serves as a warning of the savagery within.

In *Zion* this savagery is contained by a domesticating force as the Day family—mother, father, and daughter—are reunited and confront Marwood together. In an act that seems to belie the passive heroine that is assumed in melodrama, Mrs. Day is able to secure a knife in the ensuing struggle and stabs her tormentor Marwood with it. She then *"falls on her knees in front of* DAY, *and raises her clasped hands to him."*[51] Her final pose echoes one of the first stage pictures of the show, when the couple is together in their home and she enters to ask her husband's wishes. The melodramatic return to domesticity is dependent on the forceful eradication of the savage foreigner—the Mormon—who threatens the happy home.

One of the markers of the happy home in nineteenth-century rhetoric was the sacred duty of woman as mother in a patriarchal home. Here again, the Mormon man serves as an external threat to the spread of this domesticity across the nation and the world. If a woman was a slave of misguided male passion, she wasn't allowed to fill her ultimate biologically-determined domestic role as a mother. Mrs. Sigourney, in outlining some of the characteristics of full domesticity, wrote that women "reached the climax of [their] happiness" and achieved "a higher place in the scale of being" by having children.[52] In polygamous households, however, women had less-than-average numbers of children, and many didn't have children at all. Polygamy was thus perceived as destructive to a woman's major purpose in life as a mother because it limited opportunities for child-bearing.

Kaplan suggests that "understanding the imperial reach of domesticity and its relation to the foreign should help remap the critical terrain on which women's domestic fiction has been constructed . . . We can see how such narratives imagine domestic locations in complex negotiation with the foreign."[53] Anti-Mormon melodramas repeatedly staged migration between home and abroad through the juxtaposition of America and Utah as a foreign land. The agents of this juxtaposition were the bodies of men and women who were taken from their families through a false conversion, or by kidnapping. Lovers of women desired by Mormons are murdered in *Zion* and *Evelyn Gray,* and Brigham Young kidnaps Harry in *Brigham Young* to keep him from the woman Young wants to marry. The character Elder Pratt, in *The Mormons,* is willing to murder to gain his next bride. He is so jealous of Mary's preference for Eagle-Eye that he plots to kill Eagle-Eye: "I watched her when I assailed him. She loves him. Absence might cure her, perhaps—a final separation certainly will. He must be put out of the way."[54]

More often the women are the victims of forced migration. Dora in *Zion* is kidnapped and abused after her mother has been lured away by false promises. In *Zion, The Mormons,* and *Evelyn Gray,* a similar rhetoric is used to convince women to leave their homes and travel to Utah. As Elder Marwood urges in *Zion,* Mrs. Day must choose between "the delights of heaven, and the anguish of hell."⁵⁵ Joining the Mormons is painted as paradise where saints will "revel in the sweets of everlasting happiness, and sip the nectar of eternal life."⁵⁶ Mormon men always entirely deny rumors of polygamy, until the women are safely "in the walls of Zion."⁵⁷ Once there, women (and sometimes men) in melodramas are immediately forced into plural marriage against their will or better judgment.

In showing the two spheres of the domestic and the foreign, both on American soil, anti-Mormon melodrama complicates a reading of geography and gender. It also points out how nineteenth-century fictions wrestled with issues of manhood and womanhood, wherein both men and women had true natures, but were also always tainted by some foreignness within. As Julia, an escaped polygamist wife describes in *Zion*, her willingness to follow the Mormon Church came from an internal compunction. This is only discovered in her journey from "fair New England" to what seemed a promised land, but turned out to be a horror.

> About ten years ago, Marwood came to my home, a fair New England village, and commenced a revival in the interest of this Mormon church. I was young and filled with that deep religious enthusiasm, so common among the descendants of old Puritan stock. I therefore lent a willing ear to his subtle arguments. He seemed a pattern of honest manhood—in short I gave him my love. We were married and went to Salt Lake City—to me the promised land. Judge of my horror when I discovered how I have been betrayed; being only Mrs. Marwood, the seventh.⁵⁸

Mormon men seem to be able to lure the internal threats out of good women through false promises of salvation that allow the women to be taken away into sexual bondage. Mormon men also threaten the stability of the masculine private space by both the lure of unchecked lust and the need for proper society to abhor the same. The character of Brigham Young—the most frequently represented figure in anti-Mormon melodrama—is a site where these issues of manhood were focused.

Brigham Young

One of the greatest spokesmen on polygamy, and consequently a highly visible Mormon villain, was Brigham Young. During his lifetime, Young married (in one manner or another) nearly sixty women—the numbers vary in different sources. Johnson discusses the nature of these marriages in "Determining and Defining 'Wife': The Brigham Young Households": "Twenty-one of Brigham Young's fifty-five wives had never been married, six were separated or divorced from their husbands, sixteen were widows, and six had living husbands from whom divorces had apparently not been obtained. Marital information is unavailable for six."⁵⁹

Church records document time-and-all-eternity marriages between Young and twenty-seven women, sixteen of whom bore him a total of fifty-seven children. Once in Salt Lake City, he established his wives in the Lion House, a residence with different rooms for each of his wives and their children. He had women married or "sealed" to him almost until his death at age 76; when he died his oldest daughter was fifty-two years old, and his youngest was seven. His highly visible position as the Governor of Utah Territory and President of the Church, his openly polygamous lifestyle, and some celebrated divorce cases made him an iconic figure of polygamy. In anti-Mormon melodramas, he is the ultimate example of the lusty old man who wants young wives to fulfill his sexual fantasies. Demonizing Young as a dramatic character allowed popular culture to explore the possibility of sexual transgression, while reaffirming the opposing characteristics of American manhood.[60]

Herbert Sussmann argues that the pressure on the nineteenth-century man was to control a constant flow of energies in the body through self-regulation. Medical and philosophical wisdom advised that it was dangerous to repress these energies or to let them flow unchecked. Sussman states, "Early Victorians defined maleness as the possession of an innate, distinctively male energy that, in contrast to Freud, did not represent as necessarily sexualized, but as an inchoate force that could be expressed in a variety of ways, only one of which is sexual."[61] This mirrors cultural historian Michael S. Kimmel's assessment that the postbellum man's manhood was entirely self-making; men were responsible for their own success in guiding their energies towards success and masculinity.

Kimmel outlines how this shift in perception led to great anxieties in the performance of masculinity. In 1800, 80% of the men in America were farmers; by 1880, only 50% worked in agriculture. There is a parallel slip in percentages of self-employed men. Kimmel reasons, "Manhood had meant autonomy and self-control, but now fewer and fewer American men owned their own shops, controlled their own labor, owned their own farms."[62] The frontier was receding, so there was no escape from increased urbanization and the commodification of men brought about by the industrialization of labor. The conflict here is one of self-control and ownership—issues that both exacerbated and provided solutions for the late nineteenth-century man. Men were changed into products themselves and suffered a loss of self-control as they lost ownership of what used to signify value—labor and land. To replace this loss, a new measure of success emerged, and that was one of conspicuous consumption. Men who could purchase more were more manly.

Kimmell suggests that racism, anti-feminism, and nativism fed off of these trends:

> American manhood had earlier been grounded upon the exclusion of blacks and women, the non-native-born (immigrants) and the genuinely native-born (Indians), each on the premise that they weren't "real" Americans and couldn't by definition, be real men. But they were also more virile, more potent, more sexually active.[63]

While Kimmel focuses on Indians and Blacks as major sites of sexual anxiety, Mormon men were also perceived as threats. Fear about emasculation was exacerbated by excessive sex in those already not perceived as American. For example, Brigham Young's voracious need for more wives reveals his superior masculinity as he is able to gain the highly valued cultural capital of a virtuous women not just once, but upwards of sixty times.

Fig. 2.1 "The Mormon Problem Solved." A Wood engraving first published in Frank Leslie's Illustrated Newspaper (1871). The cartoon shows Brigham Young, with large group of wives and children, saying to Ulysses S. Grant, "I must submit to your laws—but what shall I do with all these!" Grant replying, "Do as I do—give them offices." The satire here is directed at President Grant, but the image of countless wives from old to young and innumerable children illustrates public opinion about Young's family. Courtesy of the Library of Congress, Prints and Photographs Division, LC-USZ62–65461.

Young's perceived sexual prowess was additionally troubling as he justified his sexual appetite in religious terms. In *Brigham Young,* he tries to convince Alice that she should wed him. He first attempts to lure her with promises of power and wealth. Then he explains that marriage to him is her only hope of eternal salvation: "I am your Lord, and I will be your husband, and you will be my wife. I will give you an exaltation above all the saints. By marriage you shall be sanctified unto the Lord Jehovah."[64] He refers to himself throughout this interview as the Lord's mouthpiece, his chosen servant, and an anointed prophet.

Young's claim to spiritual knowledge and feelings that overwhelm Alice's womanly intuitions disrupts masculine self-control that was necessary to keep sexuality in check. While she may argue that her young lover Harry will give her a "faithful heart, rich in love," Alice does not deny the religious and sexual dominance of the prophet. She can only temper it by recognizing its deviance: "Oh, I hate this man! . . .—this vile and sensual prophet!"[65] Young may have an undisputed religious calling, but he uses it in an inappropriate way. It is only after she has renewed her convictions towards Harry that she is able to regain a sense of the balance misaligned by Young: "*Now I am a woman*, I am free, and will prove that woman can be constant to her love."[66]

In allowing that polygamy is sexually gratifying for men, its representation in anti-Mormon melodrama becomes a loophole for behavior desirable to, yet unbecoming of the American man. Ralph Waldo Emerson recognized this tension in popular constructions of Mormon villains: "Nothing is so hypocritical as the abuse in all the journals,—& at the South, especially,—of Mormonism & Free-Love Socialism. These men who write the paragraphs in the 'Herald & Observer,' have just come from their brothel, or in Carolina, from their Mulattoes [sic]."[67] In criminalizing Young's behavior, authors of anti-Mormon melodramas validated societal restrictions on their own sexual desires, or as Givens puts it, reaffirmed that their sense of "self-denial [was] a necessary and valuable offering."[68]

The staged representation of the villainous Mormon man was a direct response to the cultural anxieties in American society, as anti-Mormon melodramas provided a space to enjoy and condemn transgressive sexual practices. Fears about the conduct of Mormon men put the appropriate behavior expected of American manhood in sharp relief. They also congratulate American men on adherence to strict moral codes while allowing them the titillation of viewing deviant practices. By showing all Mormon men to be evil, society reaffirmed what it meant to be a real American man. He was virile, yet restrained, willing to follow the spiritual example set by wives, but still firmly in economic and social control, and married for procreation, not for sexual gratification. This was the type of social order that late nineteenth-century America, still reeling from the horrors of the Civil War and the corruption of Reconstruction, craved. Characterizing the Mormon rapist successfully established the appropriate characteristics for the patriarchal man, and codified his role in the American family structure. The Mormon rapist was also a necessary evil that provided victim heroines a villain to resist.

II. THIS DEGRADING BONDAGE

> Our day has seen a glorious breaking of fetters. The slave-pens of the South have become a nightmare of the past; the auction-block and whipping-post have given place to the church and schoolhouse; and the songs of emancipated millions are heard through our land. Shall we not then hope that the hour is come to loose the bonds of a cruel slavery whose chains have cut into the very hearts of thousands of our sisters—a slavery which debases and degrades womanhood, motherhood, and the family.
>
> —Harriet Beecher Stowe, preface to *Tell It All*

The image of enslaved polygamous wives touched a real chord with American audiences. Primarily, it stood as an absolute affront to the notion that a woman was the sweet guardian of the home by instead turning the "home" into a prison where women were raped and abused. After Marwood captures Dora, he intends to force her to become his thirteenth wife. Lucy, Mrs. Marwood the eleventh, is assigned to bring Dora sustenance and they converse about their plights. Dora asks Lucy if she is one of Marwood's wives, and Lucy responds, "I reckon it would be nearer right to say I'm one of his *white niggers*—that's about what we all are . . ."[69]

As the conversation continues, Lucy's description of her life sounds like a description of a plantation slave. She says she can't run away, since all who escape either "don't make it out" or are hunted down and brought back. Punishments for misbehaving wives are starvation, "double duty in the kitchen, or in the field," or whipping.[70] Lucy, however, points out that since there is no escape, Dora will come around eventually, and that all the women "must make the best of it."[71]

Dora observes that Lucy and other Mormon wives in the play are so enslaved that they do not even realize the horror of their situation, "that poor creature is trying to make the best of her sad lot; her spirit is crushed—she is an abject slave to a vile master. He owns her body and soul . . . Her womanhood is gone; her mind is benumbed, and the apathy of despair has seized upon her."[72] Lucy's particular use of "white niggers" was a sharp racial insult, even in the nineteenth century. It not only makes the connection clear between plural wives and slaves, but in its offensiveness—that white women might be treated as "niggers"—forces audiences to be doubly troubled.

The treatment of the women as slaves is clearly problematic. The image invoked by calling white women "niggers" offended pro-slavery sensibilities in which the connection between white women and slaves was a particular affront, and it offended anti-slavery sensibilities that recognized the slur for what it was.[73] Both types of audiences (pro-and anti-slavery) had access to anti-Mormon melodramas and the melodramas' relative success across the nation points to the fear of polygamy in its own right, outside the battle for abolition. The ties between slavery and polygamy only served to heighten the stakes. Additionally, the sexual slavery of polygamy allowed audiences a tantalizing glimpse into a world of bondage and pain. This pornographic peek reveals what Lisa Z. Sigel calls the social imaginary of sexuality, or pornography that "elaborates the possibilities of sex."[74]

At the same time, the idea of slavery also opened up the possibility for escape and agency for women, or what Rosemarie Bank calls "the second face of the idol." In her essay, Bank elaborates how the female characters that populated melodramas of the nineteenth and early twentieth century had more than one aspect to them, more than the ideal: "chaste, virtuous, nurturer of home and family, charitable servant and defender of the weak and downtrodden, loving wife, sister, sweetheart, and mother, loyal friend, and cornerstone of a stable, productive, and decent society."[75] Based on her analysis of a sample of melodramas from across the century, Bank identifies three ways that women revealed another side to their characters: they worked at jobs outside the home, they actively solved their own problems, and they defined the moral climate of the world of the play. In doing so, she challenges "the view of these characters as uniformly passive, helpless, naïve, irrational, and uninventive."[76]

Bank's call to reconsider women in melodramas resonates with women in anti-Mormon melodramas. While none work outside the home, all take their problems into their own hands, and with this agency may serve as the heroes of the play in their own right. Additionally, the women function as the moral center to anti-Mormon melodrama, not only in their rhetorical speeches, or the examples they set of righteous behavior, but also for choosing the appropriate use of their own bodies in a monogamous relationship. If women in these plays are victims, they are victims through resistance—with but a few notable exceptions women are enslaved because they refuse to participate in polygamy so the Mormon villain resorts to bondage and violence in order to keep them in unwanted "marriages."

Equating polygamy with slavery also brings to the forefront the ties between sex and violence inherent in anti-Mormon melodramas. The frequently evoked imagery of bondage, chains, and imprisonment creates eroticization of polygamy that is all the more powerful for its enactment upon white bodies. It doesn't matter if the images actually reflected the reality of the situation—it only mattered if audiences thought that they did. In imagining polygamy as slavery, audiences could be horrified, enjoy the horror, but also heed the warning to avoid this destructive sexual practice that was anathema to the patriarchal family structure.

The Pornography of Polygamy

Harriet Beecher Stowe, after her publication of *Uncle Tom's Cabin*, turned her eye to freeing her "sister-slaves." In a preface to *Tell It All: The Story of a Life's Experience in Mormonism* by Mrs. T. B. H. Stenhouse, Stowe urges that "every happy wife and mother who reads these lines give her sympathy, prayers, and efforts to free her sisters from this degrading bondage."[77] The rhetorical pairing of slavery and polygamy was first publicly made at the 1856 Republican national convention, when party members referred to the two institutions as the "twin relics of barbarism."[78] It gained popularity in literature and performance as both language and actions made the connections between the two clear to audiences.

The rhetoric in *Zion* and other anti-Mormon melodramas goes even further to suggest that polygamy is more than physical slavery but is also emotional and mental bondage. As Dora observed in her conversation above, Marwood owns his wives "body and soul." Julia Marwood, another one of his wives, makes this point clear: "My life for years has been a living death, blackened with infamy . . . I will perish in the forest, on the mountains, anywhere, rather than return to that *physical and moral slavery*."[79]

The enacted terror of the enslaved white woman is not entirely a criticism. In sensational melodrama, it was also strangely compelling to both male and female audiences who were given a carefully controlled glimpse into a pornographic fantasy of bondage and rape. In her work on the differences between eroticism and pornography, Gloria Steinem argues that pornography is any depiction with sexual elements,

> . . . in which there is clear force, or an unequal power that spells coercion. It may be very blatant, with weapons of torture or bondage, wounds and bruises, some clear humiliation . . . It may be much more subtle: a physical attitude of conqueror and victim, the use of race or class difference to imply the same thing . . . [T]here is no sense of equal choice or equal power . . . pornography is about power and sex-as-weapon . . . its message is violence, dominance, or conquest.[80]

While this is clearly not the only definition of pornography, Steinem's focus on the unequal power balance portrayed through sexual representation provides insight into the particular fantasy being staged in anti-Mormon melodramas.[81]

In his work *Slavery, Empathy, and Pornography* (2003), Marcus Wood uses a close reading of John Gabriel Stedman's *Narrative of a Five Years Expedition Against the Revolted Negroes of Surinam* to discuss the literary function of slavery as pornography. In it, he suggests that the white male gaze (here Stedman's) is unerringly attracted to the vision of a beaten slave woman. Audiences to sensational melodramas would have found it nearly impossible to miss the vision of the polygamous slave wife, as theatre can literally focus attention on the most powerful images through design, lighting effects, and stage composition.

The play *Zion* makes the connections between slavery and polygamy clear both in dialogue and action. When Julia, one of Marwoods's wives, manages to escape into the wilderness, she literally runs into Mr. Day, who is on his way to Salt Lake City to seek revenge. She describes how she was held "a prisoner—constantly watched" and has seen "maniacs wander about the streets, pitiful wrecks of glorious womanhood; ruined by Mormon cruelty."[82] In other plays, the connection is more subtle, but pointed up through the use of stagecraft. In *The Mormons*, none of the women are kidnapped or literally enslaved. The state of polygamy is made clear, however. Polygamous wives, in the character Eagle-Eye's view, are "wretched victims of Mormon brutality, to whose sufferings the records of modern days afford no parallel" and are "condemned to [be] degraded, trampled on and despised."[83] This is made real after Mrs. Woodville stops her husband's wedding, and then is pulled from her husband's embrace. As discussed earlier, the final tableau for this act has Mrs. Woodville kneeling in position of ultimate submission.

In *Evelyn Gray*, two Mormon Elders are discussing how to best discipline their wives. The character John D. Lee offers, "I tell you how I do, George, when my wimmin' commence any sich doins among themselves. I take 'em one by one an' tie 'em to a bedpost an' give 'em a first-rate hummin'. That takes the fight out of 'em every time."[84] The physical violence of the whipping ("hummin"), is sexualized by the fact that Lee ties the women to a bed first. The placement of this violence in the bedroom enforces the connections between bondage, sex, and violence.

Women in a variety of melodramas faced physical danger and threats to virtue. In others, the villain may try to bend heroines to their will through soft words or deception. The active role that many heroines take, however, keeps her pure or allows her to escape actual harm. Bank records that these deeds of women in melodramas range from:

> ... exposure of the corruption, to bringing the police, to tying up the villain or untying the hero, and so on, for examples of female courage and inventiveness abound in these plays, even though the characters are in most respects conventional women of the times. Indeed, the picture of a heroine slapping the villain smartly across the cheek or telling him off in public is a salutary antidote to the posters of heroines as victims.[85]

What sets women in anti-Mormon melodramas apart is that in every single extant play, there is either a lead character or a secondary one who was not able to escape, but has in fact been seduced or raped into polygamy. Some of these women, like Julia Marwood in *Zion,* escape after rape to tell their tales, but even in this play, she leaves behind women who are still in bondage. The result is a patina of slavery and pornography that hangs over every relationship, even the ones that resemble the villain/heroine relationship in other melodramas.

This is true in *Brigham Young,* where the character Young describes in detail the role of the dominant lover to Harry. Young has decided that Harry must pretend to make love to Amelia so that she will be occupied while he woos and weds Alice. He instructs Harry:

> Emulate me. Let my example be your guide. Even propose elopement with her. Run me down; abuse me; make her crazy for you. Go on your knees; implore, rave, weep, pray; kiss her hands, her lips; ravish her lips with kisses; distract her with your vows of love until she yields, all tears, soul and body to your amorous arms.[86]

Stage directions for later love scenes in the play suggest that audiences saw quite a bit of this male-dominant lovemaking. As Harry takes Brigham's advice, he leads Amelia to a chair so that he can lean down at her to convince her of his love. Then he *"kneels . . . and takes her hand, fervently kissing it"* and in doing so, drives her to yield to his embrace.

This scene could be reenacted in any number of melodramas that played throughout the century. However, the image here is complicated by the physical presence of Brigham Young, a man known to audiences as the head polygamist of Mormondom. Additionally, the character Brigham Young has already kidnapped two young lovers; the man with the intent of having him killed, and the woman with the intent of keeping her captive as a plural wife. It would be impossible to divorce these previous actions of the character Young from his less coercive lovemaking.

Even more visually compelling is a similar scene between Brigham, Alice, his daughter Lotty, and one of his wives, Harriet. They have come to beg him not to continue with his plans to marry Lotty off as a plural wife and take Alice as his newest wife. Each woman in turn kneels before Brigham in supplication. The stage directions indicate that most of the scene is played in this composition, with Brigham standing above, talking down to, and touching three women who kneel at his feet. Returning to Wood's analysis of representations of African slavery, he suggests that an audience's view shifts between "an objectifying gaze that tends to animalize and dehumanize the black female body as 'object' and 'creature' and a highly wrought sentimentalized empathy which clothes the black victim in an elaborately romanticized diction."[87] The same process is at play in anti-Mormon melodramas. Rather than a black female body, however, the victims of polygamy are white, middle-class, and Christian. The elevation of the social and racial status of the enslaved makes the violence more titillating and more troubling.

Madwomen and Heroines

The fantasy of the enslaved woman created a situation that troubled gender ideologies of the time and allowed audiences a glimpse at the fascinating horrors of male sexuality run amok. In the play *Zion*, Mrs. Day begins in a life of perfect domesticity. She is a loving housewife, devoted to her family, but more importantly, to her spiritual life. She is convinced that her eternal salvation is dependant on her acceptance of the Mormon Church and her relocation to Zion. She is torn between her duties as a wife and mother and her new religious convictions. Mr. Day is a patient and loving husband who attempts to instruct his wife about the truth of Mormonism. Ignoring his council, Mrs. Day agrees to accompany Elder Marwood to Utah. She laments:

> My heart sinks at what I am doing—but I cannot retract I must go on ... Oh, if I only dare tell my husband all—no, no, I dare not, he would spurn me. This act severs my connection with all I hold most dear ... Farewell my home, beneath your shelter I have been the happiest of the happy. I have basked in the light of love and rejoiced. Years have come and gone freighted with joy; I have loved and been beloved—but now to all the past, farewell—to my old life—to my old love—to my old home farewell—farewell forever.[88]

The titular "Zion," however, turns out to be the slavery and prostitution of Salt Lake City where she is forced to become Marwood's eighth wife.

Mrs. Day's fate is a direct consequence of her actions: she rejects the counsel of her good husband, leaves her duties as a wife and mother, and follows a falsely spiritual man to her downfall. She in effect, denies her nature as a woman. The trials and travails of Mrs. Day illustrate the fears of the nation about women and their role in the family and in society. Anti-Mormon melodrama confront these fears by providing representations of two types of women: abused victims who never escape (either literally or figuratively) the horrors of polygamy, and heroines who actively fight against this fate and secure their own futures as wives in monogamous relationships.

Women who have been forced into plural marriages and are unable to escape remain until they have either become deadened to all delicate sensibilities, or have been driven mad. The extreme victimization of women in these situations serves as a warning to America that true women cannot exist in the bonds of polygamy. The image of degraded wives runs through most anti-Mormon melodramas with wives lamenting the tears, toils, agonies, woe, shame, horrors, seduction, slavery, and torment of polygamy. Even nature recognizes the evil of Utah where women are made such victims. Mrs. Day describes the scene outside her prison window as: "Black, cheerless, starless night anon swoops down and in seeming pity obscures the light of reason."[89]

In *Brigham Young,* three wives of Brigham all slip so far into despair that they consider suicide. For Clara, the despair has led to madness. With deep irony, and clutching a vial of poison, she exclaims:

> Why, I am not mad! How could I be mad and live in this heavenly life of happiness! O, what a sweet heaven to be the wife of the great and holy prophet. Oh, I have been in heaven so long that I want to go to hell! I am too happy here. I want to burn in hell! I am ashamed to be so happy when all my sisters are so wretched. Oh, sister Harriet, I must drink to the happiness of the prophet and his new bride . . . (*After pausing a moment—then laughing hysterically*) O, now I must drink this sweet poison to the health of my Lord and Prophet![90]

For Emeline, the threats of suicide come from the great emotional blow that Brigham wants yet another bride. Falling on his breast and weeping, she cries, "The Lord's will be done! But the Lord is unkind to let me live! I want to die! I must die! My heart is broken, and I don't want to live any longer!"[91] Amelia is the most rational of these wives and the most deadly in her intent. She also has a vial of poison that she threatens to use if Brigham is not willing to renounce his intentions to marry Alice. Amelia is willing, too, to place blame where it belongs—not on the victim heroine, but on the villainous Brigham. She warns him, "Refuse to renew your oath and I will drink this, and you will be my murderer."[92]

When Emeline tries to take the vial from her, Amelia turns on her to remind her of the reality of their situation. "There is enough for both of us, drink after me. Why should we live the slaves, the prostitutes of this vile man! Let us no longer be subject to his monstrous and hellish will! Let us be true women! Let us be an example for our wretched sisters in this vile hell of sin and iniquity! I can happily die for the honor of my sex!"[93] Amelia, however, quickly reveals in an aside to Emeline that she is just playing a part in order to force Brigham to her will. In manipulating Brigham Young with threats as a means to serve as an example of action for other women, Amelia becomes a melodramatic heroine.

Mary, one of the heroines of *The Mormons,* is another example of a heroine who appropriately resists. She is a gentle and lovely girl who inspires the love not only of Elder Pratt (who desires her for a plural wife) but also Eagle-Eye. A woodsman and tracker bent on revenge, Eagle Eye is inspired by Mary to dream a traditional life of home and family. This introduction to Mary establishes her innate goodness that has prompted a wandering man to consider settling down and devoting himself to his duties as husband and father. She first speaks out against polygamy in no uncertain terms when Alice, Brigham Young's daughter, comes to congratulate her on the marriage that she didn't know was taking place:

> ALICE: I presume that I am to be invited to the wedding, Miss Mary.
> MARY: Wedding! Whose, pray?
> ALICE: Yours, with Elder Pratt.
> MARY: Nonsense, you'll never be present at that wedding, I promise you.[94]

Mary later puts action to her words when she rescues Eagle Eye's stolen rifle from the Mormons and sneaks it to him so that they can escape. She is not entirely independent, though. When she and Eagle Eye are captured by Mormons to prevent their escape, Eagle Eye asks if she could cut the cords that bind him. She replies that she is unable, and then faints from the terror of it all. It is up to Eagle Eye to exert both mental and physical prowess to trick the Mormons into loosing his hands so that he can overpower them. Mrs. Woodville, in the same play, is even bolder in her resistance to polygamy. When she learns that her husband is taking a second wife, she invades the sacred male space of the Mormon Temple to convince her husband he should stop. She is successful both for her persuasive language and in her unwillingness to give in to the Mormons; she has to be physically dragged away from her husband.

In creating a fantasy of victims to Mormon lusts and in celebrating the women who resisted, anti-Mormon melodramas reinforced the importance of American domesticity against foreign threats. It is this vision that Mrs. Day holds dear after all of her tortures in *Zion*: "Remember? Yes, I remember the lowly home-like cottage, covered with clinging vines, and filled with love and peace. I remember—oh, how well I remember my loving daughter; my noble husband, I remember—and the remembrance sears my brain."[95] Even in the world of the play, this domestic scene is a happy dream, and in holding the vision up as a model of American happiness, the play urges the audience to yearn for it as well. This image is made topsy-turvy by Mormon women real and dramatized, who didn't fit the model of the true woman.

III. A GREATER ANOMALY

> Utah is the land of marvel. She gives us, first, polygamy, which seems to be an outrage against "woman's right," and then offers it to the nation as a "Female Suffrage Bill." ... Was there ever a greater anomaly known in the history of society?
>
> —*The Phrenological Journal*, November 1871

In a scene of comic relief in *Evelyn Gray*, the character Elder George Q. Cannon has gotten into a fight with his four wives that devolves into a catfight between "No. 1 and No. 4, agin [sic] No. 2 an' No. 3." Several men witnessing the fight even place bets on the winner. Humiliated by their behavior, Cannon rounds up his wives and instructs them to "Go, now, you hags, wash your faces and get dressed. I want you to come along to the polls and vote." When Wife No. 2 questions for whom they should vote, Cannon responds, "Never mind, I'll tell you."[96] This image of the voting Mormon woman whose political opinions are dictated by her husband was a significant trend in popular representation. Like the melodramatic scene, however, the issue was generally treated through humor rather than invective. It was also a representation that responded directly to the growing Mormon woman's movement.

From its foundation, women were a part of the Church of Jesus Christ of Latter-day Saints and participated in its administration. In 1842, Joseph Smith established the Relief Society, a women's organization devoted to charity, education, and religious sisterhood. Under the direction of his wife, Emma Smith, the Society grew rapidly in Nauvoo, but declined in activity during the years of relocation to Utah. In 1866, Brigham Young called his wife and former Nauvoo society secretary Eliza R. Snow to rebuild the Relief Society. Aided by a circle of "leading sisters," she oversaw the establishment of more than 300 local chapters before her death in 1887.

Snow's twenty-year administration of the Relief Society illustrates the opportunities for women created and supported by the nineteenth-century Church. Under her management the women purchased properties and built Relief Society halls, maintained and controlled their own funds; they also built granaries to support a grain-storage program and established cooperative and commission stores. The Society operated schools for nurses and midwives in the intermountain area, provided scholarships for women to attend medical schools, and operated a hospital. They published a widely-read newspaper, *The Woman's Exponent*, staged mass meetings to express their views on political issues, and lobbied for women's suffrage.

The content of the *Exponent* points to the broad impact of the woman's movement on Utah women, and on their contributions at local and national levels. Each issue (twice a month from 1872–1914) consisted of sections on women's health, education, and professional advancement. Letters expressed opinions on sexual, economic, and legal issues. Frequently the *Exponent* reprinted pertinent articles from women's publications in other parts of the country. The "Notes and News" and "Woman's Record" features reported on triumphs of women globally.[97] While the local work of the Relief Society might have continued unnoticed by the rest of the country, the Church's vocal participation in the suffrage movement brought Mormon women to the center of the suffrage debate.

The treatment of Mormon women in anti-Mormon melodramas played with American concerns about women's rights by devaluing them through humor. There is a linked phenomenon here of belief and practice. Women who are lured into Mormonism, whether they end up as madwomen or active heroines, all reject the religious belief along with their rejection of polygamy. Women who maintain a belief in the practice are depicted on stage as actively

Fig. 2.2 "Representative Women in Zion." Composite of 20 photoprints on lithograph by Graphic Co., N.Y. (1883). Head and shoulders portraits of 20 women leaders of the Mormon Church including Bathsheba Smith, Phoebe Woodruff, Zina Huntington Young, Sarah M. Kimball and Emeline B. Wells, surrounded by the decorative iconography of women's material culture. Courtesy of the Library of Congress, Prints and Photographs Division, LC-USZ62–89018

Mormon and remarkably ridiculous. It is these characters, as Mormon women, that promote women's rights. The result is a complicated dismissal of both polygamy and suffrage through caricature and physical comedy.

Pathetically Homely Creatures

An intricate political tangle of suffrage, polygamy, and statehood placed Utah as a contested space for a number of national groups—women's rights organizations, political parties, state and federal legislatures. Wyoming was the first territory to grant suffrage in 1869, a move that gave the rights to vote and hold office to its 1000 female citizens. When Utah followed suit six months later, the impact was much larger. Not only were there a large enough number of newly franchised women to have a significant political impact, they actually exercised their rights quickly and decisively. While Wyoming enfranchised women months before Utah did, Utah women participated in a vote first. The first woman to cast a ballot was Seraph Young, a niece of Brigham Young. She voted during municipal elections in Salt Lake City in 1870 and became the first woman to legally vote in the United States.

At first, there was national support for suffrage in Utah. Women's rights advocates across the country felt sure that this remarkable event would finally allow Mormon women to throw off the shackle of polygamy. However, Greeley's "joyful trust" that American women would not be reduced to harem slavery remained unfulfilled. Instead, in a move unanticipated by Greeley's hope for the solution to the "problem of Women's sphere and destiny," Mormon women used their new political clout to promote women's rights to education, to careers, and to practice marriage according to their choice.[98] And they chose polygamy.

It is ironic that America was willing to support suffrage in Utah as long as the women immediately used this public power to conform to an American ideal of domesticity. Instead, suffrage seemed to open the floodgate to major anxieties about nineteenth-century Mormonism's liberal view of gender equality.[99] Brigham Young preached:

> ... We have sisters here who, if they had the privilege of studying, would make just as good mathematicians or accountants as any man; and we think they ought to have the privilege to study these branches of knowledge that they may develop the powers with which they are endowed. We believe that women are useful not only to sweep houses, wash dishes, make beds, and raise babies, but that they should stand behind the counter, study law or physic [medicine], or become good bookkeepers and be able to do the business in any counting house, and this to enlarge their sphere of usefulness for the benefit of society at large. In following these things they but answer the design of their creation.[100]

In addition to organizing an effective suffrage campaign, Mormon women were encouraged to learn trades, become educated, and serve as contributing members of society.

In anti-Mormon melodrama, however, the agency of Mormon women characters is undercut by their ridiculousness. One view of Mormon women on stage that echoed satirical writing of the period, was that Mormon women were all physically unattractive and were political active as a way of compensating for their lack of other, more obvious virtues. The writings of famous satirists such as Mark Twain and Artemus Ward created an enormously popular view of the ugly Mormon woman. In his 1872 publication *Roughing It,* Twain famously suggests that his first-hand experience seeing women in polygamy changed his mind about the evils of the practice:

> Then I was touched. My heart was wiser than my head. It warmed toward these poor, ungainly, and pathetically "homely" creatures, and as I turned to hide the generous moisture in my eyes, I said, "no—the man that married one of them has done an act of Christian charity which entitles him to the kindly applause of mankind, not their harsh censure—and the man that marries sixty of them has done a deed of open-handed generosity so sublime that the nations should stand uncovered in his presence and worship in silence."[101]

Robert Norris, a New York journalist, expresses a similar opinion in the melodrama *Evelyn Gray* when he remarks: "The Mormon women have evidently been supplied with a gracious, providential bulwark against temptation in their homeliness."[102]

It seems reasonable to assume that these comments about the appearance of Mormon women functions, as Eric A. Eliason argues, as "internal requirements of his joke" rather than as actual observations.[103] Travel writer Sir Richard Burton found Mormon women of the day to be great beauties, with "noble regular features, the lofty, thoughtful brow, the clear transparent complexion, the long silky hair, and greatest of all, the smile of the American woman."[104] Eliason supposes that "evaluations of Mormon women's attractiveness seem to have more to do with the rhetorical goals of the evaluator than with any objective reality."[105] In melodrama, one such rhetorical goal of writing comic Mormon women was to discredit the opinions and beliefs of these women who were unattractive, uneducated, and ridiculous. The comic effect of these characters counteracts any actual validity to women's logic, activities, and political aspirations and assuages fears about their effectiveness.

In *The Mormons*, the thirteen wives of Timothy Noggs hold family councils to discuss problems, jointly raise all their children, and band together against their husband. They share the household duties, as described in the stage directions, "*Discovered the various Mrs. Noggs, engaged in knitting, sewing, ironing, washing, and other domestic occupations.*"[106] Although the women clearly take care of the home, they also organize themselves into a delegation that proposes motions for household rules, seconds the motions, votes, and passes resolutions. By the end of the play, they have united against their husband, tied him up, tarred and feathered him, and sent him packing, all on the outcome of their vote.

The comic Mrs. Noggs (plural) in *The Mormons* are a rag-tag bunch of women of different nationalities with foreign accents and short tempers. They are united only in their proper use of Parliamentary Procedure and in their disgust with their husband, Mr. Noggs. Chatterina ("Mrs. Noggs No. 1") is called on to be the convention speaker. She suggests that their collective husband is a lazy man, dishonest, and that he needs straightening out. The content of her speech, however, is mediated by her accent and poor use of grammar:

> And he's got to be taken in hand, and his bristles combed the wrong way, and his kinks taken out—which he is a kinky man by nature, being of the porkypine gender—and requiring straightening out for the good of his health. And it's my opinion that we are the women to do it, if we strive. And with them observations, Mrs. Cheerwoman and fellow wives, I squat.[107]

Her suggestion is nominated, seconded, and voted upon unanimously. The revolt of these wives, portrayed seriously, would be a shocking displacement of the male role of savior and protector of female virtue. In making the entire subplot comic relief, the actions of the women are confirmed as unthinkable—women don't really behave in this way, and it's funny to think that they might.

Twiss, one of the character Brigham Young's wives in *Brigham Young*, is another such figure. She, as her name onomatopoetically suggests, is a flighty, silly gossip who revels in the intrigues of plural marriage—keeping up to date on who the "favorites" are, or who the next wife will be. From her bustling interference in others' lives, to her long-winded chattiness, to the opinions of the more credible characters around her, she is drawn as an absurd woman. Harry, the hero of the play, states in an aside that he doesn't trust her,[108] and Alice refers to her as a "poor, innocent, dupe."[109] Her easy acceptance of polygamy is both invalidated by her character, and serves as a mark against her—since she doesn't mind being a plural wife, and is frankly supportive of Young taking more wives, her opinion doesn't matter. As a comic character, her opinion (including her opinion of polygamy) is likewise ridiculous. Comic characters like Twiss serve a variety of purposes in anti-Mormon melodramas—they approve of polygamy, they push for social change, they lobby for suffrage—but their transgressive potential is mediated by their function as comic relief rather than a legitimate opposing point of view.

The characterization of some Mormon women as both ugly and manly is a physical manifestation of their personality traits that are outside the purview of true womanhood. Representations of Mormon women's rights on stage were negated by their comic use. Staging the mockery of suffrage confirmed that a woman's place is in the home. To be otherwise is for women to become, as Bridgit Noggs describes, "one of the b'ys."[110] Humor in anti-Mormon melodramas was an effective tool in treating the fear about Mormon women as an affront to the patriarchal family structure.

Women, Men, and Mormons

In anti-Mormon melodramas, women are portrayed as abused slaves, as victims of rape and bondage, as resistant heroines who fight against polygamy, or as mannish political leaders—homely women who vote, are ridiculously violent against men, and far from submissive. Victim characters suffer the consequences of their loss of virtue with characteristic melodramatic death by suicide or insanity, or they are deluded converts to a dark religion who have been betrayed by their natural sense of Christian piety. Heroines are rewarded for their active fight against polygamy with the promise of a happy monogamous marriage to an ideal American man. Fighting against these domesticating forces is the Mormon rapist who, as performed in *Zion*, adheres to a false religion "founded and maintained, for the sole purpose of pandering to the lust and cupidity of man."[111] The Mormon villain was a dark sexual fantasy that both validated men's concerns about emasculation and suggested the inappropriateness of giving away self-control.

The issues of consumer culture, slavery, and women's rights that were wrestled with at the end of the nineteenth century point to the difficulty in reading men and women exclusively through the doctrine of separate spheres. Instead, anti-Mormon melodramas rhetorically linked polygamy and slavery in order to justify moral outrage against sexual practices that were in fact a savagery already imbedded in American culture. In an extremely sensational style, the plays created a space where gender issues were inverted, transgressed, but also reaffirmed. In doing so, they set up a model of appropriate Christian marriage as a key aspect of American identity.

Characterizing polygamy on stage provided clear models of behavior that suggested appropriate gendered behavior for both men and women. Sometimes the relationships between adherence to the ideal of domesticity and rewards and punishments are clear. Mrs. Day leaves her husband, her home, and her child. She abandons her primary duties as a woman. The negative consequence is painted in no uncertain terms—she is raped, abused, and driven to madness and violence. On the other hand, Eagle Eye, a true man who honors all women and protects them against dishonor and violence is rewarded for his goodness. Early in *The Mormons* he dreams "of a cabin by the old riverside, in my native place—my roving habits laid by—a loving wife and chirping infants at the fireside."[112] His actions throughout the play prove him worthy of the dream and the final tableau of the production reunites him with Mary. Their loving embrace suggests a future just as he has envisioned.

Other times, the relationship is more complicated. In *Brigham Young*, Amelia is Young's last and greatest love. She is a polygamous wife who, during the course of the play, alternates between displaying attributes of a true woman and behaving in a manner altogether unbecoming of a true woman. When she is falsely seduced by Harry, she never abandons her principle responsibility to her home and husband. Even after Harry points out that she is not Young's lawful wife, and that her "happiness is a myth," she remains true to her responsibilities. As she explains, "Do you suppose I am abandoned in my heart, and in my nature so depraved that any flattering tongue can lure me into shame? What improprieties have you seen in me to give you warrantable hope I could be won to forfeit virtue and respect?"[113]

She justifies her rejection of Harry's suit not because she is happy with her lot as a polygamous wife, but because it is not in her "nature" to betray the trust of her husband. Her behavior resonates with the advice of countless books to women in the nineteenth century that clearly assign responsibility for peace in the home and in marital relationships. In Daniel Wise's 1854 book, *Bridal Greetings: A Marriage Gift in Which the Mutual Duties of Husband and Wife are Familiarly Illustrated and Enforced*, he gives a number of scenarios to show that it is the wife's responsibility to keep peace in the home, no matter the behavior of the husband. Madame Adorna, the fictional heroine of the Wise's book, is a paragon of this principle: "She bore the outbreaks of her husband's temper with Christian submission; she devoted herself to the task of making his home attractive and delightful."[114]

Initially, Amelia submits to her husband's eccentricities, accepts her role as a plural wife, and models behavior of what could be read as an exemplary true woman. Once she learns, however, that she has been falsely seduced, she rejects that "nature" and, in fact, takes over her husband's role. Young has imprisoned Harry, but Amelia frees him into her custody: "You shall be my prisoner, now, not the Prophet's. I will secret you and be your keeper."[115] Taking over the male role in the machinations of the play allows her to rave against her husband, threaten violence against him, and speak her mind without hesitation. Her confrontation with Young is a moment of transgression where the gender standards are reversed.

Amelia describes her behavior as a "performance," which it was, in two ways. The actress playing the role provided a staged possibility for behavior unbecoming of a woman that breaks the anticipated consequences of that behavior. The character of Amelia is also play-acting a gender reversal. Her confession that she is playing a part makes her behavior safe for audiences, and suggests that the gendered behavior preached by the doctrine of separate spheres is a construction, fractured, and fluid.[116] Instead, Amelia stands as the melodramatic heroine of the piece, having acted to preserve her own virtue and bending her husband to her will.

Feminist theorist Lisa Tickner suggests, "we have no unmediated access to the real. It is through representation that we know the world."[117] The gendered world of nineteenth-century America was known by the way in which it was represented in popular culture. The characterization of these women, men, and Mormons in anti-Mormon melodramas allowed the ideal to be enacted. Although the representations were at times complicated, the conclusion of these plays invariably reinforced the dominance of monogamy, the importance of home and family, and reinstated specific gender identity.

As with other polygamous characters represented on the melodramatic stage, Amelia's reconciliation with her husband is staged in a way that reestablishes gender norms. Young forgives the trouble she has caused, and she forgives him and *"kneels at his feet."*[118] While other wives are dramatized in this piece (Emmeline, the first wife; Clara, Lotty's mother; Twiss; Harriet; Hetty), Young's vow that he will be faithful to Amelia alone confirms his primary relationship with one woman. The final tableau of the play emphasizes this monogamy and privileges normative marriage relationships. The stage directions explain: *"Talbot and many of the wives up stage. Frank and Lott, R[ight]. Brigham and Amelia, C[enter]. Harry and Alice, L[eft]."*[119] Brigham Young and Amelia are the center focus of the audience's eye as a couple whose vow to be faithful to one another is cemented by the last line of the play: a reaffirming "And the Lord be with us."[120] The Lord approves of this relationship, and Young's willingness to only be with Amelia brings him back into the acceptable Christian fold.

This ending suggests a realignment of the binary of the public/private sphere wherein the poetic justice of the piece is the unification of Young and Amelia in a new monogamous domestic relationship that brings them back into the American fold. The historical reality of Brigham Young's marriage to Amelia further complicates his capitulation at the end of the play and presents a hopeful end to polygamy that would alleviate the foreign threat of Mormondom from the heart of the West.

The Mormon Church's efforts to find a place for polygamy in America ultimately proved unsuccessful. The popular vilification of plural marriage in political legislation, sensational histories, lurid novels, satirical reports, and anti-Mormon melodramas was an overwhelming representation. Pressures from the government, growing concerns from Mormon men and women alike about the viability of the practice, and finally, a formal announcement from the Church's president in 1890 ended the official practice of polygamy. The sexual politics that promoted a patriarchal family of monogamy prevailed and Utah was granted statehood. By the outbreak of the First World War, Mormonism had firmly established a dominant literature promoting the Church as the defender of the very system that destroyed its early practice of polygamy.

3 Murderers
The Necessity of Honorable Violence

> Them ar Mormons mean murder an' massacretion.
> —Bill Williams, in *Fonda*

> Americans have a deep belief in the moral necessity of violence and ... this belief accounts for the paradox of an ostensibly peace-loving and lawful people being so obsessed with violence.
> —John Cawelti, "Myths of Violence"

The popular stereotype of the "Wild West" is based in the reality of the methods by which America enlarged her border: the conflicts that arose between settlers and the uncharted land itself, between settlers and indigenous peoples already inhabiting the land, and between various groups of settlers. The geographic and cultural distance between the West and the centralized federal government in the East exacerbated these conflicts. The portrayal of frontier violence in popular culture emphasizes the basic goodness of the "civilizing" settlers, and the evil intents of those that oppose them, generally Indians or outlaws. In the late nineteenth century, however, concerns about the threat of violence were centered on another, perhaps even more threatening group: the Mormons.

The history of the Mormon Church is littered with violent encounters. Many were perpetrated against the Mormons, who suffered vigilante persecution in New York, Ohio, Illinois, and Missouri. The Battle of Crooked River between Mormons and the Missouri militia was the catalyst for the Mormon War in Missouri that included Governor Lilburn Boggs' "Extermination Order," against the Mormons and culminated in the Haun's Mill Massacre (1838) where U.S. militia killed seventeen Mormons. Shortly thereafter, both Joseph and Hyrum Smith were assassinated by a mob (1844). Even after the exodus to Utah, violence remained part of the Mormon experience. Almost immediately, President James Buchanan sent federal troops to quell a perceived uprising, an event now referred to as the Utah War (1857–1858).

Mormons were responsible for violence as well. The greatest causalities in the Utah War came from the Mountain Meadows Massacre (1857) where Mormons, aided by Native Americans, killed roughly 125 settlers. The same year, a group of six men, the Aiken party, were murdered in central Utah. Although the perpetrators were well known in the area, they were not indicted until years later, and only one lived to make it to trial where he was acquitted.[1] The Mormon militia, Mormon vigilantes, and allegedly secret Mormon enforcers were also documented committing acts of violence throughout the early days of the Church. For nearly two decades, both those who opposed the Mormons and the Mormons themselves resorted to violence as a measure of maintaining control over what they each perceived to be their rights and privileges as Americans.

In his work *Vigilantism: Political History of Private Power in America* (1990), William C. Culberson points out that one of the prevailing notions in American political thought is that the abuse of freedom is part of the price of its use. Different groups throughout America's history have walked a fine line between legitimate and criminal acts of violence in the name of upholding freedom.[2] John Cawelti makes a similar observation in his study, "Myths of Violence in American Popular Culture." Cawelti wrestles with the seeming paradox between American's penchant for violent stories and their pride in being a "non-violent, law-abiding people." He resolves the issue in suggesting that Americans must believe "that their dedication to law and peace [is] not sufficient or complete enough unless it [is] tested by their willingness to commit criminal and even violent actions in support of their crusades."[3]

Observations of this phenomenon in practical history and popular culture suggest that violence can serve both as an evil and as a moral necessity. What defines which type of violence is being enacted is dependant largely on the way that the violence is represented. In turn, the way the violence is represented is dependant almost exclusively on the legitimizing moral opinion of the popular majority. Culberson argues:

> The line dividing violent acts from criminal acts is a matter of cohesive social values, aspirations, and the tests of time that define motives for political or private purposes. For the source of social cohesion is not the Constitution or written laws, but a consensus regarding the dominant norms and values of society.[4]

However, as Bill in Jack Crawford's *Fonda* suggests, Mormon representations on stage focused on a particular type of violence: "murder and massecration," perpetrated by Mormon outlaws that established a clear line between good and bad violence. The differentiation between types of violence in melodramas such as *The Danites, Fonda, The Mormons, Evelyn Gray,* or *Treason, Stratagems and Spoils* evidences assumptions about who is justified in using violence, how it can be used appropriately, and why its use is necessary. The late nineteenth century in America was a period of expansion, Civil War, Industrial Revolution, and reconstruction that required citizens to demonstrate their commitment to the development of a better civilization. Conformity to civilization required action, and as

Culberson states, "Aggression is a defense, opposition is a protection, and assertion is an expression to maintain social values from harm by ephemeral alien forces."[5]

Anti-Mormon melodramas were a tool in providing these ephemeral alien forces with tangibility in the form of murdering Mormons who refused to follow the laws dictated by the legal institution of the nation and by the complex customs that pervade and control a community. In these plays, melodramatic heroes emerged as the ideal example of Americans who were honorable in their motivations, followed national laws, community rules, and worked to preserve the family unit. The juxtaposition of villainous Mormons and American heroes represent how the appropriate use of violence is an integral part of American identity.

In his essay "A Critique of Violence," Walter Benjamin provides a number of insights into the ways in which violence functions in society. He suggests a complex relationship between violence and lawmaking: "All violence as a means is either lawmaking or law-preserving . . . It follows, however, that all violence as a means, even in the most favorable case, is implicated in the problematic nature of law itself."[6] He observes that violence functions not just to uphold, but to *make* laws by closely analyzing a number of different types of violence: strikes, police work, capital punishment, and military action. While Benjamin's work is specifically focused on twentieth-century formations, his central thesis on the relationship between violence, morality, and the law provides a fascinating insight into the use of violence in nineteenth-century America. His ideas about the lawmaking function of violence are especially applicable to the frontier, where the challenge of establishing new communities forced an application of violence to create, uphold, and defend societal rules and regulations.

Benjamin points out that the process from violence to law does not erase the violence, but in fact, strengthens its potential usefulness:

> For the function of violence in lawmaking is two fold, in the sense that lawmaking pursues as its end, with violence as the means, *what* is to be established as law, but at the moment of instatement does not dismiss violence; rather, at this very moment of lawmaking, it specifically establishes as law not an end unalloyed by violence, but one necessarily and intimately bound to it, under the title of power.[7]

This observation, that violence is not only the means to establish laws, but is a necessary condition of actual lawmaking, opens up the possibility for the notion of "honorable violence," or socially acceptable use of aggression for the maintenance of nation, community, and family.

Honorable violence is my phrase, not Benjamin's. A parallel concept in "The Critique of Violence" is Benjamin's idea of "justice," or "the principle of all divine end making."[8] I base my notion of honorable violence on this justice which infers, for Benjamin, that "every conceivable solution to human problems . . . remains impossible if violence is totally excluded in principle."[9] Here he suggests that violence is ethical, as well as legal, and therefore it stands to reason that violence can and must be used as an appropriate means to a moral end.

There is a tradition in popular literature of the outlaw hero—a protagonist who breaks certain laws in order to keep others. The attraction to outlaw heroes and the willingness to accept their lawlessness is mediated by the fact that society functions in accordance to a number of different codes of behavior. So while these characters might be outlaws by one definition, they are rarely outlaws in every sense of the term. On the American frontier in the nineteenth century, differentiating between law-abiding and outlaw citizens came as a result of adherence to three intersecting categories of law: national, community, and family.

In the wake of the Civil War, the nation rebuilt itself on the principles of united ethics; what was good for one part of the country was good for it all. State autonomy was mediated by emerging federal rules and regulations. At first glance, this may seem to be the easiest way to determine legality—an act either upholds or breaks "the" law. The fluid systems established in unorganized territories, the distance between the application of western justice and oversight of the eastern legal center, and the actual lack of any appointed government in many communities, however, complicated the relationship between violence and governmental law. Mormon violence in melodramas supported the need for federal regulation by dramatizing attacks on the United States. In doing so, consistent crimes of Mormons created a vision of the need for national lawfulness.

Another, perhaps even more pervasive law, are the unwritten codes established by society and based in the underlying ethics of an individual's personal sense of right and wrong. A community's undefined, yet guiding principles impact daily life and the administration of justice; both history and literature are marked by examples of clearly biased outcomes to trials whose juries acted on their perception of a societal code of ethics rather than procedures dictated by institutional law. The portrayal of murdering Mormons as evil Danites underlines the ways in which they are not members of the communities that they interact with, but are instead, a totally autonomous group of religious fanatics who have their own code of rule and behaviors.

The Danites were a fraternity of Mormons organized by local Mormon leaders in Missouri in 1838. A vigilante group, they both defended Mormons against violence and sought revenge against their attackers. Officially disbanded soon after its inception, rumors of a strong secret brotherhood emerged and caught hold of public imagination. In later articulation, the Danites were not a vigilante group, but a band of murderers. The belief in and horror of Mormon secret violence as disseminated in novels, newspapers, and melodramas suggested boundaries that separated justified vigilantism from murder.

A final vision of the law springs from the second amendment to the constitution, which provides a right to bear arms. While the constitution speaks specifically of a national militia, this amendment, based on early English law, presumes the right to self-defense in the bearing of arms (US Const., Amend. II). Legal precedence in the nineteenth century grew up around this point, specifically, the right to bear arms in self-defense. Particularly on the violent frontier, the notion of self-defense allowed citizens to "stand their ground" and protect themselves and their families with violence. In protection of home and hearth, violent self-defense was therefore not only appropriate, but also lawful. In anti-Mormon melodramas, on the other hand, Mormon villains seek out women and children as victims of violence and take obscene pleasure in their murders. The contrast between violence to protect the weak and violence that targets the weak provides yet another line defining honorable violence in America.

The way in which heroes and villains were portrayed in the nineteenth century encodes a belief deeply embedded in American identity: violence is a necessary evil. So while anxieties about violence emerge in popular culture, the solution to restore peace is violence as well. At the height of Manifest Destiny, violent conflicts were a necessary condition of America's moral obligation to bring law and order to the continent. In the wake of the Civil War, honorable violence can be seen as the violence that defends a united nation as opposed to violence that seeks to tear it apart.

I. VIOLENCE AND THE NATION

> It's either one or the other. It's Columbia or Deseret, Washington or Zion, Uncle Sam or Brigham Young... We are the one and only true church, and we are bound to die or rule over the whole world.
>
> —Brigham Young, in the play *Evelyn Gray*

Rob Norris, the character of a young journalist from New York City who travels to Salt Lake City in *Evelyn Gray,* sets up an interesting juxtaposition in his opening lines of the play between the wild land of savages and the beautiful land of cities which dot that land. He states:

> Amid the arrows of the savages,
> I stand, upon the eastern gateway of
> An empire, stretching hence from sea to sea,
> For many thousand miles of broad expanse,
> Where in the stead of pristine wilderness,
> Infested by wild beasts and men like wild,
> A thousand cities shadow now their spires
> In the white sheen of garden-bordered lakes,
> And rivers, skirted by the rushing trains.

> The heavenly air of freedom gently blows
> Over the golden grainfields with their fruit
> Waving and rip'ning in the gladsome sun.[10]

It is "the heavenly air of freedom" that is both the reason for and the result of this civilization. Civilization is not just a political necessity, but according to Norris, is a religious imperative. It is this imperative that provided the Doctrine of Manifest Destiny with the double justification of geo-political and divine right to take over the North American continent. Mormons complicated this process with their attempts to create alliances with and even convert their native neighbors. Mormon-Indian relations appear in anti-Mormon melodrama as a united stumbling block to the advance of civilization across the nation.

Norris celebrates the American "empire, stretching hence from sea to sea." Writing *Evelyn Gray; or, A History of Our Western Turks* in 1890, author Herman Isadore Stern would have been a witness to a nation recovering from the Civil War. An impossibly long play (236 pages at first printing), this tragedy follows the fictional character of Evelyn Gray through years of Mormon history and doctrine packed into an action-filled plot. Many of the Mormon characters in the play are based on real-life figures and their dialogue expands upon published Mormon sermons. Events in the play include the Martin and Willie Handcart disaster, from which Evelyn barely escapes alive, to the Mountain Meadows Massacre, that she does not.

Evelyn is aided in her attempts to flee the Mormons by her fiancé, James St. Clair, and his best friend, Norris. Evelyn's romance is complicated by the interference of an actress of ill-repute who stars on the Salt Lake Theatre stage and the machinations of the violent Danites. A final massacre kills off all of the beloved characters in the play, including Evelyn, James, her parents, the Irish comic sidekick, and the actress. Norris, also fatally wounded, is left alone on stage to reflect on the evils of the murderous Mormons.

Set before the Civil War, the play's rhetoric evidences concern over the soon-to-come conflict. Boasting of an uninterrupted empire foregrounded national fears of any group that would divide the nation. After the return of the Confederacy to the Union, the greatest threat came from the Mormons who made no secret of their desire to create a State of Deseret to house their kingdom of God on earth. Congressional control kept the state from forming, but did not ease concerns, evidenced in anti-Mormon melodrama and in newspapers across the country, that the Mormons would eventually make literal their kingdom and would attempt to secede from the nation.

Frontier melodramas, with their exciting use of violence as a means of plot resolution and spectacular staging, may have provided nineteenth-century audiences with an exaggerated view of the predominance of violence in the American West. At the same time, the situations of violence responded to audiences' concerns over national threats, both real and perceived. In anti-Mormon melodramas, specifically, Mormons are the threat against which American heroes emerge, willing to eradicate those forces that would halt the progress of civilization and destroy the primacy of "one nation under God."

Manifest Destiny

The growing power of the Mormon theocracy in the West was a concern that was enhanced by Mormon resistance to federal sovereignty. Mormon settlements across the nation and Mormon control of the major East-West passages through the Great Basin was in direct opposition to the doctrine of Manifest Destiny that proclaimed the dominance of the United States over the entire country. As one newspaperman in 1872 suggested to his readers, civilization was occurring "without agency of our government, without responsibility of our people—in natural flow of events, the spontaneous working of principles, and the adaptation of the tendencies and wants of the human race to the elemental circumstances in the midst of which they find themselves placed."[11]

The civilizing of the continent was only able to occur due to policies such as President Andrew Jackson's Indian Removal Act (December 1831). This authorized Congress to initiate treaties with Native Americans to remove them from their tribal homes and relocate them to lands further West. For incompatible societies, such as the tribes of Native Americans, Americans felt perfectly justified in forceful establishment of civilization. Using violence as a tool to bring about peace (or in other words, compelling freedom) was less of a paradox in the nineteenth century than it may seem today. It is in fact, one of the central features of frontier melodrama. Roger Hall discusses violence first as one of the primary contradictions that "are given theatrical shape in frontier melodrama." Building on Gary A. Richardson's assertion that the violence in frontier plays is the rule rather than the exception, Hall concludes that the "guns, knives, and rifles typically carried by the characters furnished a fundamental aspect of their bearing."[12] This fundamental aspect of frontier melodrama was more than evident in anti-Mormon melodrama where violence is countered by violence; these both were a reflection of national philosophies and policies.

Inexorably linked to the philosophy of Manifest Destiny were the politics of Popular Sovereignty, a policy promoted by Stephen A. Douglass, who advised that newly formed territories and states should decide for themselves their position on slavery. A significant feature in the 1848 presidential campaign, the policy suggested generally that all legitimate political authority within society is obtained by consent of the subject population. As the United States government legalized "civilizing" the continent and provided opportunities for immigrants to establish communities, they validated the Westward expansion of Anglo settlers who had decided for themselves where they wanted to live. Meanwhile, each individual's lawmaking efforts in the West were a vote of confidence in and a support of a federal government that was serving the needs of American citizens.

The doctrines of Manifest Destiny and Popular Sovereignty mediated the aftermath of expansion and the introduction of civilization to lands previously seen as wild and unsettled. As is seen in the lines from *Evelyn Grey* above, America is not just the acquired land—"thousands of miles of broad expanse"—but is the civilization that is built upon the land—"Where in the stead of pristine wilderness/Infested by wild beasts and men like wild/A thousand cities shadow now their spires."[13] For Norris, as for the rest of the country, America was defined by the civilizing institutions and laws that were established within her borders. An article in the *Democratic Review* in 1845 emphasized: "Already the advance guard of the irresistible army of Anglo-Saxon emigration has begun to pour down upon it armed with the plow and the rifle, and marking its trail with schools and colleges, courts and representative halls, mills and meeting houses."[14]

The character Rob Norris's vision of the West in *Evelyn Gray* is untroubled by Indians, whose arrows have been tamed by the "empire" of the United States.[15] It is, however, troubled by the political machinations and violent behaviors of the Mormons and their stronghold in Salt Lake City that provided an oasis for criminals and a prison for deluded converts. In a reprise of his poetic introduction to America at the beginning of the play, he closes the show with another vision of America. The hopeful land of "waving grainfields" is darkly tainted by the existence of "Western Turks," who have raped and massacred an entire wagon train of innocents. Norris recovers from his wounds enough to cry to God for vengeance:

> But what of thee, my loved America,
> Who harborest unknown in hidden lap
> This ghastly thing, whereat the devils laugh.
> Can no one help thee expiate this curse?[16]

Norris then calls upon the mountains, the sky, and the sun to testify of Mormon brutality to heaven so that God can punish them for their sins. Comparison between the two poetic scenes is striking. America is a land of flowing rivers, gently blowing breezes, and shining sun. America with Mormons is a somber witness to the atrocities of inconceivable violence that makes devils laugh with joy.

Mormons were not going along with the "natural flow of events" identified as the impetus for civilization. They were insular, resistant to integration with the surrounding population, and voted as a bloc. Popular representation painted them as violent outlaws who defended their kingdom with deadly force. More frighteningly, they colluded with savage Indian tribes and borrowed from them weapons and methods of cruelty. In the play, Norris was not just shot and brained, he was also scalped by Mormons.

Mormons and Indians

Mormon relationships with Native Americans must be understood in context of their belief that Native Americans are God's chosen people on the American continent.[17] Stemming from doctrine established in *The Book of Mormon*, Mormons believed that the native inhabitants of the Americas were "Lamanites," descendants of the Biblical tribe of Joseph and inheritors of the blessings of Israel. As a result, from the beginnings of the Church, Mormons made overtures to Native American tribes by sending missionaries to befriend and convert them. They also manipulated this same relationship by using Indians to further their own causes. For example, Mormon district military commanders in August 1857 were ordered to "instruct the Indians that our enemies are also their enemies."[18]

Early missionary efforts in the tribes in Iowa and Missouri were successful enough that Indian agents became concerned that Mormons were, in fact, using conversion as a mask to join with Native Americans in rebellion against the United States. Agent Henry King, an interpreter between Joseph Smith and Potawatomi chiefs reported to Iowa governor John Chambers, "It seems evident, from all that I can learn . . . that a grand conspiracy is about to be entered into between the *Mormons and the Indians* to destroy all white settlements on the Frontier."[19]

Mormon policy in the Great Basin continued in an ostensibly friendly manner. While Brigham Young met with chiefs of local tribes to secure permission to settle land and share crops and livestock, inevitable disputes over boundaries and rights occurred. In their chapter on Mormons and Native Americans, Arrington and Bitton suggest that from the Mormon arrival in the Salt Lake valley until the Indian removals in the late 1860s, Mormon policy was politely contradictory.[20] On one hand, Mormons continued to believe that Native Americans were part of the Lord's elect and should be treated as spiritual equals. On the other hand, Mormons actively pursued the development of the State of Deseret for and on behalf of white settlers. This included the forced removal of Indians from Mormon lands and resulted in growing hostilities between the two peoples.[21]

In his work, *Making Space on the American Frontier,* W. Paul Reeve articulates that the Mormon Indian policy "was not only caught between visions of Indian redemption and the need for Zion land, but also between divergent Indian doctrines." These were exacerbated by local leaders who would modify "Young's advice to suit local circumstances as well as [their] own vision of colonization."[22] For all of the Mormon efforts to treat their Indian neighbors without hostility, the prevailing attitude surrounding the interactions between Mormons and Indians remained one restricted by a cultural superiority and religious imperative.

Brigham Young evidenced the contradictory Mormon Indian policy in an address before the Utah Legislature in 1854:

> I have uniformly pursued a friendly course of policy towards them [the Indians], feeling convinced that independent of the question of exercising humanity towards so degraded and ignorant a race of people, it was manifestly more economical and less expensive, to feed and clothe, than to fight them.[23]

While Young is willing to pursue a "friendly course of policy," it was only in service of civilizing an "ignorant race of people." For Young, this was also a chillingly practical solution—it was less expensive to woo than to fight. Avoiding an Indian war, however, directly conflicted with the more commonly accepted adage—"the only good Indian is a dead Indian"—that supported the important doctrine of Manifest Destiny. Mormons, in this way, were directly opposing established methods for supporting the nation. Additionally, the initially friendly relationship between Mormons and many tribes suggested a unity that was dangerous to others on the frontier. The resulting rumors were of a Mormon-Native American military alliance that would prove a valid threat to Westward expansion. That these rumors may have been based in fact does not alter the exaggerated representation of the villainous implications of a Mormon-Indian alliance in anti-Mormon melodramas.

In *Fonda*, there is a staged collusion between Mormons and Piute Sam, "Chief of the Mormon Indian allies," to massacre the wagon train. The same is true in *The Danites*, where miners save a young girl "half-dead with hunger and fright" who tried to find refuge in the camp. The miners try to protect her, however, as one miner relates: "The Danites came burstin' in upon us, leadin' the Injins, and all of 'em a shootin' at that poor, helpless baby, that never did anybody any harm."[24] Here the Indians are not even central to the story, but neither are they remarkable for their presence. It is no surprise to the miners that Indians would abet Mormons in their murder plots.

The collaboration between Mormons and Indians is such an integral aspect of frontier lore that the two groups begin to take on one another's characteristics. Ruth, a "black Republican" in *Fonda* responds to a child's question if God makes Mormons by saying, "no honey, de debil makes dem—dem and de Indians."[25] Both being made of the devil, it is unsurprising that Mormons end up in the same place as Indians after this life. Ruth's friend John H., promises his lady friend that he will protect her and will see that all the Mormons are "ready to pitch their tents in the happy hunting grounds of the hereafter."[26]

To nineteenth-century audiences, perhaps the most horrifying collapse between Indians and Mormons is the repeated image of the scalping Mormon. In *Evelyn Gray*, Brigham Young himself professes to this form of violence: "We have lots of Jack Gentiles and I tell you I am after their scalps [*Laughter.*] O you laugh, do you? You think I am using a funny figure of speech. You think I am going to have their Gentile friends attended to. And so I am."²⁷ Captain Jack in *Fonda* understands that scalping Mormons is far from a figure of speech and promises his friend Bill: "Should you fall by the hand of Indian or Mormon and I ever strike the miscreant's trail, if I don't wipe him out, he can have my scalp to keep yours company."²⁸ Whether killed by Mormons or Indians, the prize is a scalp. The national concerns about collusion between the Mormon kingdom and Native American tribes were formed and fixed by their telling and retelling in popular culture. While images such as scalping, attacks shared between Mormons and Indians, or actual reenactments of plots between the two groups furthered national concerns.

Treasonous Campaigns

In 1857, President Buchanan, wrestling with the growing risk of secession from Southern states and convinced by reports of an emerging Mormon kingdom in the West, focused his energies towards Utah. He determined to replace territorial Governor Brigham Young with a non-Mormon official. He ordered a 2,500-man federal army, under the command of Colonel Albert Sydney Johnston, to Utah to wrest power away from Brigham Young, by force if necessary. The conflicts of the Utah War were marked by exaggerated rumors on both sides about the violence each intended for the other. The concerns that led to this war were enacted in various melodramas that confirmed that the Mormon Church was engaged in treasonous campaigns against the United States.

As with many of the threats countered by violence in anti-Mormon melodramas, the basis of the fears was grounded in reality. In this case, as David Bigler outlines, in December 1856, Utah lawmakers:

> . . . drew up and sent to President-elect Buchanan a series of resolutions vowing to resist any effort by federal officials to ignore territorial laws or impose federal laws 'which [were] inapplicable and of right not in force in this territory.'²⁹ Buchanan received the defiant decrees soon after his inauguration in March 1857 and referred them to Interior Secretary Jacob Thompson. Thompson stamped the Mormon doctrine of nullification "a declaration of war."³⁰

Johnston's approaching army led Young to declare martial law in the territory, and at his orders Mormon militia engaged in guerilla tactics intended to slow the progress of the expedition and force them to winter over in Wyoming. While these tactics achieved their purpose they did not ultimately stop the advance of the army. When it became clear that the army would continue into Utah, but that they meant no harm to its citizens, a compromise was reached. Brigham Young voluntarily stepped down as territorial governor and in the spring of 1858, President Buchanan issued a "Proclamation of Pardon."

In his work, *Forgotten Kingdom* (1998), David L. Bigler analyzes the conflicts between Federal and Mormon politics in the Utah Territory. He concludes that Mormons established "the most singular form of government ever seen on American Soil."[31] Almost immediately following their arrival in the Salt Lake Valley, the Mormons organized a provisional government modeled after their conception of a divinely organized religious kingdom. There, secular and spiritual concerns were administrated by the central authority of the priesthood of the Church, headed by a prophet-president who served as both the religious and governmental lawmaker in the territory.[32]

To this end, the Constitution of the State of Deseret (1849) was drafted in a way that provided the religious leaders of the Church authority to also function as government officials—most notably by abolishing voting by secret ballot in favor of open elections. Ecclesiastic leaders would select government leaders, and Church endorsement virtually guaranteed election.[33] The judicial system was maintained by appointment, and Brigham Young as the governor selected congregational bishops as justices of peace in all county probate courts.[34] While Brigham Young only served one four-year appointment as territorial governor and the federal government was assiduous in appointing non-Mormon federal officials in Utah, the power structure of the Church maintained nearly total legal control of the territory for over forty years.

The representation of Mormon villains on stage was not a simple vilification of Mormon violence for the sake of popular culture. It was also a direct response to an alternate form of government that threatened a national democracy. The resulting portrayal of Mormonism was focused on an antiquated system of vengeance that was typified by the staged enactment of the doctrine of "blood atonement." This principle of justice was just one of a number of rumored practices that suggested to the nation that Mormons were establishing their own government, laws, and punishments.

Introduced by Mormon apostle Jedediah Grant during an 1856 general conference of the Church, the doctrine of blood atonement preaches that there are some sins that Christ's atonement will not expiate. Sinners guilty of these crimes will need to atone for them with the shedding of their own blood. The fiery rhetoric with which the doctrine was introduced in the nineteenth century prompted a debate about its application. It was not clear if Mormons meant that in the life to come, certain sinners would be required to suffer for some of their own guilt, or if Mormons planned on killing those whom they perceived as sinners. In popular culture, however, the meaning was clear, as is illustrated by a speech of the character Brigham Young in *Evelyn Gray*.

Early in the play, Young dramatically establishes the doctrine of blood atonement as a religious imperative in a fiery monologue:

> Let's have no more palaver about the enemy. They are doomed to perish like the infernal Canaanites of old did by the sword of Israel. They are judged and will be exterminated, and their blood and rotting bones

shall manure the earth for us . . . There is not a dog of an unbeliever in the territory for whose life I would give fifteen cents . . . It is strong doctrine. It is the doctrine of the blood atonement and it is sound Mormon doctrine . . . The sword of the Almighty is unsheathed, and in spite of all howling and tears and kneeling prayers, his Prophet will spill the blood of the unfaithful.[35]

According to Young in this play, the penalty for apostasy to the Church from within or for Gentile opposition to the Church from without is a divinely-appointed bloody death.

Whether blood atonement was actually practiced in this manner during the period is a discussion that has kept theologians, scholars, and Mormon practitioners occupied since it was introduced, and continues to be an issue today.[36] The widely disseminated depiction of blood atonement as murder in popular culture from the late nineteenth century, however, illustrates that actual incidences aside, America *believed* that the Mormon Church functioned by violence. More importantly, there was a growing concern that Mormons would use violence to either secede from the nation, or attempt to take over the nation by force.

This concern was the subject of the satire *Treason, Strategems, and Spoils* (1852) written by William Lysander Adams for the Portland *Oregonian* newspaper. Adams published this work under the pseudonym "Breakspear," and dedicated it to the "Association of Gentlemen" who had contributed to a Portland publication the *Vox Populi*. The bitter tone of the dedication, the imaginary "cast-list" that made clear which Oregon politicians were being parodied, and the iambic pentameter in which it was written suggests a closet drama that was more a literary satire of territorial politics than a play for performance. The play follows the efforts of a corrupt judge to join with Brigham Young to take over the West and establish an independent country:

> You know that Utah, did some months ago,
> Assert her rights, and send her tyrants home.
> *The plan's arranged that we're to do the same.*
> Then leagued together, like two brothers true,
> We'll haste to conquer California too . . .
> My kinsman; P. P. Pratt, will hold the reigns
> Of government o'er California's sons;
> While seated on the gubernator's chair,
> The rule of Oregon, with you I'll share;
> We'll fill our seats with honor, and with pride,
> And o'er the whole, will BRIGHAM YOUNG *preside*.[37]

While the play's plot to overthrow Oregon is unsuccessful, the fear remains that Mormons would be willing to use treasonous force to tear the nation apart.

The Mormon characters in *Evelyn Gray* are all based on real characters, while the other historical figures are given pseudonyms. In particular, the second governor of Utah territory is Governor Dummings (dumb enough to believe the Mormons) and his main cohort is Judge Letcher (only in Utah for the hope of loose women). The impact of these names is to remind audiences of the character of the historical figures rather than their actual reality. Most importantly, these figures are seen as dupes of the Mormons, who convince them that they are happy to remain under the rule of the United States. It also lessens the impact of their roles, since they are obviously made-up characters.

Brigham Young and his counselors, however, are given extra authority with the use of their real names. So when the character Young confides in private of his political machinations, it seems more likely to have happened this way in actual history than if he had been made fictional through a dramaturgical device. His rhetoric is recognizably fiery, and his message ultimately disturbing:

> I'll march to Washington at the head of millions . . . I'll knock over the Washington monument, and set up my own figure there. I'll pitch the President and that everlasting babbledom of a Congress into the Potomac. I'll take their wives and daughters for my women . . . I'll make the imbecile old Pope come over, like Napoleon did, and crown me Prophet Priest and King of the New World, and there shall be no other Lord in America except Brigham Young.[38]

The power of this use of documentary positioning in anti-Mormon melodrama was one of the main features of its reception. A *Los Angles Times* book review for *Evelyn Gray* in 1890 suggests:

> In this volume the author gives some vivid pictures of the infamy of Mormonism, that twin sister of barbarism which still lingers to disgrace our modern civilization. His portrayal is sufficient to thrill to indignant protest the heart of every honest man and woman against the continuation of a system so at variance with the sacredness of virtuous marriage. The whole tragedy strikes the reader as a [sic] something possible to have been enacted in real life among the Mormons.[39]

The reviewer recognizes that the work is meant to "thrill to indignant protest"—a term that emphasizes sentimentality in tone and sensationalism in action. The impact, however, is seemingly not overwrought, but "something possible to have been enacted." Whether through the practice of blood atonement or through overt plans to take over the country, the Mormons were clearly engaging in a dishonorable use of violence and anti-Mormon melodramas were seminal in creating the "vivid pictures" that would disseminate this image to theatre-going audiences.

Standing in defense of the nation was a national force—the United States Army. In anti-Mormon melodramas, the army sometimes serves as an unseen force that troubles the Mormons and their plotting. In other plays, the army is an actual force of protection and power that thwarts the Mormons of their schemes. Whether as an omniscient presence, or a hero to the play, the army in melodramas showed how violence could and should be practiced by true Americans.

The United States Army

In *The Mormons*, a conversation between Mormon apostle Elder Pratt and Colonel Cannon illuminates the threat of the Mormons:

> PRATT. We hardly expect the army to be the willing tools of the government, in the oppression of the inoffensive Mormons?
> CANNON. Nor do I, sir, But common report gives you credit for anything but inoffensiveness, and the public mind, already excited by your polygamy, is roused to anger by the accounts of rapine [sic] and murder laid to the charge of the Danites.[40]

Here, the army is set up as the dominant law-enforcing body on the nineteenth-century frontier. Pratt is concerned that the army might be after the Mormons, but Cannon assures him that the army is not about oppression. Instead, he later reminds his soldiers, "All we have to do is to watch their actions and report. We are not to disturb them as long as they refrain from overt acts."[41] The army is a defense to the public rather than a force of violence against the Mormons.

The conflict between the two groups is striking in that Mormons are devious, hypocritical, and bloodthirsty. On the other hand, as the character Cannon describes, "the Army is no band of base marauders. Its officers are men of honor—its privates orderly and disciplined. It has been ordered to escort the Governor and other officers to this place, and if needed, to afford them its protection. Be assured, sir, it will obey those orders."[42] Indeed, serving in the army provides various heroes with a background that assures their innate goodness and willingness to fight for right.

Of all the figures that attach themselves to the mythical western frontier, perhaps none have held the American imagination as much as that of "Cowboys and Indians." A notable subset of the Cowboy category is the cavalrymen who brought order to the West. The U.S. Army regulars stationed in the West were considered a federal police force, whose job was to keep order and make peace. The very deployment of professional men of violence, however, suggested the foreknowledge of armed resistance to the settling of the frontier. In territories where hostile Indians still roamed free, civil unrest was unchecked by established laws, and land ownership was constantly in dispute, these regiments frequently used extraordinary violence to uphold the sovereignty of the United States.

Fig. 3.1 "Custer's Last Charge. Brevet Major General George A. Custer, Lieutenant Colonel 7th U.S. Cavalry. Killed in Battle with the Sioux, June 25th 1876." Lithograph by Currier & Ives (1876). Courtesy of Library of Congress, Prints and Photographs Division, LC-USZC2–2161.

Durwood Ball, author of *Army Regulars on the Western Frontier* (2001), argues that "frontier soldiering was lonely, aggravating, and punishing in good times; it became embarrassing and sometimes unbearable in the sectional cauldron."[43] Despite the harsh realities of army life on the frontier, the image of the heroic cavalryman dominated popular fiction. Illustrated newspapers such as *Harper's Weekly* or *Frank Leslie's Illustrated Newspaper* reproduced iconographic engravings of the cavalryman going into battle, saber at the ready.

In *Evelyn Gray,* James St. Clair is introduced as an ex-army scout. This provides him credentials, and his experiences in the West, along with his disgust at the treatment of Indians, prove his good character. His army service is held up as a reference for him throughout the play. Rob Norris likens his courtship of Evelyn to behaving like a good soldier and attacking without fear, while the evil John Lee curses him for being a "brave young captain."[44]

By the same token, Jack Crawford, playing himself as "Captain Jack" rose to fame on reports of his experiences as "Chief of Scouts." About ten years after his service to the Union Army in the Civil War, Crawford was appointed to the head of the Black hills rangers, a 125-man militia set on protecting Custer City (now in South Dakota). His successes in this position led to his appointment as a Scout with the army. His duties there, later reported with flourish to his audiences, included meetings with tribal chiefs, tracking hostile Indian parties, and once, traveling over 300 miles in four days to deliver army dispatches ahead of the official government courier. His years as a Scout defined his public persona and prompted one contemporary biographer to query:

> Then how are we to estimate a man who, amid the conflicts of Indian warfare ... not only acquired a fair education, but learned to commune with Nature and long for the inspiration of her divine afflatus? Has he not interesting elements in his mental constitution, such a faithfulness to the true ideals of life as to attract admiration?[45]

In *Evelyn Gray,* even the character Brigham Young recognizes the power the army holds over the nation. He dismisses a plot to ambush and defeat the approaching army because attacking them, " ... would rouse the whole country, and we would have a horde of a hundred thousand men down on us before we could look around."[46] This proves true in *The Mormons* when an entire regiment of the army steps in to rescue Eagle-Eye and Mary from the murderous hands of Rizen Sleigh and Kneeland Whine, two Danite assassins. The stage directions call for a magnificent tableau spread across the stage with the Danites surrounded by Colonel Cannon and his soldiers, who *"take aim with carbines"* as a *"trumpet sounds."*[47]

The defeat of the Mormons at the hands of the army provided a clear visual image for audiences that fixed for them the necessity of violence on the frontier. This "peace-keeping" body illustrates that in order for America to be protected as a union even after the Civil War, violence continued to be necessary. Additionally, the setting of anti-Mormon melodramas shows the importance of "civilizing" the continent for the growing numbers of American immigrants who were arriving to find homes in the West. Mormons were potential threats to both the project of Manifest Destiny and to the healing of the nation. In characterizing Mormons as clearly dishonorable, the possibility of honorable violence emerges with the army as its most legitimate force. A different hero emerges when Mormons practice violence not on a national scale, but in communities where right and wrong is dictated more by popular accord than legal dictates.

II. VIOLENCE AND THE COMMUNITY

> *Fool! Defend yourself against the destroying angels? Whistle against the winds of the Sierras, but defy not the Danites of the Church!*
> —Bill Hickman, a Danite Chief in *Danites in the Sierras*

The anti-Mormon melodrama *Fonda; or, The Trapper's Dream* (1877) was written by Captain Jack Crawford, the "Poet-Scout of the West," who also staged and starred in the California touring production in 1877.[48] According to an introduction to a lecture series featuring Crawford, *Fonda* "was a pronounced success. He had no money and no manager, yet with a company of fifteen people, made a ten weeks' tour through California."[49] This account clearly painted a picture to impress the audiences eager for Captain Jack's stories of the West. *Fonda* was successful enough, though, to catch the eye of Alfred Dampier, the manager of the Theatre Royal Melbourne, who offered to co-produce *Fonda* in Australia. The tour never materialized, but this first play by Crawford led to two other pseudo-autobiographical plays featuring the heroic Captain Jack.

In *Fonda*, Captain Jack joins up with an emigrant train that has stopped near Salt Lake City for supplies. There, he encounters Fonda, a "waif hunted by the Mormons." The Mormons attempt to convince the wagon train to convert and stay in Utah, but settlers rally around Captain Jack and continue on their way, bringing Fonda with them. Further along their journey, Jack leaves to visit a beloved trapper friend. In his absence, Elder Force, a missionary who also joined the train, leads the emigrants to a desert wilderness in order to stage the Mountain Meadows massacre. Jack and his trapper friend return just in time to halt the massacre, rescue Fonda, and serve the Mormons their just reward. Reunited at last, Fonda and Jack profess their love for one another and head out for their new life in California.

Playing himself, Jack Crawford's presence on stage lent the characterization an air of legitimacy, as he was already renowned as an Indian Scout, a poet, and an actor in Buffalo Bill's Wild West shows. A true American hero playing a melodramatic hero doubled the impact of the character. On the other side of the coin are the Danite assassins, who are portrayed as outsiders to the community of settlers because of how and why they use violence.

The emigrants in *Fonda* make it clear that Mormons are guided by conventions and rules of conduct that are diametrically opposed to the codes that guide Americans. The old cowboy John Henry's opinion is that "Mormons are a slippery set."[50] Jack Crawford is more pointed: "There goes a true Mormon—a treacherous, licentious villain. What is to be the future of such a creed and people? Will their doctrines spread and flourish until they become a power and might in the great Western nation?"[51] In both of these comments, Mormons, by nature of their personalities (slippery, treacherous, licentious) and conventions (a separate creed and doctrine) are not the same as the Americans who encounter them. In this clear distinction, Mormon villainy serves as a foil to define the ethical American community.

Crawford's portrayal of a Mormon network of spies and mysterious Danite plots responds directly to the characterization of Danites in anti-Mormon literature as a secret band of hired assassins who avenge murders of Mormons (especially those of Joseph and Hyrum Smith). They also enforce the Mormon dominance of the Utah Territory. The characterization of the secret band of Danites, however, is complicated by the wide participation of men in secret brotherhoods such as the Freemasons or the Knights of the Golden Circle. These brotherhoods were a major part of American society and had a material impact on the use of violence to maintain political or socioeconomic control. The representation of this Mormon brotherhood on stage showed how secret violence was acceptable in the community as long as it furthered agreed-upon social goals. Mormon violence as represented in fiction, however, was only in service of a personal religious agenda that worked towards the destruction of community peace and social harmony.

The Danites

In the spring and summer of 1838, growing persecution of the Mormons in Caldwell County, Missouri concerned Mormon families who had recently been forced out of Jackson and Clay counties. Rather than allow the theft, vandalism, and terrorism to grow into violence and expulsion, a group of Mormon men banded together under the name of the "Brothers of Gideon" and organized a resistance to the threat. Their initial purpose was to force a number of Mormon dissenters to leave Missouri rather than support and inflame Missouri mobs. Finding support in the fiery rhetoric of Church leader Sidney Rigdon, the Brothers of Gideon were successful in driving out the dissenters.[52]

The achievement of the Brothers of Gideon's initial purpose gave strength to continued vigilante activities by the group. Events such as the Haun's Mill Massacre gave further resolve to Mormons who, fearful for their safety, moved to engage in active defense of their communities.[53] Sampson Avard, a disaffected member of the Church, came to front as the head of a new organization, the Daughters of Zion, later called the Danites. The group evolved from their initial purpose of defending Mormon settlements from mob attacks to promoting eye-for-eye retribution for theft, plunder, harassment, or violence against Mormons. After recruiting additional members, the Danites boasted a significant membership of Mormon men in Missouri. Many of these were simultaneously members of the Missouri Mormon militia, a detail that blurs the identities and the actions of the two groups.

Eventually Sampson Avard was arrested for illegal activities and brought up on charges.[54] By 1839, other Church members were jailed for alleged support of the Danite raids. Avard and several leading members of the Danite band were excommunicated, and the Danites were disbanded. The mystique of a secret organization dedicated to violence and crime, however, merely gained more currency as time moved on, and Danites became internationally known for their crimes.[55] By 1900, roughly sixty anti-Mormon novels had been written in America that featured these evil Danites. In literature, these "Destroying Angels" of the Church abused, raped, mutilated, murdered, plundered, and pillaged in the name of God. In real life, they were so elusive that they avoided any concrete evidence of their existence.

In 1877, two different autobiographical accounts were published that claimed to reveal all of the secrets of the "rapine and murders" of the Danites. The first was *Mormonism Unveiled,* the autobiography of John D. Lee, who was convicted as the leader of the Mountain Meadows Massacre, and the other was *Brigham's Destroying Angel,* the autobiography of "Wild Bill" Hickman.[56] The advertisements for these publications emphasize the "revelations" of these two different "Danite Chiefs." John D. Lee's varied confessions and Bill Hickman's account agree so closely with each other and with the representation of Danites so prevalent in popular culture that there wasn't much left to reveal.

The stories about the Danites as recorded in these books point to an interesting phenomenon. It is difficult to prove the negative corollary of existence—if something doesn't exist, there are no records because there was no organization. With secret organizations, however, the lack of records does not prove non-existence; the lack can be explained by the dire secrecy upon which the whole organization is based. Lee's description of Danite initiations emphasizes this point:

> The members of this order were placed under the most sacred obligations that language could invent. They were sworn to stand by and sustain each other. *Sustain, protect, defend,* and *obey* the leaders of the Church, under any and *all circumstances unto death*; and to disobey the orders the leaders of the Church, or divulge the name of a Danite to an outsider, or to make public any of the secrets of the order of Danites, was to be punished with death.[57]

There was no proof of Danite activity because revealing even the name of a Danite would result in death. Deficient evidence of actual Mormon murders could easily be justified by the nature of the execution.

The pervasive representation of secret violence of the Danites, however, suggested that Mormon murders were, by their very hidden nature, clearly dishonorable. If Danite killings were in any sense justifiable by law, popular wisdom suggested that they would be done in the open, where the rightness of the violence could be seen and judged by the community. Instead, Danites hid their crimes, aware themselves that their crimes were socially unacceptable.

Secret Brotherhoods

Joaquin Miller's *The Danites in the Sierras* (1876) was the most commercially successful anti-Mormon melodrama. Set in the "glorious climate of

California," a group of rough yet honorable miners are troubled by the arrival of two Mormon Danites. The Danites are hunting Nancy Williams, the daughter of one of the men who killed Joseph Smith, and have followed her trail to the camp. Not realizing Nancy is disguised as Billy, the youngest miner, they murder a newly-remarried Widow and her baby, thinking she is the woman they seek. The Widow's husband, Sandy, discovers Nancy's secret, defends her and overcomes the Danites, and is united with Nancy in love at the end of the play.[58]

On September 1, 1877, the *Spirit of the Times* published a detailed report and analysis of the premiere of *The Danites*:

> It was not surprising that the New Broadway was crowded to excess, notwithstanding the heat, on Wednesday week last. The opening of a new theatre and the production of a new play by a well-known writer were, unquestionably, sufficient attractions to excuse curiosity, although the thermometer stood close on a hundred. Most persons, we believe, anticipated a dead failure for the drama, having little to no faith in the dramatic ability of that eccentric poet of the Sierras, Mr. Joaquin Miller. They were, in a certain sense, agreeably disappointed. The play proved to possess more than ordinary merit, and if it is not a great work, it is decidedly not a very bad one.[59]

It was heralded by the *New York Mirror* as "the best, probably, of any play of native authorship now before the public."[60]

Surprising in a time when Mormon problems in Utah were making daily headlines, contemporary reviews of the first run of the show were uninterested in the style in which the villains, the titular Danites, were drawn. The *Spirit of the Times* review mentions in passing that the Danites, or "'Avenging Angels,' are a fanatical and secret society of men, whose object in life is to avenge the violent death of a Mormon prophet." The *New York Times* is more specific: "'The Danites,' [are] an offshoot of Mormondom, who, as an organized body, combine religion, murder, and rapine [sic] in their everyday life."[61]

Over the course of its presentation on a number of New York stages (the Broadway, the Grand Opera House, the Brooklyn Academy of Music, the Park Theater) reception of *The Danites* changed. By the time it began its four-week engagement at the top-ranked Booth's Theatre two years later in January 1879, the play had become:

> That best of American plays . . . It strikes a keynote of American life and character and combines humor, pathos, and poetry in agreeable proportions. One cannot conceive of anything more thrillingly and truly dramatic than the spectacle of a weak but noble woman pursued by the avenging, unsated, semi-religious fervor and fury of a mighty organization.[62]

Fig. 3.2 McKee Rankin as Sandy in *The Danites*. London Photographic and Stereographic Company. Courtesy of the Laurence Senelick Collection of Theatrical Imagery.

This *New York Mirror* review (1879) reflects a distinct shift in the way the subject of Mormon murders was treated. This later critic perceived the fanatical religious violence represented in *The Danites* as a "keynote of American life."[63]

While no evidence of the Danite band exists past Avard's trial in 1838, the popular belief in a secret Mormon band to which any type of violence and perversion could be attributed was both convenient and far-reaching.

Robert Norris, a New York reporter in *Evelyn Gray*, assures his friend that while many other negative stories about the Mormons are clear exaggerations, "the Danites are assuredly no myths."⁶⁴ The representation of Danites in *Evelyn Gray* proves Norris's point; throughout the play Danites drink, cuss, steal, and murder with a watchful eye towards Johnston's approaching army that has been sent to bring them down. The army is even an ineffective deterrent to this elusive band of outlaws.

In *Evelyn Gray*, for example, a Gentile judge in Utah attempts to try Danites for murder, but the Church arranges to force him out of town and the Mormon who testified in the trial, "was politely stopped and entertained on the way by some of the tribe of Dan."⁶⁵ The murdered man here is not given a name or a background; his only existence is his absence. By the same token, lack of factual evidence in the construction of the Danites was in fact a benefit of the stereotype. It allowed any offense to be laid at the feet of the Danites whose secret nature covered all proof of the crime.⁶⁶ Additionally, the context of this Danite murder—as a way to silence a witness in a federal court case—shows the murder to clearly be illegal. From this construction, a code of violence begins to emerge. Secret brotherhoods that mask their violent acts are not honorable by the very token of the secret nature of the crime.

The secrets of the Danites revealed on stage made for some of the most thrilling moments in anti-Mormon melodramas. The Salt Lake Temple becomes the setting for Danite meetings in a conflation of yet another secret of the Mormon Church: the temple ceremony. Staged in half of the extant melodramas, the temple ceremony variously serves as comic relief (as in *Deseret Deserted*), as a highly ritualized religious event (as in *Evelyn Gray*), or (as in *The Mormons*) a dark meeting of Danites sworn to violence and treason. Eagle Eye witnesses the "endowment" in *The Mormons*, having discovered "both passwords and grips."⁶⁷ The scene is the "*Interior of the Endowment House, Salt Lake City. An altar, C[enter]. Discovered, Young, at altar in white. Mormons in black, with hoods, grouped around him bearing torches.*"⁶⁸

What follows is a ceremony complete with secret knocks, eerie music, ritualized movement, swords, crowns, death threats, and oaths to the Church. The Mormons swear to "pay immediate, implicit, and unquestioning obedience to [Church rulers'] demands," to "sacrifice to the will or interest of the church, your nearest relative, your dearest friend, or even life itself," and "to cherish constant enmity towards the government and people of the United States." The punishment for breaking any of these oaths confirms the violent nature of the Mormons and provides an existence for the Danites: "Under the penalty of having your heart torn from your breast by the destroying angels of Dan, your body quartered, your flesh burned to ashes and scattered to the four winds of heaven, and your name taken from the Book of Life."⁶⁹ This scene is effective and affecting in its depiction of the horrors of the secret brotherhood of the Danites. Audiences viewing it would have been left no options but to perceive the Mormons as murderers bent on the destruction of not just the nation generally, but the very communities that they valued.

The regulation of the conduct of the vast majority of people depends largely on the constraints of conscious or unconscious obedience to all kinds of imperatives. When certain groups choose not to behave in a manner that is consistent with these rules, their behavior is necessarily unethical according to the socially constructed codes of conduct on the frontier. More appropriate were those brotherhoods whose participation in acts of violence served to protect the community or further its collective interests.

Band of Brothers

The Danites opens with the Judge and Limber Tim lounging in a saloon and recounting the story of the recent murder of three miners. The way in which the miners are described gives a clue as to characteristics that mark a decent American. Although they kept to themselves, they were "good miners and good neighbors, too, and was a makin' money like mud." They were "strong, healthy, handsome fellows" whose only flaw was that they had been some of the "hundred masked men" that killed the Mormon Prophet, "Joe Smith."[70] The telling of the story makes it clear that the sympathies of Judge and Tim are with the three miners—their quiet, hard-working ways and their physical attributes recommend them to their peers.

A "long-haired stranger chap," assumed to be a Danite, joins up with the three "fine, hearty fellows," and each dies by an unfortunate mishap; the first has a rope break and drop him down a shaft, the second is drowned when water floods into the mine, and the third is found mysteriously dead. Judge and Tim reason that the Danite had killed all three of the men for being part of the Illinois mob that killed Joseph Smith. Even their participation is excused by the miners because the later behavior of the three showed themselves to be a true band of brothers.

As the *Spirit* reviewer of *The Danites* suggested, the miners "are represented as marvelous specimens of low depravity, combined with almost supernaturally heroic virtues." The dialect they use may be strange to audiences less familiar with western metaphor (and offensive to several critics, including the *Spirit* reviewer, who stated: "The name of the Deity should not be invoked upon the stage").[71] The ways in which the miners drink moderately, defend virtue fiercely, and act directly, however, created a spirit of camaraderie that celebrated the positive aspects of organized brotherhoods.

In his work on secret rituals and manhood, Mark C. Carnes cites an 1897 study that found that at least one in every six men in late nineteenth-century

America belonged to a fraternal organization of one kind or another.[72] This same study concluded that the immense participation in secret organizations was due to:

> [A] peculiar fascination in the unreality of the initiation, an allurement about fine 'team' work, a charm of deep potency in the unrestricted, out-of-the-world atmosphere which surrounds the scenes where men are knit together by the closest tie, [and] bound by the most solemn obligations to maintain secrecy.[73]

Clearly, secret fraternities were a large part of American society; the power that they were presumed to have was both attractive and troubling.

Most secret brotherhoods were not perceived as being directly involved in crime and murder. Instead, they were socio-political groups. Some, such as the Union League (a patriotic organization supportive of the Lincoln administration) and the rival Knights of the Golden Circle (a Copperhead antiwar society), had their objectives in political activism. These groups raised morale for their causes, planned for the election of local and national candidates, and furthered agendas that ranged from inciting army desertion to establishing reading rooms with party propaganda.[74] Others, like the Freemasons, the Odd Fellows, the Sons of Temperance, the Grangers, and the Holy and Noble Order of the Knights of Labor, were formed to serve perceived needs in society. For some this was a lack of male-centered spirituality; for others, it was a need for organized labor unions to protect laborers and/or provide insurance.

Despite the wide differences in aims and style, these organizations held a few things in common not only with each other, but also with the Danites. First, they were all secret societies whose oaths, signs, and covenants were both indications of membership and promises never to reveal the secrets. Second, the meetings of the fraternities were largely based on rituals in word, action, and dress. Third, all of the groups were intentionally and exclusively male. Finally, all of the organizations served both a political and social function. For the overtly political groups, the ritual basis of the meetings provided a shared experience that united men as brothers. The social groups, whose activities may have been almost entirely ritualistic, still suggested a political agenda by their very existence.

For Danites, the political agenda, particularly as seen through the eyes of sensational popular literature, was clear. They were a group of assassins, initially hunting down the mob that killed Joseph Smith and later serving to mete out blood atonement punishment or to murder any who opposed the rise of Mormonism. The Danites' sole purpose was the disruption of the community. Conversely, almost all of the other secret brotherhoods had a political agenda that attempted to improve the external community—providing insurance, organizing labor unions, making charitable donations, assuring job security, and more.[75] Friendships and fraternities like these in anti-Mormon melodramas benefited from comparison to the evil Danites. More importantly, it reassured audience members that their own membership in secret societies was in fact honorable.

The trappers Jack Crawford and Uncle Bill in the play *Fonda* suggest a brotherhood that serves as a model for appropriate male social interaction that also defends the community. Uncle Bill, in rejecting society except for those that frequent his trading post, hints to adventures that cannot be recorded because they are hidden by his solitude and secretive nature. It is not until he meets Jack that he shares with someone the tales of his life. The process of bringing Jack into the trapper fold bonds the two men together as family. As Jack describes Bill, "there is one who's expecting me—one who loves me with all the pride and fondness of a father."[76] Their bond is solidified through their joint defense of the emigrants during the Mountain Meadows massacre.

Defense is also the unifying bond of Sandy and the miners in *The Danites*. In the final act of the play, these brothers band together in a vigilante group to seek out the murderers of the Widow and her child. When the Danites are finally revealed through their disguises, the miners quickly disarm them and take them off-stage to their deaths. Their punishment at the end of the play is hanging, and vigilantes carry out the execution.

Sandy and the other miners who defend Nancy, shun the Mormon evil, and restore order, are ultimately American in their willingness to, as Calweti suggests, "face extreme situations of violence with trust in [their] own individual judgment backed up by a willingness to place [their lives] on the line at the proper moment."[77] The miners participate in the second, psuedo-secret vigilante group that is only open to the men in the Sierras and is bound by sacred promises. They are violent, but their violence builds the community rather than tears it apart.

The violence of these bands of brothers is acceptable because it responds to the communally-agreed codes of crime and punishment. In the final scenes of *Fonda,* the Danites are hauled offstage to be cowhided, tarred, and feathered—and one character reasons, they "deserved all they got." Another replies, "well, they got it whether they deserved it or not, and if Captain Jack and Fonda hadn't begged so hard for them, we'd a swung 'em where the coyotes could never reach 'em."[78] The violent death of the Danites by hanging would have been socially acceptable violence, but the hero of the piece is able to mediate the punishment away from death. The heroic solution is a vicious beating, which is acceptable because the American citizens in the play agree that it was the best thing to do.

A wide range of influences impacts the conduct of people. On the American frontier, perhaps the least of these was formal law that came slowly from the East and sometimes didn't even address western living in conditions that were incomprehensible to federal lawmakers. Community conduct was therefore impacted as much by laws dictated by religious or cultural demands as by governmental ones. In the late nineteenth century, there was an explosion of secret brotherhoods that grew up around notions of right and wrong that were culturally, rather than legally, established. These socio-political groups furthered the needs of the community as perceived by it and in doing so, cemented the notions of honor, ritual, and defense already in circulation.

The Danites were brothers in a secret fraternity, but one that functioned entirely outside community approbation. As seen in anti-Mormon melodrama, these assassins were murderers whose only loyalties were to each other and the Mormon empire. In sensationalizing their violence, melodramas showed the limits of how violence could be used and validated the need for other bands of brothers that honorably upheld a community's living laws. Perhaps the most important of these was the protection of the weak and the innocent who were the special targets of Mormon murderers.

III. VIOLENCE AND THE FAMILY

> Good God Almighty, what's this? O, my darlins. Wife, wife!—Dead, she's dead, and so's the boy, killed by the same bullet. Great lord in heaven, who done this?
>
> —Levi Savage, on seeing his family slaughtered by Mormons in *Evelyn Gray*

In colonial America, the family structure was intrinsically connected to the agrarian economic system. These patriarchal families were led by fathers who not only ran the family business, but also took the lead in spiritual and educational growth. The system was upheld by common law that suggested fathers had a moral, but not a legal, responsibility to support their children and that fathers had an unlimited right to their children's labor and earnings. The nineteenth century saw a change towards individualism in the urban family, as children were no longer assumed to follow immediately in the family business. Instead, education was perceived as the means of future livelihood.

Family focus in the late nineteenth century shifted from production towards socialization. Rather than making goods or providing services, families were training children to become successful in a commercial society. Courts revised family law towards our modern notions of responsibility and care; it became a legal mandate for parents to support their offspring, and see to their children's welfare.[79] Roles that once were thought to exclusively belong to the father were spread out among a variety of other people and institutions. Mothers held the moral authority in the home and took on larger responsibilities for overseeing aspects of the education of children. Schools claimed the position of training children for the future, and the courts took over the job of defining and defending a child's welfare.

While the rhetoric driving the new conception of the family was disseminated on the frontier, the realities of life suggested a more practical view of "defending the family." In addition to being the home of hard-working and upstanding Americans furthering the glories of Manifest Destiny, the frontier was also peopled by a different segment of society—outlaws, deserters, Indians, and rebels. The dangers of the frontier were based in reality, but had also been greatly exaggerated in popular culture. It was this popular opinion, however, that suggested the vital importance of physical protection against those that would molest the family.

The frontier was also not alone in the huge threat from perceived dangers. In the North, there was a growing influx of immigrants, as well as African Americans who were made free persons through the war, but were still not necessarily welcome in the neighborhood. The South was inundated with disaffected former Southern soldiers. As Cathy Luchetti argues in her work *Children of the West: Family Life on the Frontier* (2001), these were lawless men,

> . . . only marginally conversant with such truths as the "sacred duty" of motherhood, so touted by ministers and polemicists of the eastern establishment. In fact, they raided, plundered, and robbed at will, often seeing women and children as ideal ransom opportunities, striking terror in to the lives of the vulnerable and undefended.[80]

In the post-war years, there was even legal precedence for taking back, taking over, or taking away lands and homes from families.

Mormons, believed to have secret bands of assassins and to be a threat to the United States, were another group on the frontier that threatened home and family. According to popular rumor, not only were Mormon men enslaving women into polygamy, they were practicing violence against women and children for pleasure and for profit. Nowhere is this made more clear than in the melodramatic stagings of the Mountain Meadows Massacre.

The Mountain Meadows Massacre

In September of 1857, the Fancher wagon train, a group of Arkansas pioneers on its way to California stopped in Southern Utah for water and fuel. Tension over the approaching army had prompted renewed efforts on behalf of the Mormons to make alliances with Native American tribes. Both Paiute Indians and Mormons ran into difficulties with the Fancher party, which culminated in a battle with losses on both sides.[81] After the initial skirmish, the wagon train surrendered and under a flag of truce, a group of men—variously described as Paiute renegades, Mormons dressed as Indians, or a combination of Indians and Mormons—attacked and killed nearly 130 men, women, and children. The massacre was particularly heinous because of the indiscriminant use of violence. Children were shot out of mothers' arms, women were scalped, and teenagers were cut with hatchets.

After several years of investigation, numerous accounts of the events, official Church involvement, and two trials, Bishop John D. Lee was convicted and executed for instigating the massacre. Author Juanita Brooks concludes in her extensively researched account of the Mountain Meadows Massacre that the "complete—the absolute—truth of the affair can probably never be evaluated by any human being; attempts to understand the forces which culminated in it and those which were set into motion by it are all very inadequate at best."[82]

There remain two distinct theories of responsibility for the massacre. The first, a position held officially by the LDS Church, and supported by the exhaustively researched *Massacre at Mountain Meadows* (2008) is that the massacre was perpetrated by an independent and isolated community of Mormons.[83] Young's public instruction to the Southern Utah Saints of how they should treat the Fancher train supports this. He wrote, in part: "In regard to the emigration trains passing through our settlements, we must not interfere with them until they are first notified to keep away. You must not meddle with them. The Indians we expect will do as they please but you should try and preserve good feelings with them."[84] Unfortunately, this missive arrived in Southern Utah a day after the attack. The second theory of responsibility, a position supported by Lee's confessions, made popular in nineteenth-century literature, and still held by some historians today, was that Brigham Young ordered the massacre.

At the time of the massacre, the truth of the affair in popular culture, however, was clear—it was horrific proof of the murderous rumors about Mormons. William Bishop, an attorney to John D. Lee wrote in the preface to Lee's *Confessions*:

> The Mountain Meadows Massacre stands without a parallel amongst the crimes that stain the pages of American history. It was a crime committed without cause or justification of any kind to relieve it of its fearful character. Over one hundred and twenty men, women and children were . . . murdered in cold blood, and left nude and mangled upon the plain. All this was done by a band of fanatics, who had no cause of complaint against the emigrants, except that the authorities of the Mormon Church had decided that all the emigrants who were old enough to talk, should die—revenge for alleged insults to Brigham Young, and the booty of the plundered train being the inciting causes of the massacre.[85]

Bishop's interpretation of the analysis was made popular by the publication of Lee's *Confessions*, and by the rapid appearance of other exposés, novels, and dramatizations of the event. All of these accounts support a view of the massacre as an example of the fanatical violence of which Mormons were capable.

The Mountain Meadows Massacre confirmed the nation's worst fears, but unfortunately, it was in many ways, a self-fulfilling prophecy. For nearly three decades, Mormons had been in literal conflict with Americans who saw their religion as dangerous to the nation. Popular representations emphasized the violent tendencies of the Mormons, which in turn heightened the tension. The portrayal of Mormon violence in literature and on stage is particularly reprehensible as it targets those unable to defend themselves—women, children, and the elderly. The violence is doubly offensive as Mormons profit from it, both emotionally through the pleasure they take in the killings, and materially through the goods they steal from the dead.

Murders and Massecration

The first scene of the fourth act of *Evelyn Gray* is set in the "Zion's Co-operative Distillery." Bill Hickman, Porter Rockwell, Ike Hatch, Eph. Hanks and Robert T. Burton are seated at a table drinking.[86] On the wall, the name of the bar and the designation "Holiness to the Lord," surrounds an All-Seeing Eye. The conversation dramatized between these Danite leaders is an opportunity to establish the personalities and the exploits of murdering Mormons. The setting is apropos since all of the men are drinking heavily and recounting their exploits. The conversation is colored by two anxieties about uncivilized America: drunkenness and abuse of women.

The crimes that frame the characterization of these Danites illustrate how they are creating a dangerous chaos. Women were put on a pedestal as the moral guide of the home, in need of extra care and protection. At the same time, reformists lobbied for temperance or even prohibition, in large measure to keep families safe. To have drunken Mormons revel in their crimes confirms the worst fears about their threat not just to the nation, but to the very foundation of it—the family.

At the Zion's Co-operative Distillery, Burton is bragging about how he and some Danites attacked a group of unarmed settlers who had left Mormonism to establish their own community. After the group had surrendered and thrown down their arms, the Mormons entered their compound to kill them all:

> I cut [Morris] short with a ball in his throat. When he fell I gave him another . . . Then I turned and keeled his man Banks over. A women came running up . . . she got the fourth cartridge and another woman that came up blubbering to Morris, got the fifth, and it was lucky for the other that the last chamber of my six shooter was empty.[87]

The violence described here is indiscriminate, unrepentant, and excessive. It suggests a threatening savageness to the frontier that holds no life sacred, not even that of fleeing and weeping women. Rather than using violence to civilize and protect, Mormons are murdering families and doing so for pleasure.

In addition to the abuse women suffer in the horrors of polygamy, women are singled out in anti-Mormon melodramas as victims of murder. At the end of *Evelyn Gray,* a mother and her nursing child are shot dead with the same bullet, while in *Fonda,* an entire wagon train, both men and women, are attacked by Mormons and Indians. The murder of women is especially heinous in a period when women were, above all, to be protected and kept from harm. Particularly outrageous is the suggestion that Danites consider the violence of their job part of the sensual pleasure of being a Mormon.

Again in *Evelyn Gray,* the Danites agree, over another round of drinks, that "feelings and such trash" can't be part of their characters. One of them adds, "On the contrary, the harder they squeal and the harder they begs, the more fun it's fur me." Later he continues, "I think the spoils, the fun an' the feastin' orter cum to us."[88] The sense of privilege and "fun" associated with killing is contextualized here in terms of the profit (both literal and symbolic) to be made from murder. The suggestion that Danites might even take pleasure in the killing puts both the action and the actor beyond the pale. Danites are not only criminal, but also deviant human beings.

This deviance is clear in the variety of descriptors used to identify Danites. In *The Mormons,* Eagle-Eye calls them Myrmidons—a literary reference to the traitorous killers of Hector of Troy.[89] M'Fadjin, an Irish-American militia man in the same play sings a song about how the Army will overcome "Brigham Young's Cannibals."[90] Danites are called snakes, vampires, and devils. Each of these references is to other creatures that are not even considered human. This devaluation of the Mormon murderer, however, makes sense in light of their disrespect for the weak and defenseless.[91]

As a result of how Mormons misuse violence, they are portrayed as cowardly, traitorous, and possessing a murdering spirit. In *The Mormons,* the Danites don't fight fairly. They steal Eagle-Eye's pistol, and wait in ambush for him, and sabotage his rifle. Blair, the man whom Eagle-Eye has hunted for the entire play does not defend himself at the end, but instead hides behind the heroine, Mary, after he "presents a knife to her breast."[92] The Danites even recognize themselves as cowardly. Bill Hickman in *Evelyn Gray* admits: "Wen it cums to mistreatin' and murderin' wimmin, ur w'en you kin shoot people from behin' rocks or bushes you're mighty brave, but w'en you're got to stan' up an; fight men fair an' square, w'er are you then?"[93]

Mormon villains in melodramas not only profit emotionally or sensually from violence against women and children, they also profit financially. In *Evelyn Gray,* Brigham Young is portrayed as a businessman first and foremost, and most of the violence of the piece is connected to his illegal ways of gaining wealth. Just as he took over the Zion's Co-Operative Distillery by sending its owners on foreign missions, Young spends much of his time in the play looking for opportunities to despoil wagon trains. He bargains with Bill Hickman to organize the attacks: "You shall have half of all the plunder. No dickering or bickering, clean halves this time, Bill."[94] The reason for the massacre in *Fonda* is also that the slaughtered emigrant's goods "will be a rich haul":

> DAN: Do we play the old game?
> ELDER: The old game, Daniel?
> DAN: Yes. Must they all be killed?
> ELDER: Yes, Daniel, that's the safest way.
> DAN: What's your plan?
> ELDER: The Indians will do the job. All's arranged—the last payment made.[95]

The implication here is that "massacretion" was a standard operation—the old game—and that murder is more of a business transaction than an illicit activity, with organization, planning, and payment. It also is an easy haul since those to be killed are a few armed men, but many women and children.

A Manly Heart

The position of heroes who oppose Mormons on the melodramatic stage was complicated by the particular representation of actual western hero figures in popular culture. Wild Bill Hickok, Buffalo Bill Cody, Texas Jack Omohundro, and others had a large hold on the public imagination and constructed an image of the western hero that was disseminated through stage shows, reenactments, lecture, and dime novels. Most of these men, at some time in their careers, commissioned (or wrote) vehicles for this image in which they could star. The result is a number of frontier melodramas that celebrate the lives, deeds, and actual adventures of real heroes. The representation of heroes in anti-Mormon melodramas projected a use of violence that was appropriate (it had, in the audience's mind actually happened somewhere out West), and appropriable (it set up a code of conduct to standardize the use of honorable violence in America).

Captain Jack Crawford, "Poet-Scout of the West," is one of the most colorful figures in late nineteenth-century history. An Irish immigrant, he learned to read and write while convalescing in a Civil War hospital. The gold rush took him West to the Black Hills, where he failed as a miner, but thrived as a correspondent for Omaha and Cheyenne newspapers. In addition to his work as an Army Scout, he also spent a year as a performer in Buffalo Bill's Wild West Show. In 1893, he embarked on his last career as a public lecturer. He fulfilled eastern American fantasies of a western hero for audiences who loved his buckskin pants, fur-trimmed buckskin coat, wide sombrero over shoulder-length hair, and six-shooter strapped to his hip. He died in New York in 1917, leaving behind a legacy written in his collections of poems, articles, and plays, and written in public memory as a popular performer. One obituary tribute described him as "a real scout and a real poet—a man with a warrior's soul and the heart of a woman."[96]

This description served him well and served to further the character of the American hero that Crawford imaginatively created in his melodramas, each of which featured a very loosely autobiographical Captain Jack Crawford as the hero. In *Fonda,* Jack's bold defense of helpless settlers from Chopper, the Mormon, prompts a young girl fleeing from Salt Lake City to trust him with her story. She admits, "I overheard our conversation with the one who just left you, and as your words fell upon my ears something seemed to whisper to me, 'Fear not to listen, the words you hear are from a manly heart that can assist and aid you.'" Jack responds: "To assist and aid you, fair maid, or anyone who needs a friend is but in truth my nature."[97] Jack Crawford's portrayal of himself here touches on similar heroic constructions in other melodramas. Eagle-Eye (*The Mormons*), James St. Clair (*Evelyn Gray*), and Sandy (*The Danites in the Sierras*) each exhibit natural qualities that prove that American men have both a manly heart, and also "a warrior's soul."

The heroes that emerge in anti-Mormon melodramas fulfill a particular function in the formation of American identity by illustrating the necessary use of aggression. The real Jack Crawford proved this rule; he was introduced to audiences as a man who lived his life "amid the wild and exciting incidents of savage border warfare, accustomed to scenes of bloodshed and violence . . . dealing with the most vicious and depraved criminals." Captain Jack, however, had "preserved through it all an honest manhood and a character of which he is justly proud."[98] The persona created by Crawford in his lectures and in his plays was one that at once confirmed and conformed to American attitudes about violence, especially violence threatening American ideals.

In *Fonda,* Elder Force has convinced the leader of an emigrant wagon train to stop in Salt Lake City rather than continue on to California and is targeting the rest of the emigrants for conversion. Captain Jack knows better, warns them of the villainy of Elder Force, and offers them a choice. Elder Force calls for "all who are in favor of remaining with the Saints in this land of peace and plenty" to "say aye, and take your stand by the side of a Mormon Elder." Captain Jack counters with a call to "all who are determined to be true men and women," to "take your stand here, beside Jack."[99]

The portrayal of Mormon violence as criminal makes delimitation of violence clear. The violence of the Mormons is wrong, and therefore any violence that stops them must be, in its opposition, honorable. Heroes such as Jack Crawford or Eagle-Eye typify the way in which violence can be used appropriately to establish and defend the law. Eagle-Eye's quest throughout *The Mormons* is to find the seducer of his sister and to avenge her death. When he is finally able to track the man Blair down to a Danite band in Utah, Eagle-Eye kills him in an act of righteous justice: "For three long years, day by day, I have followed this mission. Ay! A mission! For he who avenges his sister's life and honor is no assassin, but heaven's own instrument."[100] Even his killing of Blair is defensible; Eagle-Eye attacks him only after he threatens Mary and Blair dies in the struggle, stabbed by his own knife.

When heroes fight or kill in anti-Mormon melodrama, their use of hostility is specific and limited. Eagle-Eye's killing of Blair is the only on-stage death of a Danite at the hands of a hero. Other Danites are killed, but it is either offstage by a nameless group of citizens (as in *The Danites*), or at the hands of another character for whom the killing does not disrupt a sense of moral identity. In *The Mormons,* for example, Dahcoma, chief of the Kioway Indians and friend to Eagle-Eye, kills a number of Danites to stop them from killing innocents. While this moral action might place him on the correct side of the law, the style of the violence does not entirely justify it. Dahcoma is a savage killer—the first act ends in a tableau with Dahcoma about to scalp the Danite he has just shot. The foreign and frightening image of scalping places Dahcoma's use of violence also as outlaw. He is better than the Mormons (he doesn't, in fact, scalp anyone), but still not a viable example of the way in which violence should be applied in America. It is only the melodramatic hero whose personality, actions, and reactions establish the appropriate use of violence in American identity.

The heroes that opposed Mormon murderers used violence that was furthered by the cause of Manifest Destiny and protected the interests of the United States. They formed bands of brothers—alliances that upheld the unwritten laws of a community. They saved women, children, and old men from harm. They also established the function of violence as not only justifiable, but necessary. The result of these violent resolutions of melodramas was to create a template that spoke to the use of force in American society. While overtly the plays preached a message that violence is a base instinct that requires repression, the way in which the message was articulated created a need for honorable violence. This aspect of American identity, enacted on the melodramatic stage and adopted in popular society, has provided a century of fictional American heroes on stage and screen. It has also created an attitude towards violence that continues to shape the nation today.

4 Turks
Appropriating Ethnicity

> Turkish polygamy with oriental beauty and chivalry is a tolerable thing, but this would make the devil hold his nose.
> —Rob Norris in *Evelyn Gray*

> The idea of representation is a theatrical one; the Orient is the stage on which the whole East is confined. On this stage will appear figures whose role it is to represent the larger whole from which they emanate. The Orient then seems to be, not an unlimited extension beyond the familiar [western] world, but rather a closed field, a theatrical stage affixed to [the West].
> —Edward Said, *Orientalism*

A political satire about Irishmen, Mormons, and suffragettes, *Deseret Deserted; or, The Last Days of Brigham Young. Being a Strictly Business Transaction, in Four Acts and Several Deeds, Involving Both Prophet and Loss* is a melodramatic spoof by the Moon Club that played at Wallack's Theatre for the entire summer season of 1858 (starting in May). Based on its success, it was published that year by Samuel French in an acting edition. The story follows the adventures of Looney O'Flab, Tom Scott, and Lucifer "Looy" Sparks. The three friends are following the trail of Sparks' wife, who ran away to join the Mormons. Once in Salt Lake City, they witness a secret temple ceremony, rescue their women, sing and dance, and incite a riot. Their exploits are interrupted only by a drunken dream of Brigham Young that makes up the second act. The play ends with a death scene worthy of Shakespeare and the necessary intervention of the stage manager to help get all the dead bodies (including that of Young) off of the stage before the inauguration of a "Republic of Women."

In Brigham Young's second act dream, he awakes in front of a garden wall, guarded by broken bottles on top, and near a door marked "Paradise." A plate on the door bears the name of Mahomet and warns, "Any Christian found trespassing on these premises will be persecuted."[1] Young disregards the sign since it "can't refer to me."[2] Young summons Mahomet, and their subsequent conversation, held under the sign banning Christians, establishes a clear delineation of identity and alterity:

MAH. Hallo! who are you? what do you want!
BRIG. My name's Young . . . I would see Mahomet and speak with him.
MAH. I am he—the real, original, and unadulterated Jacobs. [*sic*] What do you want?
BRIG. I want a free admission . . .
MAH. [*in a rage*] An American, in among my women! Never! go away!
BRIG. I am not an American. I'm a Mormon.[3]

Americans are Christians, and Mormons are neither. Geographically, Mormons were located in the western United States, as Young proves by pointing out Salt Lake City on a map Mahomet provides. Religiously, culturally, and ethnically, however, Mormons are not American, but a distinctive "mighty race—a race of pious, upright men."[4] Persuaded that Brigham Young, as a Mormon, is neither Christian nor American, Mahomet welcomes him into Paradise where Young is dressed in a turban, plied with liquors and mint juleps, and treated to a dance of the *houris* (dark-eyed virgins of perfect beauty believed to reward the blessed in Paradise).

For all of the character Young's assertion of difference, in practical reality, Mormons were impossible to differentiate from most Americans. This lack of a marker between Mormons and Americans created the very real threat of total assimilation—if Mormons seem just like their neighbors, they might spread their religion unimpeded across the nation. This threat was compounded by the influx of Mormon immigrants that bolstered the Utah population and by the isolated location of Salt Lake City. To the rest of the country, Utah was a distant land, with a growing population of foreign nationals who gave allegiance to religious directives rather than the United States of America. These foreign nationals, however, were indistinguishable from native-born Americans and therefore an even greater threat than other minority populations.

Nativism is the socio-political philosophy that evolved in mid nineteenth-century America that blamed foreigners for crime and threats of rebellion, and privileged the interests of long-standing Anglo-Saxon inhabitants or "native" Americans. In anti-Mormon melodramas, nativist concerns were revealed through representations such as the multi-national harem or the growing population of Mormons in Utah. To contain these threats, some anti-Mormon polemics utilized the popular trope of Orientalism. By collapsing Mormon and Turkish culture, anti-Mormon melodramas like *Deseret Deserted, The Mormons, Evelyn Gray, Fonda,* and *Brigham Young* showed in contrast the unified color, language, and location of American ethnicity. The articulation of Utah as a foreign place and the appropriation of an exotic race of Mormons illustrates how the right (white) ethnicity is an essential aspect of American identity.

Following the opening of the Erie Canal in 1825, the failed European revolutions of 1848, and other global socio-economic factors, emmigration to the United States from Europe rose astronomically.[5] From 1845–1854, about 2,900,000 emmigrants came to America—more than had arrived in the past seventy years combined.[6] These new arrivals were largely Roman Catholic, with large numbers coming from Ireland and Germany. An aggressive Mormon missionary effort also resulted in a significant number of emmigrants from Europe. The influx of converts built up the Mormon Church from the six founding members in 1830 to nearly 300,000 at the turn of the century; Church membership increased almost 50% every decade during the nineteenth century, due both to high birth rates within Mormon families and the Church's aggressive missionary program.[7]

Blamed for economic instability, rises in crime and disease, and moral turpitude, immigrants, including Mormon converts, were demonized as foreign threats that would destroy the country. These suspicions were justified to a certain extent by social and economic developments: the modernizing economy of manufacturing and specialized labor widened the gap between rich and poor, and made upward mobilization increasingly unlikely. Agriculture faced similar problems in addition to poor crop yields. The boom and bust cycle in financial and commodity markets, rising inflation, and rapid increases in local taxation exacerbated the fears of Americans.[8] Most troubling were the immigrant unskilled laborers willing to work for much less than the Americans currently holding the jobs.

All of these conditions led to the increasing unlikelihood that lower-class Americans could achieve the American Dream as articulated in the nineteenth century. While the specifics of the American Dream shift across time, patterns emerge that help to define some common elements: political freedom, steady income, food on the table and a roof overhead. In other words, the American Dream promised Americans—regardless of birth, class, or education—the opportunity to achieve social and economic success, or at least stability, through hard work. Political and popular discourse laid the blame for the erosion of the American Dream squarely on newly arrived immigrants like Catholics and Mormons.

Anti-Catholic sentiment was arguably the most virulent nativist prejudice of the nineteenth century. Historian John Higham argues that, "by far the oldest and—in early America—the most powerful of the anti-foreign traditions came out of the shock of the Reformation. Protestant hatred of Rome played so large a part in pre-Civil War nativist thinking that historians have sometimes regarded nativism and anti-Catholicism as more or less synonymous."[9] Higham contextualizes American anti-Catholic nativism in terms of Colonial antagonism against powerful Catholic nations of France and Spain. For Higham, this anti-Catholic sentiment, along with two other threads—fear of radical revolutionaries and belief in the primacy of the Anglo-Saxon race—are the foundational patterns that led to nineteenth-century nativism.

Other scholars have traced the impact of anti-Catholic sentiment in local and national politics (the Know-Nothings, or the American Party)[10], in nineteenth-century fiction, and in political philosophy.[11] These sources all seem to agree that the complaint against Catholics was not necessarily one of religion but one of political power. Ali Behdad makes this distinction clear:

> What motivated the Know-Nothings . . . against Catholics was not their religion, for the American Party, following the Constitution, advocated the protection of religious opinion and worship. Rather, it was Catholics' presumed affiliation with an autocratic, hierarchichal, and centralized institution that made them an anathema to American democracy and its valorization of individual rights.[12]

While there was a clear trend in anti-Mormon nativist rhetoric, it did not occupy national interest as did anti-Catholicism. Understanding how anti-Mormon nativism drew on anti-Catholic prejudices but was also distinct from them suggests a unique intersection of religion, radicalism, and race that Higham articulates as the patterns of nativism in the United States.

One parallel between the Catholics and Mormons was how detractors used a wide range of media to voice their concerns: literature, magazine serials, political cartoons, and melodramas. Catholics and Mormons were represented in these media as kidnappers, rapists, con men, thieves, traitors attempting to overthrow the government, torturers, and corruptors of youth. Another parallel is their similar concerns about allegiance and power. Catholics were perceived as privileging their obedience to the Pope and Rome, as is evidenced by tracts such as the 1855 *Startling Facts for Native Americans called "Know-nothings," or a Vivid Presentation of the Dangers to American Liberty, to be Apprehended from Foreign Influence*. This publication proclaimed that "CATHOLICS OWE NO ALLEGIANCE TO THE U. STATES!"[13] Mormons were also perceived in this way. Thirty years after the Know-Nothing tract was published, concerned citizens like Rev. Dwight Spencer, agent of the Baptist Home Missionary Office in Utah, voiced similar concerns about the Mormons. In a lecture to the Eastern District of the Central Baptist Church entitled "The Mormon Kingdom; How it is Pushing its Way West of the Rocky Mountains," he warned:

> . . . that the Mormon religion, which was thus spreading in all directions west of the Rocky Mountains, is a fruitful source of danger politically. The Mormon Church always votes solidly, and so far as all practical purposes are concerned [President] John Taylor might be allowed to cast the entire vote of the church, and thus save expense. Politicians in Utah are careful not to do anything to antagonize this vote, and for this reason it is impossible to pass any law in Utah which would tend to injure the church . . . "Let this half of the United States once

more become densely populated under these circumstances," said Mr. Spencer, "with the Mormons holding the balance of political power, and they will be able to dictate the policy of the Nation."[14]

As was discussed in the previous chapter, the theocracy established in Utah suggested Mormon allegiance to church over state and justified fears of an independent Mormon nation.

Unlike the anti-Catholic rhetoric of groups like The American Party, however, anti-Mormon prejudice was implicated by equal concerns about the religious practices of the group. Polygamy was a central feature of anti-Mormon nativist sentiment. It was this fundamental aspect of religious doctrine that prompted the larger fears about national security. While nativists may not have emphasized Catholic doctrine as a point of contention, they focused on the eradication of polygamy as a primary necessity.

The practice of polygamy was also configured as a strain of radicalism. Concerns about Catholic radicals were framed in terms that Higham argues were established with Federalist concerns that Europe's disorders at the end of the eighteenth century might also overwhelm the new world. By the nineteenth century, and with the rise in immigration this attitude resurfaced: "Perhaps a man discontented in his own country will have no settled principles or loyalty at all." For Higham, this fear of foreign radicals was a major trend in the xenophobia of nineteenth-century nativists.[15] In anti-Mormon nativism, however, immigration concerns took a back seat to the already radicalized practice of polygamy—a clearly foreign, exotic, and reprehensible practice.

The primacy of the Anglo-Saxon race as the final thread in Higham's formulation of nineteenth-century nativism is the subject of this chapter. Mormons were uniquely assigned a racial designation in dress, comportment, and language in much anti-Mormon rhetoric. The image of the Mormon Turk was drawn from the representation of the exotic East that was found in the very same media. The nineteenth century saw a rise in popularity of Orientalism in art, fashion, decoration, literature, and theatre. In these representations, the use of Oriental tropes is simultaneously pleasurable and cautionary.[16]

Analyzing Mormons as an Other in nineteenth-century America is complicated by one remarkable fact: they were outwardly indistinguishable from other Anglo-Saxon Protestants. As *Cosmopolitan* magazine warned later in 1911, Mormons were like a "viper on the hearth," a great evil that had infiltrated the sanctity of American's home.[17] The snake in this metaphor is all the more dangerous because its physical characteristics—quick, small, agile—allowed its access into the home without detection. Only after the viper is coiled on the hearth, then ready to strike from the center of the home, does the threat become apparent. Mormons were perceived as equally dangerous to the nation, able to camouflage themselves from detection and thus snake their way into the very heart of society, where they could attack with impunity.

The issues of mimicry and menace here echo similar issues in postcolonial criticism where mimicry is identified as a primary colonial strategy of control. Homi Bhabha, in his canonical essay "Of Mimicry and Man: The Ambivalence of Colonial Discourse," suggests that "colonial mimicry is the desire for a reformed, recognizable Other, as a subject of a difference that is almost the same, but not quite." In the case of colonial mimicry, the "almost same" comes in providing for the colonized access to some of the tools of power—language, religion, art, and fashion. The Other that takes advantage of these cultural markers can create a nearly perfect appearance of the colonized and in doing so, even gain limited admission to positions of power. The appearance, however, is "not quite" the same and never can be in large measure because of the visual marking of skin. As Bhabha ironically restates, the colonial mimic is "almost the same, but not white."[18]

This control of power and knowledge is dependant on the maintenance of the fixed distance between mimicry and assimilation, or what Bhabha calls "resemblance." Effectively, the Other can be allowed access to copy (resemble) but not to become. Bhabha continues, however, to show that the ways that "mimicry must continually produce its slippage, its excess, its difference" expose and disrupt the very colonial system that requires the difference.[19] There were a variety of foreign Others in the nineteenth century whose containment in popular representation reassured anxieties and suggested a unified national identity. Mormonism was exceptional among subordinate groups for the lack of recognizable difference between Mormons and Americans. Mormons, to borrow from Bhabha, were exactly the same (white), but not quite.

One method in popular culture to deal with this troublesome lack of visual distinction was to create a performance of deviance that would suggest that even if Mormons look like Americans on the outside, they are discernibly different on the inside. The gendered and violent identities discussed earlier are enacted through this mode. The performances of sexual fantasy and honorable violence in anti-Mormon melodrama—and the boundaries they established for American identity—are based on internal characteristics that reveal themselves through action. Gender in the nineteenth century was medically seen as biological and "natural," and these innate characteristics were thought to lead to definable gendered behavior. Violence was the outward sign of inner morality; personal ethics and codes of honor led to the honorable use or abuse of violence. The rhetoric of melodrama established an overt clue for audiences as to the inner workings of the characters; characters overtly stated what sentiment prompted their behavior. As such, thought and feeling were clearly linked to performed action.

Another response to the Mormon threat was to establish a clear visual difference. The resemblance issue, for the Mormon Other, was therefore inverted from Bhabha's colonial mimic. Rather than a body that cannot be entirely disguised through resemblance, Mormons already so closely resembled Americans that their home and their bodies needed a disguise. Oriental exoticism became that disguise.

Assigning Oriental attributes, costume, and style to Mormons suggests the importance of a visual marker of ethnicity. Although Catholics and other Anglo-Saxon immigrant groups might have faced particular prejudices, they still had access to rights that nonwhites simply did not. Early naturalization laws, for example, allowed free white persons to become citizens, while Asians were denied that right for nearly a century. Deliberately constructing Mormons *as* Oriental Others speaks directly to the centrality of race to American identity and underlines that in the nineteenth century, Americans were white.

The Oriental discourse that was in popular circulation during the period suggests why this particular representation was effective: one of the primary functions of such an Other group, especially one as barbarian as Mormon Turks, is to provide a need for the civilizing culture of mainstream America. To return to Bhabha, he suggests that "racist stereotypes, statements, jokes, myths . . . are the effects of disavowal that denies the difference of the Other but produce in its stead forms of authority."[20] Since Mormons were already clearly outsiders to mainstream America, portraying them as Turks also demonstrated how racial marking of any kind except white provides those of the "right" race with a mandate for civilizing authority.

As the popularity of travelogues and lectures by globe-trotting authors attest, Americans were fascinated with the exotic foreign East and were willing to absorb safely westernized products of the Orient through commercial consumption. These interactions with the East remained cautionary as story structure and moral conclusion revealed that western values of Christianity, democracy, and monogamy were better. While American audiences may have enjoyed seeing Turkish extravagance, they understood that their own way of life was not only preferable, it was morally superior.

Therefore, assigning Mormons a Turkish identity associated Mormons with a group already viewed with extreme prejudice. Terryl L. Givens suggests that "since the cultural work of dehumanizing or at least demonizing Asians had been well accomplished by the advent of Mormonism, exploiting the ready-made category was easier" than inventing a foreign identity for Mormons from scratch.[21] In collapsing Mormons and Turks into a new racial community, Mormonism was tainted by the Orientalist assumption of gross treachery, carnality, and indolence already associated with Turks. Turks, on the other hand, were made more fearful by their newly discovered geographical proximity in the Salt Lake Valley.

The particular construction of the Mormon Turk speaks directly to intertwined aspects of American ethnic identity: place and race. The way in which the East was performed onstage in the nineteenth century simultaneously represents distinct visual difference and contests that difference by its obvious construction. Behdad reminds that while America has always characterized itself as an immigrant nation, that "engaging in historical scrutiny one notices powerful strands of anti-immigrant sentiments that have played an equally fundamental role in how a nation-state is imagined in the United States."[22] Assigning Oriental attributes, costume, and style to Utah as a place and to Mormons as a race suggests the importance of a physical difference against which Americans could identify themselves. The Oriental discourse that was in popular circulation during the period suggests why this particular representation was effective.

I. ORIENTALISM IN AMERICA

> My aim, throughout this work, has been to give correct pictures of Oriental life and scenery . . . if a few of the many thousands, who can only travel by their firesides, should find my pages answer the purpose for a series of cosmoramic views—should in them behold with a clearer inward eye the hills of Palestine, the sun-gilded minarets of Damascus, or the lonely pine-forest of Phrygia—should feel, by turns, something of the inspiration and the indolence of the Orient—I shall have achieved all I designed, and more than I can justly hope.
>
> —Bayard Taylor, in the preface to
> *The Lands of the Saracens* (1855)

When poet, playwright, and renowned traveler Bayard Taylor published *The Lands of the Saracen* in 1855, he brought to America more than a simple travel journal. The detailed portrait he drew of life in the Turkish Empire was based on his total commitment to living as an Arab. His personal engagement with the subject matter translated into a writing style that worked hard to recuperate pejorative western visions of the East. In his preface to the book, he clearly states that his goal is to move his readers with "the inspiration and the indolence of the Orient."[23] He is careful, however, to wrest the term "indolence" from its Western connotation of laziness and to provide a replacement meaning: "annoyance without anger, delay without vexation, indolence without ennui, endurance without fatigue, appetite without intemperance, enjoyment without gall."[24] The resulting effort is a careful balance between faithfulness to a foreign subject, and self-reflexive alteration that responds to the preconceived expectations of Taylor's audience.

In his work on travel writing in the nineteenth century, Larzar Ziff suggests:

> Eastern physical contentment may show up Western moral nervousness, Eastern pleasure show up Western guilt, but Taylor's very ability to assert this stems from his retention of his sense of the enclosing superiority of Western culture that permits his excursions into the exotic.

Even as he indulges himself in different practices he conveys an awareness of himself as a participant in a performance that he can end whenever he wishes although the other actors cannot.[25]

Even as Taylor reconfigures "indolence" for his audiences, he relies on the common use of the term to make his work unique. Exoticism in the nineteenth century is marked by this peculiar circulation between here and there, home and foreign lands. In visual, literary, and dramatic representations, the Orient worked to fit itself to its western audience—providing enough remarkable exoticism to hold attention, while never going so far as to be unbelievable. Understanding this method of presentation and the theatrical style in which it was enacted contextualizes the processes by which anti-Mormon melodramas utilized Oriental tropes.

The exotic in the nineteenth century was encountered, recorded, and represented in a particularly dramatic way. Authors of the Orient, such as Taylor, were the artistic auteurs of the performance—in total control of the content and style of its articulation. They kept in mind their western audiences to such an extent that the image became as much a reflection of the already-imagined as an introduction to the realities of a foreign culture. On stage, the exotic Orient was a hybrid; western styles and stories were married to images of the Orient already circulating in popular culture. Additionally, the presentation of the Far East on stage provided audiences the opportunities to clearly differentiate between Americans and foreigners. The western style of eastern representation and the visual difference created by these representations on stage point to the various means by which exotic ethnicity was performed in America.

An Arabian Night Spell

It was evident from the early days of the United States that control of trade routes to Asia would be both economically and politically lucrative. Politicians lobbied for the construction of a North American road that would allow access to the East without going through Europe.[26] A public craze for goods from the East might have provided some impetus for these expanding trade routes, but the opium market demanded them. By the 1850s, all leading U.S. firms handled the sales of Turkish and West Indian opium to China, a business that reaffirmed America's dominant place in the global market. Culturally, other Oriental merchandise like silken goods, handcrafted chinaware, jade, porcelain, tea, and painted calico became highly sought after as markers of the upper class. Oriental objects accrued an enormous cultural importance among fashion-conscious Americans. The ability to literally own a piece of the East established a desire that was eventually reflected in America's imperialist agenda.[27]

The introduction of steam packets as passenger vessels in the 1830s opened access to the Orient to visits from America. As writers and artists gained access to these fascinating foreign lands, America became inundated with a new literary trope of the mystique of the Orient. As illustrated in 1853 in the popular magazine *Knickerbocker,* a particular vision of the East inundated popular culture:

> We frame ourselves a deep azure sky, and a languid alluring atmosphere; associate the luxurious ease with coffee-rooms and flower-gardens of the seraglio of Constantinople; with their tapering minarets and gold-crescents of Cairo; with the fountains within and the kiosks without Damascus—setting of silver in circlets of gold. We see grave and revered turbans sitting cross-legged on Persian carpets in baths and harems . . . we then bespread over all a sort of Arabian Night Spell.[28]

With the invocation of flower gardens, harems, and a "languid alluring atmosphere," this essay describes in words what other artists at the time were capturing in art and luxury goods. In the second half of the nineteenth

Fig. 4.1 Bayard Taylor in "A Morning in Damascus" by Thomas Hicks (1856). In this painting, created in New York City by his friend Hicks, Taylor wears the Egyptian costume he also wore on his lecture circuit. He is seen with Achmet, his servant on his Middle East travels, whose portrait is based on a daguerreotype. To paint the background view of Damascus, the artist relied on drawings made by Taylor. Courtesy of the National Portrait Gallery of the Smithsonian Institution.

century, writers traveled to the East and recorded their encounter with foreign cultures in a particular literary style that both reaffirmed already circulating images of the East and introduced new exotic traditions to assure their readers' continued interest.

Anti-Mormon melodramas drew on the pattern established in travelogues by appropriating a popular vision of the Far East that corresponded to Western expectations. Both plays and literature presented exoticism in a way that was exciting, but not too exciting—strange, but not too strange. This balancing act between adhering to already accepted visions of the Orient and introducing enough new material to keep the audiences interested emerges in anti-Mormon melodrama in plays that stage actual exoticism and those that reveal Mormon exoticism as Turkish. Travelogue authors used similar techniques.

Many of these writers were Protestant missionaries, whose accounts of their journeys were couched in the rhetoric of conversion. Others, like Bayard Taylor, made serious efforts towards objectivity and analysis in their interpretation of the Orient for American readers. Taylor, arguably the most influential of American travel writers, spent over twenty years taking various journeys abroad, recording his adventures in books and lectures.

Taylor's writings provided a more realistic record of native life, directly addressed errors of earlier Orientalist writers, and mocked the imperialist agenda. Reading his work as relatively unbiased, however, doesn't account for the way in which Taylor appropriated a popular vision of the Orient in order to market his own performance. When lecturing on the lyceum circuit of his initial travels to "The Lands of the Saracen," Taylor would wear Arabic clothes and a scimitar. Through his dramatic costume choice, Taylor was simultaneously establishing and erasing difference.

Reports of the lectures record that his appearance made women swoon.[29] The actuality of the exotic in performance caused a literal divorce from the known world. While images of the East were widely viewed in art and illustration, the performance of the difference was more powerful (presumably women did not swoon when reading travel journals in popular magazines). The act of fainting reinscribed appropriate behavior for encountering the Other: with shock, fright, and artistically performed distaste. The calculated effect of the dress shows how Taylor's exploitation of difference disseminated a particular image of himself and the Orient.

In wearing an Arabic costume to his lectures, Taylor was also erasing the boundaries between East and West. With his discernibly white body clothed as a "Saracen," he was merely wrapping himself in the trappings of exotic Otherness. Removed from the Arab body and divorced from its cultural and practical milieus, the clothing lost its referent. On Taylor's body, the garb took on a new significance, not as a true encounter with difference, but as a safely contained representation of it. The Orient, by the very nature of the lecture medium, was more readily available for public consumption, and the clothing on the wrong body reassured audiences that in the end, the differences are not too great.

Frederick N. Bohrer suggests a methodology for addressing the complex network by which exoticism functions in western culture. First, as illustrated by the Bayard Taylor anecdote above, the eastern object of exotic interest cannot be seen outside a system of circulation. At the same time, exoticism is always assimilated—it must resist expectations to a certain extent in order to be exotic, but in the end, it cannot be totally different from the audience's preconceived notions. As a result, the exotic object "is ultimately (even if only provisionally) assimilated in the very norm it begins by challenging."[30] The transformation of the East for the West requires interpretation by the audience in order for the presentation of culture to have meaning.

A similar technique is used by Taylor in his description of the temple in his melodrama, *The Prophet*. Livia, the prophet's second wife, is overcome at the sight of the newly constructed temple and poetically expresses its beauty:

> Lo! now the temple's gilded pinnacles
> The impatient sun hath kissed; across the land
> They sharply shine like arrows drawn to a head,
> And heavenward aimed![31]

The multiple sharply-pointed spires, shining under a hot sun, are not so much illustrative of the Protestant style that dominated early Mormon architecture. The description resonates more with the description that Bayard writes of mosques in his travel journals:

> In the centre [sic] of the city rose a steep, abrupt mound, crowned with the remains of the ancient citadel, and shining minarets shot up, singly or in cluster, around its base. The prevailing city and long, monotonous hills, gleamed with equal brilliancy under a sky of cloudless and intense blue. This singular monotony of coloring gave a wonderful effect to the view, which is one of the most remarkable in all the Orient.[32]

While the description is hardly a central point of *The Prophet*, the ease with which Taylor draws a visual comparison between the play's temple and a mosque speaks to the familiar way in which boundaries between Mormons and Turks were crossed in literature and performance.

Brigham Young's description of Mahomet's Paradise in *Deseret Deserted* is another fascinating example, and the only time in anti-Mormon melodrama where the Mormon/Turkish categories are entirely collapsed. Once he has been dressed in a cloak and turban, the doors to Mahomet's paradise are thrown open. With the sounding of gongs, an elaborate tableau is revealed: "Merciful Powers! what do I see—the elephant in all the developments of his artistic anatomy! Oh! the delicious creatures! Music, roses, wine—fairy shapes inhaling heavenly cobblers through ethereal straws!"³³ The elephant and the *houris* make the Oriental flavor unmistakable, while the "heavenly cobblers" suggest a particularly western brand of sweetness.

Drawing connections between eastern and Mormon religious buildings, food choices, and dress styles makes sense in a period where foreignness was generally drawn in an Oriental flair. Postcolonial historian Malini Johar Schueller traces the intersection of culture, economics, and travel to explain the prominent use of the Orient in American literature in the nineteenth century. She points out that the style in which the Orient was imagined varied across the century, but was always grounded in a juxtaposition between East and West: "Poets, dramatists, essayists, novelists, and short-story writers routinely wrote about different Orients and produced a series of literary works in which the nation was variously embodied as a vigorous, active, masculinized, and morally upright Columbia-as-empire, against a version of a decaying, passive, demasculinized, deviant, or spiritual Orient."³⁴

Although these differences were meant to be read as natural, the use of the Oriental tropes of decay and deviance in American writing was also self-aware of the constructed nature of the description. As the *Knickerbocker* article quoted earlier illustrates: we "frame ourselves" in this vision of the East and "bespread over all" of the representations an imaginative Oriental "spell." In much the same way, anti-Mormon melodrama clearly appropriated an exotic Eastern ethnicity for Mormons that was already familiar to theatre audiences while simultaneously foregrounding the constructed nature of the Mormon Turk.

Staging the Orient

Oriental studies had, by the late nineteenth century, been a focus of scholarly and popular interest for over a century. Translations of Oriental literature, like William Jones' first act of *Shakuntala* (1803), appeared in widely circulated magazines. The translation of the Rosetta stone (1822) opened up access to Egyptian literature and art; by mid century several private collectors had established extensive private Egyptian collections. Rammohan Roy, a Hindu reformist, toured the continent with a lecture on the Hindu religion in the 1820s. He excited intense interest and was reviewed by journals such as *The Christian Disciple,* and *The American Reviews.*³⁵ Raymond Schwab, a scholar in Western translations of Oriental literature, argues that the introduction and distribution of Sanskrit texts in the West, whether in print or performance, created an intellectual renaissance greater in impact than the renaissance following the arrival of Greek manuscripts in the fifteenth century.³⁶

While these literary discoveries brought legitimacy to the field of Orientalism, however, popular acceptance of Oriental music and art was more evident on stage, where costuming, make-up, and other design elements created an exotic landscape that separated the American self from the foreign Other. Performing Orientalism was a powerful means of disseminating the idea of the Far East; anti-Mormon melodramas echoed Orientalist style. Anti-Mormon melodramas were not alone in their feature of an exotic setting. Throughout the nineteenth century, there were nearly one hundred plays that either contained an Arab or Turkish character, or were set in some Eastern location.[37] Closely examining some of these also reveals a methodology for examining anti-Mormon melodramas as rich performative texts with meaning beyond that which is imbedded in the scripts alone.

Of particular interest in the United States were plays that dramatized the Tripolitan War (1800–1815). A diplomatic crisis in the Barbary States over tribute payments to protect American shipping routes from piracy led to the formation of the U.S. Navy during the war. A number of attacks from land and sea, sieges of major cities, and settlement negotiations ended both the war and tribute payments from the United States to any Barbary State. More interestingly for the American public, the war provided a perfect opportunity for the colorful juxtaposition of American and Turkish customs and characters.

Two of the more well-known plays about this conflict are Richard Penn Smith's *The Bombardment at Algiers* (1829) and *The Usurper; or, Americans at Tripoli* (1835) by Joseph Steven Jones.[38] Both of these early plays are patriotic celebrations of the bravery of American soldiers in the face of the bewildering Orient and were revived throughout the century. In *The Usurper*, Clothine is a servant to the Turkish maiden Immorina. Clothine fears the American naval prisoners being held in Tripoli because of her mistaken impression that the Americans scalp their prisoners:

> IMMO. Frankness appears to be your characteristic, Clothine, but pray inform me what are these Americans if they are not men?
> CLO. Indian! Yes indeed, Indian! That they are. They used to tell me that these Americans, that is, Indians, if they caught a man or woman, no matter which (and I'm sure this proves them not to be men) would take of the top part of his or her head in the twinkling of an eye! Oh, dear! dear! We shall all be scalped, that we shall.
> IMMO. Nay, nay, you mistake, Clothine; these Indians of whom you speak are the natives of America. They inhabit the western regions of that vast country, and are savage and barbarous like our wild Arabs. But those whom we denominate American are a civilized and polished people, enterprising, brave and hospitable.[39]

Immornia's description of the soldiers ("civilized, polished, enterprising, brave, and hospitable") establishes the American character not only in contrast to Clothine's vision of Indians, but also to the barbarous behaviors of "wild Arabs."[40]

Appropriating Ethnicity 131

This juxtaposition is made even clearer when the American soldiers are first brought to the court of the Usurper as slaves. The scene opens in a grand exotic spectacle:

SCENE 4: *Grand Hall in the palace, splendidly illuminated. Abdel Mahadi discovered seated on a throne surrounded by Officers, Guards, Slaves, male and female Dancers, etc. Banners. Chorus. At the end of the chorus, a fancy dance by one of the slaves. Turkish dance.*[41]

While there are no extant records of the design for this production, it seems reasonable to assume the scenery and costumes would correspond to Orientalist art from this period, as epitomized by the work of European artists Jean-Léon Gérôme and John Frederick Lewis and explored by American artists such as Robert Swain Gifford, Frederick Arthur Bridgman and John Singer Sargent. In her analysis of Orientalism on the early English stage, Elaine Hadley suggests, "Audiences could reasonably expect costumes of a certain richness, but rarely indicating any profound sense of cultural specificity; sets of monumentality, with fortresses and palaces amidst mountains or vast expanses of deserts; and dramatic climaxes in which armies and their horses were deployed by the awful intensity of a villain's tyrannical will."[42] Melodrama brought art to life.

Orientalist art has long been critiqued for its troubling representation of the Orient of the late nineteenth century. Many of the paintings were not composed by sight or by memory, but based on the writing of sensationalized travelogues or novels. Some painters, such as Gérôme, did spend much of their time in the East and painted scenes that would have been readily observable. One such is Gérôme's famous "The Snake Charmer" (1880). Others, such as his "An Almeh with a Pipe" (1873), are romanticized blends of authentic ethnographic detail and cultural distortion. In the Islamic societies Gérôme was purporting to document, women were not allowed in public without the protection of a male family member and a veil. Portraits like "Almeh," featuring a thinly veiled woman posing sensually in an open doorway, are probably no more culturally correct than the painting of colleagues who never traveled outside Europe.

Stage settings, costumes, and dramatic action drawn in a similar artistic style, like performance of a "Turkish dance" in *The Usurper,* allowed audiences a living glimpse into this constructed world. As John M. MacKenzie argues in *Orientalism: History, Theory and the Arts* (1995), theatre "brought together the art of stage scenery, the design of sets, costumes and props, the music of song and the instrumental pit, the architecture of both the building in which the performance took place and the fantasy world portrayed beyond the proscenium arch, and the text and characterizations of the play."[43] MacKenzie's point may seem evident, but serves as a sharp reminder of the rich text of live theatre that requires a thicker reading than does writing alone. Additionally, MacKenzie emphasizes how the image of the Orient in popular representation was always framed by the Occident; the proscenium served as a clear barrier between home and the exotic represented beyond its frame.

Sardanapalus by Byron was arguably the most popular Orientalist play of the nineteenth century. Initially staged in 1821 in England, the production was revived throughout the century both in Europe and the United States. The play, which is considered by some to be Byron's greatest dramatic achievement, follows the story of an ancient Assyrian ruler, Sardanapalus, who attempts to establish a rule of peace and prosperity rather than furthering the war agenda of his father Nimrod. When his people rebel against him, he realizes his hopes for an earthly paradise are unattainable. Supported by his brave concubine Myrrha, he takes up arms to curb the rebellion and dies with his dreams and Myrrha on a funeral pyre at the end of the play. In addition to displaying Byron's poetic genius, the subject of the play allowed for an exploration of the power and limitations of monarchy, and the setting provided an opportunity for exotic spectacle and a thrilling pyrotechnical climax.

The *New York Times* review of Charles Calvert's production of *Sardanapalus* at Booth's Theatre on 13 April 1876 illustrates the impact of theatrical arts on the presentation of the Orient. Earlier productions of the play drew their designs from recent archeological discoveries. Charles Kean's 1853 revival, for example, used the details provided in Sir Henry Layard's report of his excavations at Nineveh, which were published in 1849. MacKenzie suggests that the popularity of the archeological report might have in fact prompted the revival of the play.[44] Calvert's 1876 revival and international tour was also presented as a work of astonishing historical accuracy. The *Times* reviewer suggested:

> The mere spectacular part of the work is superb. The costumes, properties, decorations, and "stage sets" are in many respects more solidly magnificent and artistic than anything yet presented to our theatre-goers. We are not used to such accuracy in these details of archeological research nor to such care in working up the supernumerary elements forming the body of this grand picture of twenty-four centuries ago.[45]

While the reviewer took exception to Calvert's cutting of Byron's script and suggested that the addition of elaborate ballets, war scenes, and stage tricks overwhelmed the delicacy of Byron's poetry, he felt the overall production was a success because "so far as costumes, scenery, colored lights, and ballet evolutions go, nothing is left to be desired."[46]

The play was a huge success and on opening night, the crowds were so large that "standing room, even in the lobbies and hallways, was at a premium."[47] As the plot of the play is neither complex nor new and the play itself would have been familiar to audiences from other revivals, the success of the production can be attributed, as the *New York Times* reviewer suggests, to the theatrical presentation of the exotic East. The setting for *Sardanapalus*, with the elaborate scenes of harems where the ballets took place, created for them the shape and style of lands beyond their borders and reaffirmed their place as American. Anti-Mormon melodramas created the same effect as Salt Lake City was established as an exotic foreign land where the religion was more Islamic than Christian and the women all lived in harems.

II. THE OUTCAST BORDER OF THE WORLD

> I am not happy here. This seems the outcast border of the world. Society is crude, and lacks that culture which refines and elevates the soul. The men are vulgar and the women rude. Were I a man, my sojourn would be brief.
>
> —Alice in *Brigham Young*

In *Evelyn Gray,* Rob describes his travels across the Orient, evoking a similar tone to other travelogues of the time, where first-hand observation conforms to the literary style of *The Arabian Nights* already in vogue. While in the Far East, he has an opportunity to describe America to an Englishman also traveling abroad. Rob says that he then realized that he knew more about the world then he did his own country and he "blushingly confessed [his] ignorance." His English companion "got into one of his Highland rhodomontades about the snobbishness of Americans who go gadding away to foreign realms before they have seen their own glorious country." Told to go home, Rob decides to continue his travels in the "Far West" of Salt Lake City.[48]

By juxtaposing international travel to Cairo and Africa with travel to Utah, and with the play on words (Far East to Far West), a clear connection is made—Utah is a foreign land. Unlike plays set in the actual Orient, however, Utah has very little to offer in the way of brightly tiled architecture, colorful midriff-revealing costumes, sensual dances, oddly shaped pipes, turbans, incense and strange perfumes, or music of bells and pipes. In fact, the costume and set designs for most Mormon characters was almost the exact opposite. Plays like *The Mormons, Brigham Young,* and *Zion* required dark suits and beards for men, plain hairstyles and modest homespun dresses for women. The houses were modeled after log cabins on the frontier and the furniture was specifically American in its design. For example, *The Mormons* advertised that "NEW SCENERY" of life in Utah, "from actual views, will illustrate the halt of an emigrant party, with handcart, at a spring, on the prairie, by moonlight—Raising of the tents—The flower prairie. SALT LAKE CITY FROM THE MOUNTAINS" and "THE MORMON TEMPLE, with the ceremony of endowment, and sealing of a second wife—an accurate representation—Rock Canon, with much of the

United States army, wagons, mules, &c. NOGGS TARRED AND FEATHERED. PRAIRIE ON FIRE."⁴⁹ Rather than being part of a stage design, then, the connection between Utah and the Far East is made through the verbal descriptions of exotic locale.

In *Evelyn Gray*, the character Brigham Young reaffirms some of the settings of the exotic Far East—olive bowers, rose gardens, scented fountains—by connecting his Mormon and Islamic heaven:

> Mohammed . . . established a whole-sale, enterprising business. He added a new department, besides, that was a brilliant hit. I tell you his paradise, hell, purgatory, judgment, and damnation, there are the ugly bugbears that make faces and shake their fists at a fellow in the midst of his enjoyment. Mohammed swept them away for the believer, and got up a heaven of his own, and a right jolly place it is. Ah, it makes a man's mouth water to think of it, with its olive bowers, its rose gardens full of scented fountains and beautiful women, where a man can just lie down and revel like an ox in a clover meadow.⁵⁰

Since Western culture had long been suspicious of the indolence and idolatry of the Far East, connecting these to Mormonism was a short cut to prejudices against Mormons. At the same time, the proximity of the Mormon threat, in the heart of Western America, provided specifics that proved suspicions about foreign despotism and depravity. The pervasive Turkish-Mormon connection in anti-Mormon melodramas brought to mind the popular image of an Oriental setting familiar to audiences from art and theatre.

Orientalism in the Extreme Occident

In Max Adeler's comic novel of life in Salt Lake City, *The Tragedy of Thompson Dunbar, A Tale of Salt Lake City* (1879), the hero of the piece manages to gain and lose several hundred wives.⁵¹ Dunbar's adventures with this "polygamy of Turkey" establish an image of the Oriental location of Mormonism that became prevalent towards the end of the century. Later in the tale, Dunbar describes the City of Salt Lake in such a way that the location of ethnic Mormonism was made clear:

> America has no other [city] like it. Surveyed from a distance it wears a distinctly Oriental appearance. So we of the Far West who have only dreamed of the East, imagine how Damascus may look. White house shining amid rich masses of green foliage. A dome, a tower, a spire that may answer for a minaret . . . a sky of more than Oriental softness overhead.⁵²

While Salt Lake City may exist cartographically in the United States, in the cultural imagination of many Americans it was a foreign destination where "Orientalism in the extreme Occident" even altered nature to reflect its style—the Utah sky has an "Oriental softness."⁵³ Even more notably, in literature and melodramas, emphasis was placed on how Utah was isolated from the rest of the country in such a way that to visit was to journey to the "outcast border of the world."

In many ways, a distant and foreign Utah was a reality of geography. In 1870, Salt Lake City was the largest city between St. Louis and San Francisco, but it was entirely isolated from either of these population centers by the Rocky Mountains in the East and the Sierra Nevada range in the West.⁵⁴ The Mormon hesitancy to trade with, socially interact with, or vote for non-Mormons, not to mention the perception that the Mormons in Salt Lake City were attempting to break away from the United States, created an ideological as well as geographical distance. These perceptions were compounded by Mormon policies that led to violent encounters from the Utah War to the Mountain Meadows Massacre. While the completion of the transcontinental railroad a year earlier in 1869 provided direct access to Utah, Salt Lake City was more of a place to travel through on the way to California than a stopping point. As a result, the mystique of Salt Lake City as an isolated, foreign, and dangerous place persisted. Reinforcing this notion was the repeated use of Oriental descriptors and the need for characters to escape from the city.

The plays *Evelyn Gray, The Mormons, Fonda,* and *Deseret Deserted* are all framed by travel. In each case the action of the play opens to characters traveling from great distances to reach Utah. The Gray family arrives from England in *Evelyn Gray,* only to immediately "join the saintly caravan" that is traveling to the Salt Lake Valley.⁵⁵ Led by an "episcopal cameldriver" they venture into the "primitive country" of Utah—a journey so harsh that several, including Mr. Gray, die along the way.⁵⁶ *The Mormons* similarly opens mid-journey to Salt Lake City. The setting is detailed:

> *A mott of cotton wood timber, with prairie in the distance. Moon rising—a well-spring R.C., with practicable water through trap—handcarts, loaded with goods, upstage—tent, L. camp-fire, a pipe. With rifle across lap—Woodville, at a camp fire, watching Mrs. Woodville and Mary, who are engaged in cooking, and carrying victuals in and out of tent, L.—Men are engaged putting up tent, R. practicable for Pratt—the rest engaged in the usual bustle of a prairie camp.*⁵⁷

This scene is reassuringly familiar and corresponded to the vision of frontier life represented in literature and other melodramas of the time. The "practicable" set dressing of a well-spring, the tents, and the "victuals" all lend an air of reality and normalcy. This rough life is then juxtaposed from the vision of paradise the pioneers expect to find when they reach Salt Lake City.

Mrs. Woodville complains that "life on the plains is but a wearisome one at best" and that she longs "for the comforts of a home and the peace of the social circle."⁵⁸ She reinforces how this pleasant frontier scene cannot substitute for what has been promised at the end of the long journey:

> MRS. WOOD. How different the city of Zion will be! There all is peace and happiness.
> WOOD. I long for its harmony.
> MARY. And I.⁵⁹

Eagle-Eye, however, warns Mary that the notion of Salt Lake City as Zion is a myth and that instead she will find nothing there but "sensuality, hypocrisy, and murder, which form the base of the Mormon faith." He continues, "Your pure heart will be shocked with the practices at Salt Lake—your sensibilities wounded by the miseries resulting from polygamy. It will be too late then to escape the evils around you."⁶⁰

His use of the words "escape" suggests an extreme and dangerous isolation. It also echoes other verbs used in literature and theatre to describe the return journey from Utah. Alfreda Eva Bell's 1855 novel *Boadicea, The Mormon Wife, Life-scenes in Utah* was one of the most popular anti-Mormon exposés of the nineteenth century. It presents the private journal of the title character and her adventures as a Mormon wife, which include polygamy, poisoning, intrigue, and infanticide. At the end of the book, Boadicea also escapes Utah, back to the United States. Throughout the novel, there is a clear delineation between Utah and the United States, a move that erases the fact that Utah was a U. S. territory and elevates it to the status of a foreign country. Boadicea is only able to make her way back to the United States by fleeing her home, hiding in a mountain cave until some Americans find, rescue, and offer her companionship on her journey back. Eagle-Eye suggests much the same thing when he warns Mary, "It is not so easy to leave. The plains are wide—the journey toilsome—the property of the saints in Brigham's hands—and the terrible Danites in the path."⁶¹

Fonda also needs aid "to escape from this vile and wicked place."⁶² Just as in other anti-Mormon melodramas, Utah is described in *Fonda* by the Mormons as Zion, "a regular paradise . . . the garden of Eden over again, only a heap sight better."⁶³ Those who have visited and escaped describe it differently: Utah is "a wicked land," "an outlandish place," and "a modern Sodom."⁶⁴ Biblical references were frequently invoked in nineteenth-century writing to refer to a variety of places, hopes, and aversions. The metaphors, whether positive—Zion—or negative—Sodom—relied on the formal recognition of the foreign distance implied by the biblical locales. The same sense of geographical and cultural distance is maintained when these terms are applied specifically to Utah.

In *Deseret Deserted,* similar connections are made between Utah and Oriental lands. Lost in the desert near Salt Lake City, the heroes of the piece, Looney O'Flab and Tom Scott, see an animal approaching in the distance. Confused by its odd shape (up close it is revealed to be a donkey laden with petticoat hoops), they presume that since they are in Utah, it "can't be a buffalo. May be 'tis the elephant" or 'a zaybray.'"[65] The discursive links between Islam and Mormonism served to establish a view of Utah as a foreign place—difficult to reach, impossible to leave, and filled with an exotic expectation of elephants, minarets, and the sins of Sodom. Nowhere are the links made more overt than in the consistently repeated trope of the Mormon harem, a place that was foreign in the extreme.

Mormon Harems

Benjamin G. Ferris was the third Secretary of Utah Territory, sent from Washington D.C. to serve under the territorial governor, Brigham Young. His tenure lasted just six months, over the winter of 1852–1853. Based on his experiences in Salt Lake City, he was induced in 1856 to write *Utah and the Mormons; History, Government, Doctrines, Customs, and Prospects of the Latter-day Saints from Personal Observation During a Six Month's Residence at Great Salt Lake City*. He felt the Mormon question was fast becoming one of political importance to the nation and that he could reveal specifics based on his objective experiences.[66] As with others, he writes of a Salt Lake City distant and foreign where, like a "luckless navigator hemmed in by Artic ice," he had "little else to engross the attention aside from the strange and eccentric community which has established itself in that isolated region."[67]

Ferris' work treats, as the sub-title suggests, the history, government, doctrines, customs, and prospects of the Church. In his chapter on polygamy, he argues that while the Bible records some examples of polygamy, they are all examples of the sins of misguided men and that polygamy has never been a dominant aspect of any successful ancient or modern culture. He concludes:

> The modern nations of Europe are free from this scourge. It belongs now to the indolent and opium-eating Turks and Asiatics, the miserable Africans, the North American savages, and the Latter-day Saints. It is the offspring of lust, and its legitimate results are soon manifest in the rapid degeneracy of races.[68]

Of all the rhetorical connections drawn between Mormons and Muslims, the most prevalent is this—that polygamy is a shared deviant sexual practice both repellent and strangely attractive. Anti-Mormon melodramas exploit this connection with the repeated and consistent use of Oriental terms as pejorative signifiers of various aspects of polygamy: harem, bondage, seraglio, and sultana.

Of particular interest in both Orientalist art and Turkish architecture are mosaic patterns that serve as "authentic" backdrops for alluringly dressed (or underdressed) hyper-sexualized female figures. The harem was a most popular setting for paintings, a scene that allowed artists to reveal women in both commonplace daily activities and in exotic pursuits. The harem was a private domain revealed for the Western gaze, and a female space revealed as a male sexual fantasy. Books, magazine serials, articles, newspaper reports, travel writing, paintings, illustrations, sculptures, and lecture performances all presented a remarkably unified vision of a harem. Sometimes, the harem imagery is the main selling point of the play, as in *The Mormons; or, the Revolt of the Harem*, which was "produced with every aid that can be afforded by superb scenery, dresses, &c." at Wallack's Theatre in 1858.[69] The repeated use of the term harem, or words connected with it, to describe polygamous households again draws the connections between Mormonism and Islam. It also provides an elaborate image of sensuality that overlaid itself on scenes in Mormon Utah.

In *Brigham Young*, for example, the play opens as Alice discovers that the character Brigham Young wants to marry her and make her the "queen-wife of the harem."[70] Clara, one of his earlier wives, has a vision where she sees Young being married again. In her dream, the new wife sings a song of triumph:

> Dear mother farewell,
> I am going to hell
> With the prophet and all his wives
> With his sisters and brothers
> And concubine others—
> What a sweet dream of beauty our lives!
> Oh, beautiful world! Oh, beautiful life!
> I am queen of the harem—
> The great prophet's wife! I am queen over all of the harem forever!
> My heart is so happy
> For life is so sweet!
> I will never know sorrow,
> Oh, never! No never!
> I am queen over all of the harem forever![71]

The phrase "queen of the harem" suggests a double foreignness. To be a "queen" requires a system of government anathema to American democracy and the "harem" brings to mind the sexual practices of the East. The repeated and familiar trope of the indolent East was so pervasive in art and literature that this phrase, even when uttered by actresses costumed in fashions of the time, evoked an erotic atmosphere of ornamentation and excess where intertwining female bodies lounge, recline, and are exhibited for pleasure.

This is made overt in *Evelyn Gray* when Lucy Rawdon, an actress, is talking with Brigham Young about their plans to ruin a local official, Judge Lecher. Young notices:

YOUNG. You are looking very well. Do you know, Lucy, you are a very good-looking woman?
LUCY. Indeed? I thank you for your plantation compliment, but I don't consider you at all fit to judge.
YOUNG. Why not, my dear? I have traded enough in female flesh.
LUCY. Yes, that is just it. What should a being like you know about beauty? You don't see anything else in women but flesh.
YOUNG. Well, and what else are they?[72]

Here, Stern creates a particular outlook for Brigham Young that suggests that his focus on women is entirely sexual—the idea that he has "traded" in flesh underlines his role as the pasha to a harem of women. Lucy, in *The Mormons*, sees these connections as well, as she calls Amelia, his favorite wife, the "Light of the Harem" and his precious "Sultana."[73]

When Young visits the Paradise of Mahomet in *Deseret Deserted*, he and Mahomet can agree on only one thing—the importance of a doctrine that allows men to lord over women and enjoy them sexually. This is actually dramatized in the play when a group of *houris* perform a ballet. This dance literally creates the Orientalist vision of a harem on stage, with the exhibition of female bodies for the double pleasure of the gaze of Mahomet and Young, sipping mint juleps beneath a canopy, and for the audience who can see a harem come to life.

The trope of Mormon male sexual pleasure in polygamy is one that runs through most of the extant anti-Mormon melodramas. In *Brigham Young*, the character Brigham Young tries to cloak his sexual desire in religious language, but one of his wives, Hetty reveals the truth as she searches for Young to give him piece of her mind: "Where is the old flirt! Oh, you old fool! You coxcomb! You old devil! You hypocrite! Why do you send for women to tell them what you want to do! We know what you are, what you want. You want a new wife every day! You would seal and marry all the young girls in the country if you could—if you dared!"[74] Hetty's tirade follows the three associations that linked Mormon with Turkish polygamy: the hypocrisy of masking sexual excesses in a cloak of religion, the seeming endless desire for new sexual partners, and a desire for young girls.

The character Brigham Young admits as much himself when he complains to Harry that "My old wives are played out, and my younger ones are the very devils to deal with. My last wife, though young and beautiful is a she-tiger to me, and makes my life a most unhappy one; and I must punish her by taking one more young and beautiful."[75] In *Fonda* this same trope is evident. In *Fonda,* Betty advises that the widower and wagon train leader Job Elder should not listen to the preaching of the Mormon preacher in the company. If he does, she predicts, "The first thing he'll do will be to advise you to stop here and have a dozen wives; and your little innocent motherless child, you will bring up, I suppose, to marry some old bald-headed Elder."[76] As the character of Baby Elden, Job's daughter, was portrayed by a little girl on stage, this image of marriage to an old man not only furthered the trope of Mormon male lust for youth and beauty, but hinted at pedophilia.

The frequent references to multiple wives, each younger than the one before, foregrounded the sensual nature of polygamy—a marker of Western perceptions of harem culture. In drawing these discursive connections between harems and Mormon women, however, race is complicated by gender. Words like "harem" or "sultana" speak to the practice of polygamy and concubinage, which were conditions that Mormon women faced; there is a danger in reading the Mormon harem through the lens of ethnic difference that effaces the material conditions of these women. Recognizing the sites of transgression and moments of resistance enacted by Mormon women in anti-Mormon melodramas and in actual history returns agency to the polygamous body. At the same time, the parallel perceptions of Turkish and Mormon harems reveals an undeniable connection between the two cultures in the popular imagination.

In *Desert Deserted*, Young eventually requests that he be allowed to mingle in with the young and sensual *houris* who have just danced since he "might, by floating airily in a graceful attitude, produce an agreeable and cooling effect."[77] Then he is induced by Mahomet to play a few notes on a "pipe." After playing, Young again dances first by himself then with the ballet girls until he "*falls exhausted into the arms of the women. Tableau.*"[78] This final image brings the accusation of anti-Mormon literature to reality with the frozen image of Young, wearing a turban, wrapped in the arms of harem beauties.

It is an image that circulated unproblematically on and off the melodramatic stage. For example, in 1884, *Puck* published four possible solutions for the Mormon problem. In caricatures by Gillam, Keppler, Opper, and Graetz, the solution seemed to revolve around the issue of polygamy as seen by four different views. Residing side by side with representations of "traditional" marriage with a hen-pecked wife and Gillam's observation that "one wife is enough" and a sarcastic promotion of divorce is Keppler's drawing of a Mormon Harem. If it were not for the placement of the cartoon in the context of Mormonism, it would be indistinguishable from straight Orientalist illustrations.

The use of the harem trope in illustrations and anti-Mormon melodramas shows Mormonism as an unacceptable religion, non-Christian and immoral, just like the heathen practices of the Orient. The connections are not only fictional. In 1868, Madame Olympe Audouard presented several well-attended lectures on Turkey. As part of her lecture, she promised to "also make special comparison of Polygamy as its exists in Turkey, with the same institution as it exists among the Mormons. Having visited Salt Lake City, and resided there as well as in Turkey, for some time, this gifted and accomplished lady is well qualified to discuss this subject in a manner at once interesting and instructing."[79] Here, no matter the differences in style, form, and practice of polygamy between Utah and the Far East, a selling point for the lecture is the link between the two.

Fig. 4.2 "A Desperate Attempt to Solve the Mormon Question," Gillam, Keppler, Opper, and Graetz. Lithograph printed by Mayer, Merkel, and Ottmann and Published in *Puck* (1884). "Four artists who differ in style and in mind/ This courtroom on the Mormons have jointly designed/ The result of the labors is here—and what is more/ We'll remark that in Utah they laugh at all four." Courtesy of the Library of Congress, Prints and Photographs Division, LC-USZ62–94007.

Whether Utah was an isolated foreign land or Mormon homes were Oriental harems merely reinforced the rhetorical connections being drawn between Mormonism and Islam. Inventing a mythical Mecca in America, however, was not enough to sustain prejudice. The transatlantic railroad provided direct access to Salt Lake City, and more travelers were able to visit there directly. Also, as Marr argues, "For those less committed to the strict scruples of Protestant morality, the same islamicist images conjured to discredit Mormonism may have elicited more interest by augmenting its exotic allure."[80] To counteract this slippage, anti-Mormon melodramas and other works turned to race as an additional means of setting Mormons apart from Americans and in doing so, created the ethnicity of the Mormon Turk.

III. OUR WESTERN TURKS

> *I am the Prophet of a mighty race—a race of pious upright men ...*
> —Brigham Young in *Deseret Deserted*

Herman Isadore Stern was a scholar and author of a comprehensive study of Norse mythology. When he turned to an examination of American culture, his research was published in a play that he entitled *Evelyn Gray*, or, *The Victims of Our Western Turks: A Tragedy in Five Acts*. Published by the Alden Publishing Company in 1890, the book was targeted not for a scholarly, but a popular audience.[81] While the prolific use of quotes by Mormon leaders and anti-Mormon exposés, and the long didactic speeches on a wide variety of issues topical to late-nineteenth-century America make this play distinctive, even more interesting is Stern's title notion of Mormons as Western Turks.

The tactics used to create the necessary difference between Americans and Mormons were not limited to explorations of their exotic homeland. Authors such as Stern, as well as artists and scientists, constructed a physical difference that externally distinguished the two. For example, the Surgeon's General's Office determined in 1860 that the physiological characteristics of young Mormons were so distinct that they belong to a "new race":

> ... an expression compounded of sensuality, cunning, suspicion, and a smirking self-conceit. The yellow, sunken, cadaverous visage; the greenish-colored eyes; the thick, protuberant lips; the low forehead; the light, yellowish hair, and the lank, angular person, constitute an appearance so characteristic of the new race, the production of polygamy, as to distinguish them at a glance.[82]

Here, the surgeon general defines race as biology—where a group shares a common ancestry with real or imagined genetic traits that are easily distinguishable on observation. The Surgeon General points to this, when he observes that Mormons, because of their distinct physical characteristics, could be "distinguished at a glance." In addition to scientific writing, popular culture painted a picture of Mormons as a new race. In literary description, however, the physical attributes were more often borrowed from images of Eastern peoples—lazy, languid, a range of skin tones from fair to dark, black hair, curling mustaches, etc.—in other words, a Western Turk. On stage, Mormons were rarely put into costume or makeup that suggested this hybrid race. But the frequently invoked rhetorical connections between Mormons and Turks literally colored the gaze of audiences with the Oriental style with which they were familiar.

An introductory photo to *Boadicea; The Mormon Wife*, illustrates Mormons in this Eastern style. Here, Herbert and Boadicea are seen making love beneath a crescent moon. This sign of Islam in the sky sets the tone for the scene, which is framed in a pointed arch, reminiscent of Eastern architecture. Both lovers are dressed, not in the fashions of the time (1850s) but are instead wearing clothing suggestive of harem garb: Herbert wears a tunic and close fitting leggings and is shod with pointed-toed Turkish slippers, while Boadicea wears a loose turban on her head over a loose gown, draped with a shawl around her waist. While their names suggest the most European of traditions (Boadicea was a British Warrior queen), their appearance in this illustration leaves no doubt as to their exotic foreignness.

Appropriating Ethnicity 143

Fig. 4.3 The courtship of Herbert and Boadicea from Alfreda Eva Bell's exposé *Boadicea; The Mormon Wife. Life Scenes in Utah*. This illustration appears opposite the table of contents and lends authority to the overall tale. Courtesy of the Photographic Archives, Harold B. Lee Library, BYU, Provo, UT.

The formation and performance of American identity depends absolutely on groups who are denied entrance into the community. In the nineteenth century, these Others were rejected from national acceptance on the basis of racial distinction, national difference, or religious deviation. Any one of these traits that placed a group outside of mainstream characteristics was cause for public concern, and was reflected in popular culture in intolerance that ranged from gentle mockery to legislated discrimination. When two or more of these dimensions overlapped, the anxieties about and the bigotry against them multiplied exponentially. Mormons were obviously a religious Other and the Church's aggressive missionary work led to an influx of immigrants from different nations. The appropriation of a new race for Mormons cemented their difference and legitimized political and social concerns about them.

While the issue of what constitutes the American identity has always (and still is) widely debated, the mid nineteenth century was witness to a particularly vocal political movement whose aims were to define authentic Americanism and bar all those not "native" to the country from legal participation. Through melodrama, race could be tried on, metaphorically or even literally as a costume. Enacting the reality of a Western Turk on stage allowed the actors to remove their markings and return to authentic "Americanness" and the audience to congratulate itself for not being a part of this community of difference. Anti-Mormon melodramas foregrounded the issue of race by focusing on the multi-national make-up of the Mormon community and by using discursive and theatrical means to invent a new race.

The Motley Crowd

When immigration to America peaked in 1854, nearly three quarters of the immigrants were from Ireland and Germany and most were unskilled laborers fleeing poverty in their homelands.[83] Rob Norris underlines this point when he shares with the audience of *Evelyn Gray* his vision of immigrants traveling West: "Ah, what a motley crowd! It seems indeed, As if all Europe opened wide her gates to send her prisoned populace abroad."[84] The phrase "prisoned populace" underscores the concerns with the quality of immigrants, while his subsequent division of immigrants into national tribes reaffirms cultural stereotypes of the day. On the docks, he sees the "sturdy German," "the Hollander serene and stolid," "The hot Italian . . . dark-eyed and swarthy," "Swedes from Odin's mystic Northland cold," "green Erin's denizens," and the "Roman and Gaul, Teuton and Scandinave [sic], Celt and Slav."[85]

The commentary about immigrants, particularly Mormon immigrants, embedded in anti-Mormon melodrama evidences the same three nativist threads articulated by John Higham: a fear of religious authority usurping national law, a fear of radical revolutionaries, and a sense of Anglo-Saxon racial superiority. The intersection of these three notions played right into the hands of nativists who were convinced that Mormon immigrants were a direct threat to the nation. Imagining the Mormon Turk helped to unify and identify a dangerous community that was made up of a range of nationalities. Between 1846 and 1887, over 85,000 converts emigrated from Europe to Utah. They were drawn predominantly from Great Britan and Scandinavia, with smaller numbers from France, Italy, and Germany.[86] The construction of Mormons as melodramatic villains wrestled with these issues of immigration and what they suggested about a Mormon race.

In her examination of anti-Catholicism in nineteenth-century fiction, Susan M. Griffin points out the Catholic villain served a rhetorical function nearly identical to that of the Mormon villain—that writers evoked the dangers of Catholicism in order to promote a Protestant national identity. It is difficult to reduce this function to a binary of us/them, American/Catholic, however, because of the multiplicity of Catholic evils that emerged in literature. Griffin explains:

> The Catholic hegemony that Protestant polemic insistently "discovers" is belied by the very multiplicity of the Catholic groups and practices attacked: Jesuits, Carmelites, Irish immigrant families, Italian peasants, Spanish clergy, Archbishop Hughes, Cardinal Wiseman, Pope Pious IX. Similarly, the variety of Protestant identities in the period . . . are distinct and diverse. Yet "Roman Catholic" serves as a useful construct through which they can write the religion that each sees as constitutive of national identity.[87]

The rhetorical and decorative devices used to create an imagined Catholic community, however, were not to homogenize all Catholics into a racially marked group. Instead, other images consolidated the variety of Catholic groups—the black costumes of monks and nuns, with an emphasis on the hoods and cowls that covered heads and masked faces, the predominant use of crosses as decoration, architectural detail, or jewelry, opulent settings that featured the riches of Rome, or the white clerical collar of priests that set them apart, regardless of racial designation (Italian Jesuit or Spanish Inquisitor).

Mormons, on the other hand, had no religious symbols that could be manipulated to identify them. They worshiped in homes or unremarkable churches, they avoided the use of crosses or other religious iconography, and Church leaders were all lay people who dressed in fashions of the day. As the Church added to its ranks members from a variety of nations, discovering a unified Mormon image became even more difficult. The fact that such disparate peoples from so many nations were willing to come together under a single creed pointed to the frightening power of the Church and its ability to bend its membership to its will. In *Evelyn Gray,* Brigham Young suggests that he has manipulated the doctrine of the Church specifically to bring a larger international membership under his control.

> BRIGHAM YOUNG. If we fix it so that people will believe it then it will be the truth. That's my maxim. And they do believe in it. Just see how they are coming from England, Denmark, Germany, Sweden, Ireland and Hungary.
> HEBER C. KIMBALL: Considering that it is an American invention, there are few Americans patronizing it.
> YOUNG. They will come, Brother Heber, they will come, never fear.
> KIMBALL. I'm afraid they're too dogged fond of their religion and their republic.[88]

Kimball's response once again makes the division between Mormons and Americans clear—Americans won't join the Church because they love true religion and the United States. Foreign interests are necessary to the Church to bolster their power and subsequent threat to America.

The multi-cultural nature of the Church is seen in plays where the harems of polygamous wives have representations from a variety of cultures. In *The Mormons,* Councilman Noggs has married thirteen different women, many of whom come from across Europe. Bridgit Noggs, "No. 3," for example, is designated in the cast of characters as "from Ireland" and Trudchen Noggs, "No. 4," is "from Yarmany [sic]." The accents of the other wives suggest nationalities from England (Betsey Noggs, No. 8) to the American Deep South (Hepsey Melinda Noggs, No. 2).

These nationalities are marked on stage by both accent and racial stereotypes. For example, one of the wives suggests to Bridgit: "I'm as good looking as you are, any day—you Irish trollop! I don't see what Nogg's eyes were about when he married you, anyhow. You must have set fire to his heart with your hair."[89] This observation of her physical characteristic of flaming red hair is underscored by her heavy Irish accent, written into the script phonetically: "Av you mean the childer, they're packed in yon bids as snig as herrings in a cask."[90]

Trudchen, on the other hand, doesn't even speak English, but instead interjects her opinions in German, with "Yaw" for yes and "Nein" for no,[91] while English Betsey refers to Noggs as the "chap" she married.[92] These linguistic signifiers are clear markers to the audience of the range of nationalities brought not just into Mormonism, but also into the same household through polygamy. Noggs is obviously American—he is a New York Alderman who converted to Mormonism as it appealed to his prurient and fraudulent desires. While he is not the hero of the play, he is sympathetic to the audiences both as the major comic figure and as a man beleaguered by too many women who have usurped his authority.

In *Evelyn Gray,* Elder Pratt has the same difficulty with his wives causing problems with their complaints and squabbles. His ingenious solution is modeled after the lessons of the Tower of Babel. First, he divorces all his English-speaking wives, then he explains: "I went to work and picked me out new ones from all the different foreign proselytes in Utah, a Dutch wife, a Danish wife, a Welsh wife, a German wife, a French wife, a English wife, a Mexican wife, and a Indian, and had 'em all sealed to me in one day." Since the wives can't talk to each other, his house remains quiet and peaceful. Pratt congratulates himself on his idea: "It works like a charm. I'm going to keep adding new ones, just as we get converts from new countries."[93]

Unfortunately for Noggs, his wives can speak to one another and in the final act of *The Mormons*, the thirteen wives have him tarred and feathered. This rebellion of a disparate group of women from a number of nations is exactly the fear America held about Mormons generally. While there may be some infighting due to ethnic differences, in the end a common goal (for the Noggs wives—hatred of their husband; for the Mormons—obedience to a higher Church power) creates a new community of Saints loyal only to each other. The influx of immigrants insured that this community was rapidly growing and might wield real political power. In this context, the efforts to create a race to further mark Mormons as foreign are even more urgent.

Mormon Turks

On the stage, the Mormon Turk was created in three ways. First, as with the rhetorical connections between Islam and Mormonism that invented Utah as foreign place, race was created through language. Second, the acts of Mormons were carefully scripted to suggest a behavior style more in keeping with the lethargic, sensual world of the Orient than with American thrift and morality. Third, in limited examples, the Mormon Turk is actually embodied on stage through costume choices that make race clear.

Rhetorically, the connections between Mormons and Turks were both subtle and overt. As has been discussed earlier, the trope of the harem with Mormon wives as sultanas brought to audience imaginations the circulating tropes of the Oriental woman. In a similar way, Brigham Young, a major figure in many anti-Mormon melodramas is called Mahomet or the Lord of the Harem. Connections between Mormonism and Islam colored the otherwise "American" bodies on stage playing Mormons.

Writers intent on debunking the myth of Mormonism connected Mormonism and Islam in order to reveal both to be non-Christian and anti-American.[94] Parallels were drawn between the visions of Muhammad and Joseph Smith, between Muhammad's devotion to his first wife Khadija and the relationship between Smith and his wife Emma, and between the *haijrah* of Muhammad's flight from Mecca and the Mormon's migration to Utah (called the Mormon hegira by some early sources). Doctrinally, comparisons were drawn between visionary prophets, scriptures (Qur'an and the Book of Mormon), and polygamy. In anti-Mormon melodramas, there was an emphasis on how both religions picture the world they live in and the paradise to come.

The suggestion that Mormons were Turks was reinforced by the popular belief that Mormons themselves drew parallels between Islam and their own religion. In his work on American Islamicism, Timothy Marr suggests that anti-Mormon and anti-Islamic sentiment benefited from historical evidence that Joseph Smith and Brigham Young both might have likened themselves to Muhammad. He quotes the testimony of a number of excommunicated Mormons who claimed to have heard Joseph Smith, for example, say that "he would be a second Mohammed to this generation . . . that like Mohammed, whose motto in treating for peace was 'the Alcoran or the Sword,' so would it be eventually with us, 'Joseph Smith or the Sword.'"[95]

In *Evelyn Gray*, Brigham Young plots in a similar way. He also describes how he longs for some of the reforms of Islam that he has yet been able to implement. He states that "Mohammed was a much smarter fellow than the shave-pated Pope," as he was able to play to the natural instincts of man and reward lust and sin with religious approbation.[96] Mormonism, Young argues, does the same, and has even taken a cue from Mohammad's paradise into its own doctrine. In *Deseret Deserted,* Muhammad and Brigham Young see in each other kindred souls who have each separately come to the same "first idea" of having multiple wives.

Race itself comes into question as it relates to other ethnicities. In a fascinating exchange between Baby and her mammy Ruth, in the play *Fonda*, race is constructed through the intersection of morality and color:

BABY: Ruth, are the Mormons any kin to Indians?
RUTH: Ef day ain't dey orter be fur dey's a heap sight wusser, heaps of it.
BABY: Are the Mormons like us, Ruth?
RUTH: No indeed, honey—we's white folks.
BABY: Ruth, what is a Mormon?
RUTH: Why dey's a lot of heafin Hottentots dat does nuffin but go 'round hunting up wives.[97]

As Baby, a white child, and Ruth, a self-proclaimed "black Republican," are Protestant Americans; they are both, in Ruth's estimation, white. Mormons, on the other hand, are either Indians or worse—heathen Hottentots. The parallel here suggests that white is both a skin color and a moral state and that the moral state takes precedence in an understanding of race. Ruth, though she may have black skin, is "white" because she is a good person. Mormons are not just dark-skinned like Indians, but are in fact "black" because of their moral depravity.

In addition to these discursive parallels, the behavior of Mormons reveals itself as hearkening less to American than Oriental practices. In particular, Mormon characters are drawn as indolent and lustful. In a telling scene in *Brigham Young*, Young exemplifies these qualities as he illustrates for his secretary Harry how to woo a woman:

Go on your knees; implore, rave, weep, pray; kiss her hands, her lips; ravish her lips with kisses; distract her with your woes of love until she yields, all tears, soul and body to your amorous arms. If you fail to be less than myself in this, you are unworthy to have been my pupil.[98]

While the image of a bewhiskered Brigham Young enacting this scene of extreme sensuality may have been more comic than sincere, the actions here prove the foreignness of Mormon daily life, and the unrelenting focus on physical gratification. As Alice emphasizes later in the play, Young is a "vile and sensual prophet!"—the very characteristics commonly attributed to Asians in Orientalist discourse. Brigham Young in this scene and in other melodramas would have been costumed in such a way to correspond to daguerreotypes and sketches of Young that appeared in newspapers, magazines, and exposés. His un-American behavior would have seemed all the more distasteful for his apparent normalcy.

A similar technique was used in *Zion*. The acting edition of the play details staging suggestions on the first page of the script: a list of characters, playing time, necessary props, stage directions, and costume advice. Under the heading "Costumes Modern," each of the characters is described in detail. All of the Mormon women characters are described as wearing a "plain dark dress, full skirt." The directions add that "This dress should be distinctive, a sort of Mormon uniform." Parallels to the popular discourse of Orientalism are therefore not drawn through design, but through rhetorical devices that linked Mormonism to Islam, Brigham Young to Mahomet, and polygamy to harem slavery. These comparisons allowed the audience to understand that the "Mormon uniform" they saw on stage was as foreign to American life as would be a woman wearing harem pants and a veil.

In some representations, however, notable exceptions to this prove the rule—audiences were more than willing to accept Mormon Turks not only in discursive parallels or action, but also in full costume. The best example of the Mormon Turk comes from the melodramatic burlesque *Blue Beard*.[99] Unlike anti-Mormon plays that used the names of actual Mormons (Brigham and Amelia Young, Elder Pratt, John D. Lee, Twiss), *Blue Beard* creates an entirely fictional world of a Utah seraglio lorded over by an obviously Turkish Mormon.

In the late summer of 1871, Wallack's Theatre hosted the return of Lydia Thompson and her Blondes in a burlesque entitled *Blue Beard; or, the Mormon, the Maiden, and the Little Militaire*. It was wildly successful, playing to sold-out houses for the rest of the season, and it served as the centerpiece of Lydia Thompson's national tour that followed: through Pennsylvania, to St Louis, New Orleans, and Philadelphia, where it closed on 11 May 1872. Critics loved the show as well. Reactions to burlesques such as those of Lydia Thompson's Blondes were generally torn between approbation of the highly popular format and condemnation of the "indecent" entertainment. *Blue Beard,* however, was received by general acclaims as a performance of a "higher order of merit." The script was praised as "far superior," and the company as possessing "sterling talent and ripe experience." The actresses did not "appeal to sensuality" in either "style or manner." The plot was "good of its kind, full of vile puns and much romping." Lydia Thompson was singled out for her performance as Selim, the Sous-Lieutenant of Saphis, who saves the heroine from the clutches of the evil Blue Beard.[100]

The drawings for sheet music from the *Blue Beard* feature illustrations drawn from the production. The realistic drawings of Lydia Thompson suggest a relatively accurate portrayal of scenes from the production. Central to these images is the title character, whose waist-length beard, harem pants, Turkish slippers and scimitar leave no question as to his race. The women in the harem are gathered around him, dressed in similarly Turkish style, with harem pants and long tunics. A similar collapse is made in *Deseret Deserted* when Brigham Young is invited into the paradise of Muhammad. In order to join him appropriately, Young is dressed in "a gigantic turban and cloak."[101]

The effect of this costume practice is to fix the idea of the Mormon Turk on audiences in an indelible way. Even in a burlesque or a melodramatic satire, where the costumes are exaggerated and the characterizations are ridiculous, the use of turbans on the head of Mormons was a direct line to the existing cultural understanding of the dominant culture that wears a turban. As Andrew Sofer points out: "no recognizable object arrives on stage innocent. Objects bring their own historical, cultural, and ideological baggage on stage with them."[102] In the case of Mormon Turks, the rhetorical, behavioral, and costumed connections between Mormons and Turks built upon the already circulating stereotypes of both cultures.

The invention of a foreign place and an exotic race cemented the popular distancing of Mormons from Americans and reaffirmed the primacy of white America. Analyzing melodrama as a representational practice by which identity was constructed in late nineteenth-century America reveals the way in which the rehearsal, performance, and repetition of behaviors function to disseminate cultural mores. Even if it was not performed, selecting the mechanism of theatre to write his polemic about Mormonism in America gave Stern, the author of *Evelyn Gray*, a powerful literary tool. The carefully drawn characters, the explicit stage directions, and the active form of the drama painted an unmistakable picture of normative America in the face of terrible difference. Particularly, in calling Mormons "our Western Turks," Stern suggests a culture of foreignness that is dark, violent, mysterious, and sexual.

Constructing a representation of Mormon ethnic difference served multiple purposes. It justified anxieties about Mormons already in circulation and validated intolerance against Mormons already in practice. It provided an explanation for the promotion of difference by the Mormons themselves. It provided a solution for the "Mormon problem" that had already been established in the philosophical/political rhetoric of dominance over the Orient. Most importantly, it created a vision of difference that was easily contained. Erasing the boundaries between Mormons and Turks, even portraying Mormons *as* Turks presented a vision of alterity that was exotic, foreign, and clearly un-American. At the same time, the obviously western bodies that performed Orient here reassured audiences that the differences were not so great. The importance of ethnic identity in defining Americans and others is reaffirmed by the collapse of East and West, where Mormons could be seen as not American.

The fact remained, however, that for all of the rhetorical and theatrical devices used to disseminate the image of the Mormon Turk, Mormons still looked like the mainstream population of the United States. And since Mormons actually did look like Americans, the only thing that kept them separate was the practice of polygamy and their public desire for a Mormon Kingdom. By the end of the century, however, these two threats had been neutralized. The Woodruff Manifesto (1890) repealed the commandment for polygamy and new Church policy dictated the excommunication of those who practiced it. The Manifesto was a major step towards national approbation, which came in the form of statehood in 1896. The Manifesto removed polygamy and statehood signaled the end of threats of a literal Mormon political kingdom in the West. Mormons were then free to refashion themselves in popular culture in an entirely new way—as the most American of Americans.

Conclusion
The Paradox of Identity

> There goes a true Mormon—a treacherous, licentious villain. What is to be the future of such a creed and people?
>
> —Captain Jack in *Fonda*

Examining the performance of American identity in anti-Mormon melodrama is complicated by a number of contradictions. One central paradox of identity, for example, is that the formation of what is perceived as a unified national community is dependent upon that which the community rejects. Representing Mormons as religiously, sexually, ethically, and ethnically other in late nineteenth-century America had the effect of placing them so far outside normative culture that, citizenship aside, they were not perceived as American. The *New York Times* review for *One Hundred Wives* makes this clear. The reviewer argues that the story of the melodrama "has the specific and avowed object of arousing the American people to a sense of the enormities practiced by the Latter Day [sic] Saints under the cloak of their false religion."[1]

Using anti-Mormon melodramas from 1850–1890 as primary texts, I have traced the way in which the representation of Mormons in popular culture responded to cultural anxieties in circulation during the late nineteenth century. Mormons were perceived and represented to be a group distinct from the American mainstream. The melodramatic stage was a space where these two communities (American and Mormon) could be performed, where concerns could be played out, where solutions could be put forward, and resolutions could be proposed. The juxtaposition between American and Mormon characters was not a simple binary of good/evil, honorable/corrupt, us/them, but was an intimate relationship that focused particularly on the contested sites of sexual imagination, honorable violence, and ethnicity.

In the play *The Mormons*, a number of different groups are represented. There are the Mormons (Brigham Young and several apostles, the newly converted Woodvilles, Timothy Noggs and his thirteen wives), the Danites (Skinner Hyde, Rizan Sleigh, Kneeland Whine, and their duplicitous leader Godfrey Blair), the Gentiles (Eagle Eye, Whiskey Jake, Captain Cannon of the U.S. Army), Chief Dahcoma and the Kioway Indians, and a single Irishman, (Sergeant M'Fadjin). Despite the variety of the representation, the observations of M'Fadjin make it clear what internal and external attributes make up American identity.

Conclusion 153

M'Fadjin represents himself throughout the play as a man who combines "all the rashness and impetuosity of an Amerykin, with the coolness and caution of an Irishman."[2] Eagle Eye points out to him that he is not an American, he's an Irishman. M'Fadjin responds, "Av I aint an Amerykin who is? Maybe it's the brogue that's puzzlin' you?"[3] M'Fadjin clearly articulates that it is not the outward and easily identifiable characteristics of ethnicity, but his inner characteristics that define him. He is an honorable member of the army, respectful of authority, impatient with Mormon hypocrisy, loyal to his wife, and proud of being an American. The fact that he has a heavy Irish brogue, and at times is unintelligible to his companions, doesn't alter his perception of himself as "good owld Amerykin stock."[4]

His position in the melodrama as a comic Irish stereotype, however, questions his unfailing representation of himself. Susan Bennett, in her work on theatre audiences, suggests that an audience's experience of theatre is modeled on two frames; the outer frame contains theatre as a cultural construct defined by the selection of material for production and the spectator's definitions and expectations of performance. The inner frame contains the theatrical event itself and the audience's experience of the fictional stage world. Bennett proposes that it is the intersection of the two frames that forms both the audience's cultural understanding and their experience of theatre: "Cultural assumptions affect performances, and performances rewrite cultural assumptions."[5] The cultural assumptions about Irish immigrants in nineteenth-century America suggest that M'Fadjin is not to be trusted and therefore his assessment of what it means to be American doesn't include him.

At the same time, his protection of innocents from violence, his disrespect of Mormon leaders, and his participation in the capture of the villainous Danites show him to be an honorable character. If he is comic, he is a comic hero. The complex performance of identity by M'Fadjin brings into question cultural assumptions about the Irish and by extension, other minorities. To take one example, Dahcoma in *The Mormons* is represented as both foreign, and yet morally correct by his use of violence. He functions as a loyal companion to Eagle Eye, and his warning to the army saves the Woodvilles, Mary Blandford, and Eagle Eye from death at the hands of the Danites. His methods of fidelity to Eagle Eye, however, include threatening to scalp their enemies, which keeps him from being aligned too closely with the other heroes of the piece. The meaning created in the piece for the audience is the intersection of Bennett's two frames of reception at the point where difference is ultimately created by the Mormons.

M'Fadjin enunciates this difference through his comparison between the Mormon and Gentile characters. He suggests that he and his army companion are "four daycent min . . . Amerykins, ivery mother's son of them—an we're a match for fifty haythen Turks, so we are."[6] The distinction here is both religious and cultural—Mormons are heathens and Oriental, and therefore easy to overcome through honorable violence that is justifiable for the protection of the nation. By separating himself from the Mormons in this way, M'Fadjin suggests a reading of American identity that is implicated by the fact that he, too, is an outsider. The representation of Mormonism on the melodramatic stage helped to perform American identity. The processes of representation as illustrated by the character of M'Fadjin in *The Mormons* resonate with other tactics used in anti-Mormon melodramas.

An examination of the representation of outsiders on the frontier articulates how Mormon doctrine, particularly its adoption of the sacred mission of America for its own purposes, created a particularly troublesome group. "The Mormon Problem," or "The Mormon Question," as it was sometimes called, was addressed in performance by the vilification of Mormonism, emphasizing those beliefs and practices that set it apart from Protestant Christianity. Christianity during the time of the Second Great Awakening was itself a problem—new religions were growing up over night, and churches publicly battled for new converts. Politics, culture, and even melodrama were impacted by the religious sentiment of the nation. Examining these two particular sites of Christian control—the vision of the nation, and the performance of religion—suggest anxieties of mainstream America about the location of Christianity in the formation of national identity.

I also consider the melodramatic genre as a literary form and suggest that the melodramatic mode could be used to analyze the religious culture of the period. Melodrama had a very particular performance style; this is evident in how its conventions are mocked in *Deseret Deserted*. In the Act IV climax of the play, the heroes are captured by Brigham Young and are about to be killed. In an effort to escape this fate, they try three different structural resolutions familiar to audiences of standard melodrama. First, "Looy" Sparks, *"advancing dramatically,"* fakes a surprising discovery that could free him:

SPARKS. Stop! is your name Young?
BRIG. Yes! you knew that before.
SPARKS. Brigham Young?
BRIG. Yes.
SPARKS. Are you he who seven years ago, upon a dark and gloomy night, when it rained and hailed, and lightened, and blew and snew, walked down a narrow road, bordered on either side by ruined walls, and stopping at a wayside inn, where the landlord was a man with a red nose, called for a drink? Say quickly, oh! in pity say, are you the man?
BRIG. Well, I think it's probable that I might have gone down such a road at night, and had a drink. I remember going to old Tucker's grocery.
SPARKS. Tucker's grocery? That is the spot. You are my father! [*tries to embrace him*].[7]

Young sees through the "humbug," and Sparks is disappointed that his ploy does not work although he had "seen it answer admirably on the stage."[8]

The men next try singing a song in hopes that the musical performance, another generally accepted signpost of melodrama, will distract the Mormons so that they can escape. When this also fails they resort to a duel, which allows the heroes and the villains to face off in a climactic display of violence in which the "three chief Mormons are slain."[9] This parody of melodrama establishes the dominance of criticism that has elucidated its form.

The exaggerated acting style called for by these situations, and the requisite poetic justice that concludes the battle resonates with the message of the Second Great Awakening. The Christian sentiment that dominated the performance of worship established a simple world-view in which the righteous life of a true believer guaranteed a heavenly reward, just as sin promised a dark punishment. The dissemination of this Christian melodramatic mode prompted the establishment of institutions to govern religious practice and inspired an explosion of new religions that reconsidered Protestant traditions.

Mormonism was one of these, but it was not alone. The 1844 edition of the *History of All Christian Sects* lists, alongside the more orthodox religions of Episcopalians, Presbyterians, and Universalists, a number of more radical denominations: "Dunkers, Sabbatarians, Hicksites, Shakers, Sandemanians, Swedenborgians, Campbellites, Bereans, come-Outers, Millenarians, Millerites, Wilkinsonians, and Mormonites."[10] The representation of Mormonism in melodrama clarifies a growing concern with the alternate ways of believing and the impact those beliefs had on the moral center of the nation.

The resulting conclusion was the rejection of heterodoxy in favor of the more established and easily discernable Protestant religion as a marker of American identity. "Americans" were Baptists, Methodists, Presbyterians, and possibly Congregationalists. They worshiped God on Sundays, and practiced a careful balance between following ecclesiastical leadership and seeking personal witnesses to guide daily life. Americans believed Charles G. Finney when he admonished them:

> Believer in Christ, the Lord hath set you apart for himself, separated you from the rest of the world; but you are only set apart as "holiness to the Lord": this must be written plainly upon you; and if the Lord has written his name upon you, you are safe, not else. And let me say to every one in this house, Don't you expect to be forgiven, don't you expect to be pardoned, unless you will consent to be separated from your sins, and have the name of the Lord Jesus Christ written upon your hearts.[11]

The salvation of humankind was guaranteed only to those Christians who had accepted a Protestant Christ, and as such, Americans, were set apart from the rest of the world by their sacred place in God's plan.

Encounters between Christian America and groups like Mormons that trespassed on her vision and mission created an anxiety that was articulated in popular fiction, public forums, and on stage. Mormons especially were resistant to efforts to geographically contain them or religiously explain them, and their extreme vilification in melodramas points to the contested site of national Christian identity. One of the ways in which representations of Mormons played out these concerns was in the sexual politics of the period.

Popular culture of the nineteenth century was inundated with representations that clearly delineated appropriate gendered behavior and more importantly, established the family as the primary unit of American society. Enacting these gendered behaviors in a context that included a comparison to Mormons reveals that how the family was organized impacted an aspect of American identity. The late nineteenth century saw a number of movements that questioned the absolute structure of a patriarchal family. Women's involvement in reform movements—suffrage, abolition, and temperance to name a few—problematized the notion of the True Woman. The establishment of religious and social orders that tested the boundaries of sexual propriety through the practices of polygamy, free love, or complex marriage provided alternate models for the family.

The representations of gender on the melodramatic stage, especially in plays featuring Mormons, were complex. Women could be portrayed as powerful, educated, victimized, or sexually promiscuous, and their interactions with men explored the possibilities and consequences of certain gendered behaviors. The character of Marian in *Deseret Deserted* moves between these various gender possibilities and suggests how the identity of American women was constructed and reified through melodramatic performance. Marian is a convert to Mormonism who "caught a fit of the revival," and after quarreling with her lover Looy Sparks, moves to Salt Lake City. She realizes her mistake when faced with a forced marriage to a Mormon elder, and so plans an escape from Utah. Her victimization is suggested, but never enacted. Instead, she transforms into the leader of a petticoat army of other victimized women, taking on masculine tools (a policeman's whistle and baton) and attributes (organizing a military campaign and fighting to save the male heroes at the end of the play).

Under her leadership the women establish "The Republic of Woman" in the "Valley of the Silver Torrent."[12] This spectacular finale concludes the play, and intimates the possibility of alternate gendered behavior for both men and women. However, the performance of deviance is compromised by what Judith Butler calls the "appearance of substance."[13] In her discussion of parody, Butler suggests that the imitation of particular gestures, movements, and styles of bodily performance has a relationship to the "original" that foregrounds how the original is itself a constructed performance.[14] Marian's adoption of masculine attributes questions the very nature of the original male identity that she copies.

However, Butler argues that "gender is a norm that can never be internalized; 'the internal' is a surface signification, and gender norms are finally phatasmatic, impossible to embody."[15] As such, Marian's performance of deviant behavior does not allow her to take on those characteristics internally. Miss Mary Gannon, the actress performing the role in 1858, was doing just that: performing. The cultural weight of normative gender practices is not, in fact, instituted at the end of the play. Instead the comic inversion of male and female characters is a point of superficial gender play that is meant to cause laughter in the audience because of the ridiculousness of its notion. Nineteenth-century gender roles are also reaffirmed in the plot, for Marian promises the women a normative reward for their valiant service in her army:

> Mormons, countrywomen, and free lovers, hear me for my cause, and leave off drinking that you may hear. You complain that this nun-like life of celibacy is irksome to you. You shall have none of it. I would not for worlds that you should waste your sweetness on the Deseret air. To all of my soldiers who are not engaged or married—I propose a gift enterprise of husbands, varying in value from one to twenty thousand dollars.[16]

The Republic of Woman is one where the women can be organized into socially acceptable relationships with the men of their choice, and Marian is reunited with her beloved Looy.

The way in which gender deviance was treated in popular culture mirrored the reaffirmation of specific gender roles and family structures. These were established at the end of anti-Mormon melodramas, but were also complicated by women of action and agency. Still, the only family model acceptable as American in these plays was a monogamous one, headed by a husband and spiritually guided by a wife whose primary responsibility was child rearing and domestic chores.

Americans were also law-abiding and peace-loving citizens. This aspect of American identity, however, was troubled by Mormon characters on the melodramatic stage. On the surface, the plays preached a message that violence is a base instinct that requires suppression; Mormon murderers served to provide the variety of ways in which violence is destructive to society. The solution enacted in the plays to stop violence, however, was the use of violence. On the stage, heroes behaved in ways that demonstrated the positive use of aggression. This characterization responded to a larger message of the necessity of honorable violence to social control. American identity is therefore not just defined by the societal abhorrence of lawlessness and desires for peace, but intimately tied to the use of violence to maintain order.

There are two distinct representations of violence in plays such as *Zion*, and their juxtaposition sets up the boundaries of criminal and honorable violence. They establish how violence can be used appropriately to maintain social control. The first is the violence used by the Mormons. As with other depictions, Mormons in this play are clearly dishonorable: they fight against the established government, oppose community-determined rules, and cause the destruction of the family unit through kidnapping and violence against women and children. The specter of the Mountain Meadows Massacre hangs heavy over this piece—the insane Mrs. Day dreams of its horrors, and the evil Gorham revels in its memory, "it was a good job, and I enjoyed it." Elder Marwood and Gorham agree that "a little rough usage" of women is another "good thing," and they kidnap and abuse women that do not willingly obey them.[17]

Even more troubling are the reasons given for Mormon violence in this play. Gorham and Marwood make it clear that events such as the Mountain Meadows Massacre, the enslavement of women, and the murder of dissenters were part of a larger plan:

> I believe in setting up an Independent Empire, and defending it; we ought to do it and cut every Gentile's throat, who comes nosing around here . . . A war between the North and South, is the only thing that will save us. We must encourage a war as much as possible, and defend our borders to the death. We must stir up the Redskins, and get them on the war path; that will take the attention of the government, until the big war comes on. If all this does not stop Gentile interferance [sic], our rifles will.[18]

The threat of treasonous Mormon violence enunciated in this and other plays points to the concerns of the nation over the growing power of Mormon theocracy. It reveals a concern about how and why violence should be used in the nation.

Heroic characters such as Eagle-Eye in *The Mormons*, Captain Jack in *Fonda*, and Sandy in *The Danites* all serve as models for the honorable use of violence. Even Tom Scott, Luny O'Flab, and Looy Sparks, the comic heroes of *Deseret Deserted* are heroes. During their imprisonment, they "show the true American grit" by violently defending themselves.[19] For the men, this grit comes in their inventive attempts to escape hanging (as described earlier in this section), and in their willingness to use violence in an appropriate way:

> SPARKS. [*To Brigham.*] You're a coward, to take advantage of a fellow in this way.
> BRIG. It's a lie.
> SPARKS. [I]f this rope was not round my neck, I'd prove it upon your body, pestiferous caitiff!
> BRIG. What, do you defy me to mortal combat?
> SPARKS. Aye, to the death![20]

It is not that Sparks, with his American grit, is pacifistic. What characterizes him as American is how he is violent as a public act of protection and defense. A similar process of differentiation comes with the women's military exercises against the Mormons. Under Marian's direction, they bear arms, rush to the defense of their men, and overthrow the Mormons who have been oppressing them.

The use of violence by women in this piece is exceptional in anti-Mormon melodrama, but it emphasizes the extraordinary separation between types of violence. Women, for whom power and physical aggression was unnatural in the nineteenth century, are still more correct in their use of it than are the Mormons. The Republic of Woman established at the end of the play reaffirms the way in which their violence is necessary to maintaining social control. By overthrowing the rule of the Mormon men, the women are able to establish a better government that, while inverted, still reiterates that honorable violence is a necessary aspect of American identity.

Finally, the phenomenon of the Mormon Turk focuses a number of concerns about race and place that were at play in the nineteenth century. The way in which the Orient was performed onstage at once embodies visual difference and challenges that difference by its obvious construction. The Oriental discourse that was in popular circulation during the period in what was read, purchased, and believed provided a framework to control encounters with the Mormon Other. Characterizing Mormons by Oriental dress, culture, and physical features points to the importance of a visual marker of difference against which Americans could identify themselves and demonstrates how race, of any kind other than Anglo-Saxon, automatically places a group beyond the borders of American identity.

In his seminal work on the origins and spread of nationalism, Benedict Anderson argues that the nation is "an imaged political community." For Anderson it is "*imagined* because the members of even the smallest nation will never know most of their fellow-members, meet them, or even hear for them, yet in the minds of each lives the image of their communion."[21] The performance of a unified American identity in society and on the melodramatic stage provided an imagined unity by creatively juxtaposing normalcy and deviance in such a way that the difference between the two was unmistakable.

The margins against which the interior is defined are unstable and as their boundaries shift, the shape of the center must change to adapt. The relationship between Mormons and Americans was not fixed; instead, popular culture was constantly experimenting with, adjusting, and defending changing borders. This fluid realignment of expectations demonstrates how both the margins and the center are dependent upon one another: the central paradox of identity. It also troubles the paradox by illustrating the absolute impossibility of fixing a stable national identity.

Identity can, however, be performed, and has been performed in various ways, times, and mediums throughout history. Focusing on the particular representation of Mormons on the melodramatic stage reveals how different representational practices—from religious to political to melodramatic—facilitated the construction of an American identity. The way in which the Mormon community was constructed in these plays suggests the importance of the representation of transgression. Mormons were an important Other against whose image a vision of American identity was formed and disseminated. Exploring how the culture and society of nineteenth-century America was represented, contested, and inverted in society and on the melodramatic stage reveals the impact of performance as a creator of identity. Specifically analyzing the portrayal of Mormons as rapists, murderers, and Turks in late nineteenth-century melodrama illustrates how the contested sites of religion, sexuality, violence, and race helped to perform a unified American identity.

Notes

NOTES TO THE INTRODUCTION

1. As one *New York Times* review pointed out, the play was "produced elsewhere with success, and was originally brought out, we believe, in Philadelphia," (February 15, 1881). The production they refer to here played at the Arch Street Theatre, Philadelphia in October of 1880. ("The Theatres, Entertainments Last Evening with *Life Among the Mormons* and *100 Wives*," *The North American,* October 19, 1880).
2. "One Hundred Wives," *New York Times,* February 15, 1881.
3. Ibid.
4. "One Hundred Wives," *The Daily Inter-Ocean,* October 21, 1880.
5. See Emmanuel Levinas, *Totality and Infinity,* trans. Alphonso Lingis (The Hague: M.Nijhoff Publishers, 1979); Michel Foucault, *Archeology of Knowledge,* trans. A. M. Sheridan Smith (New York: Pantheon Books, 1972); Homi Bhabha, *The Location of Culture* (London: Routledge, 1994); Michel de Certeau, *Heterologies: Discourse on the Other,* trans. Brian Massumi (Minneapolis: University of Minnesota Press, 1906).
6. Michel Foucault, *The Archeology of Knowledge,* trans. A. M. Sheridan Smith (New York: Pantheon Books, 1972), 13.
7. Homi K. Bhaba, *Nation and Narration* (New York: Routledge, 1990), 4.
8. The First Great Awakening (or sometimes just the Great Awakening) was a remarkable period of religious revival in the United States and occurred in the 1730s and 1740s. The Second Great Awakening was marked by an overt evangelism and calls for spiritual and social reforms, and peaked in the early 19th century. For an introduction to these two Awakenings, see Barry Hankins, *The Second Great Awakening and the Transcendentalists* (Westport, CT: Greenwood Press, 2004).
9. Throughout this book I use the phrase "the Church" as an abbreviation for the longer name the Church of Jesus Christ of Latter-day Saints. In this application, I am referring to the Church as the organizational structure of the LDS religion rather than public perceptions of it, which I label Mormonism.
10. For example, during the time of the Civil War, anti-Mormon graphic images fell out of favor and almost entirely disappeared from national publication. After the war, national interest returned to Mormons and polygamy. Even the death of Brigham Young in 1877 did nothing to shift focus away from the topic of Mormon plural marriage. See Gary L. Bunker and Davis Bitton, *The Mormon Graphic Image, 1834–1914,* (Salt Lake City: University of Utah Press, 1983), 10, 34, 45.
11. Ibid., 10.
12. Ibid., 148.

13. Terryl L. Givens, *The Viper at the Hearth: Mormons, Myths, and the Construction of Heresy* (New York: Oxford University Press, 1997), 22–23.
14. Ibid., 23.
15. The official name of the Mormon Church is the Church of Jesus Christ of Latter-day Saints (LDS). The term Mormon comes from *The Book of Mormon*, a scripture sacred to LDS beliefs, and was initially used in the nineteenth century as an insult. Its frequent use by both non-members and members of the Church themselves, however, established "Mormon" as the recognizable name both of the Church and of its members. Recent LDS leaders have requested that the nickname be dropped, in order to emphasize Jesus Christ as the titular head of the religion. Here, however, I use the terms Mormon, Mormonism, and Mormondom throughout. For me, this is a more appropriate appellation for the time period, and its creation and use foregrounds the constructed nature of Mormon identity.
16. *Anti-Mormon Almanac, for 1842 : containing, besides the usual astronomical calculations, a variety of interesting and important facts, showing the treasonable tendency and the wicked imposture of that great delusion, advocated by a sect, lately risen up, in the United States, calling themselves Mormons, or Latter Day Saints. With quotations from their writings and from public document no. 189, published by order of Congress, February 15, 1841, showing that Mormonism authorizes the crimes of theft, robbery, high treason, and murder; together with the number of the sect, their views, character of their leaders &c., &c.* (New-York : Sold wholesale and retail at the Health Book Store, 126 Fulton Street, 1841).
17. See Richard Bushman, *Rough Stone Rolling: A Cultural Biography of Mormonism's Founder* (New York: Alfred A. Knopf, 2005), 427–429, 509–510, 532–523, 541–542 for details on the Illinois Anti-Mormon Party (1842–1844); Merle W. Wells, "The Idaho Anti-Mormon Test Oath, 1874–1892," *The Pacific Historical Review* 24:3 (August 1955): 235–252 for details on the Idaho Anti-Mormon Party; Helen Magdalene Cortez, "The Rise of the Liberal Party in Utah" (Masters Thesis, University of California, Berkeley, 1929) for details on the self-proclaimed anti-Mormon Liberal Party in Utah.
18. Bureau of the Census, *Historical Statistics of the United States, Colonial Times to 1957* (Washington D.C.: Government Printing Office, 1961), 206.
19. In his 1826 Phi Beta Kappa speech at Cambridge Massachusetts, Joseph Story heralded: "This is the age of reading." He continued that in light of the growing love and power of reading, that it was unsurprising "that reading should cease to be a mere luxury, and should be classed among the necessaries of life." William J. Gilmore, *Reading Becomes a Necessity of Life: Material and Cultural Life in Rural New England, 1780–1835* (Knoxville: University of Tennessee Press, 1989), 19–20. This source includes a detailed study of reading in early nineteenth century America.
20. "The Mormon Cowboy" is included in a number of anthologies of popular music of the period, the most comprehensive of which is: Guy William Logsdon, ed., *"The Whorehouse Bells Were Ringing" and Other Songs Cowboys Sing* (Urbana: University of Illinois Press, 1989). "The Mormon Coon" is a song from 1905, a bit after the period I am studying here, but is available both in sheet music (author Smith) and in an original phonograph sound recording.
21. "The Mormon Love Song," *Nick Nax,* July 1858.
22. Gary L. Bunker and Davis Bitton, "Illustrated Periodical Images of Mormons, 1850–1860," *Dialogue: A Journal of Mormon Thought* 10.3 (1977): 84.
23. The Mormon Battalion's 2000-mile march from Leavenworth, Kansas to San Diego is perhaps the most ironic footnote in Mormon America history.

Determined to leave the United States, whose government not only denied protection to the Saints, but who had in fact legalized violence against it, the first pioneers were heading into Mexico Territory. They had not yet reached the border when they were stopped by a general dispatch from President Polk, who asked for volunteers to fight in the Mexican-American War. The pioneers unanimously voted to support the request, and 500 men left on what is recorded as the longest foot-march in American military history. The Battalion never saw battle, but disbanded around Sutter's Mill, where several of the Mormon men discovered gold. Many stayed on to mine for gold, while others returned to their families in the Salt Lake Valley. The resulting border shifts that came with the peace treaty of the war deeded the land of the Utah Valley back into the control of the United States.
24. Deut. 14:2 (KJV).
25. Following the direct revelation that he received in these visits, Joseph Smith founded The Church of Jesus Christ of Latter-day Saints on April 6, 1830 in Fayette, New York. The beliefs of the Church of Jesus Christ of Latter-day Saints were articulated in thirteen "Articles of Faith" published by Joseph Smith. The "Articles of Faith" are included at the end of *The Doctrine and Covenants*—an LDS scriptural collection of the revelations received by Joseph Smith and other early prophets of the Church. The major points enunciated in the work are a belief in God, the Eternal Father, in His Son, Jesus Christ, and in the Holy Ghost as three separate and distinct beings; a rejection of the doctrine of original sin with the belief that that humans will be punished for their own sins, and not for Adam's transgression; a belief in continuing revelation from God to worthy members who are called and set apart for that responsibility; and a belief in both *The Bible* and *The Book of Mormon* as the word of God. The Church established an aggressive missionary program and early leaders of the Church devoted years at a time to spreading this gospel internationally.
26. Givens makes a compelling argument that Joseph Smith was not alone in his claims to prophetic visions, or new scriptures. Other heterodoxies of the time made similar pronouncements, and often times set up communities more overtly radical than LDS communities. The extreme reaction to the LDS message, according to Givens, is the hyper-ordinary style in which it was conceived and presented. Joseph Smith's message erased the boundaries between the sacred and the profane, in its conception of anthropomorphized angels and divinity, and in the practical language of its revelations. For further discussion, see "'This Great Modern Abomination': Orthodoxy and Heresy in American Religion," Chapter 5 in Terryl L. Givens, *The Viper at the Hearth: Mormons, Myths, and the Construction of Heresy* (New York: Oxford University Press, 1997).
27. The way in which Mormon history has been recorded over the years has been complicated by the extreme polemic evidenced in almost all of the early histories—either pro-Mormon (written by Church members, and supported by the Church institution) or anti-Mormon (written to discredit the "official" history). Recently, however, scholarship from writers both from within and without the Church has matured and the sections of Mormon history recounted in this chapter are drawn from a number of these sources. The most comprehensive work is B. H. Roberts's *A Comprehensive History of the Church of Jesus Christ of Latter-day Saints*. In six volumes, it provides enormous detail, but is also written from a noticeably sympathetic point of view. For the best accounts of the early Mormon Church, see Arrington and Bitton, *The Mormon Experience;* Jan Shipps, *Mormonism: The Story of a New Religious Tradition;* and Klaus J. Hansen, *Mormonism and the American*

Experience. The references to historical events in the early Church I make throughout this chapter are based on primary sources and the records found in these works. I only footnote anomalous records not agreed upon by these and other sources.

28. Gov. Lilburn W. Boggs, *Executive Order* (Jefferson: 27 October, 1838), 1.
29. Roger D. Launius and John E. Hallwas, *Kingdom on the Mississippi Revisited: Nauvoo in Mormon History* (Urbana: University of Illinois Press: 1996), 75.
30. David L. Bigler, *Forgotten Kingdom: The Mormon Theocracy in the American West, 1847–1896* (Spokane, WA: The Arthur H. Clark Co., 1998), 51.
31. Leonard J. Arrington and Davis Bitton, *The Mormon Experience: A History of the Latter-day Saints*, (New York: Vintage Books, 1980), 110.
32. *Hymns of the Church of Jesus Christ of Latter-day Saints* (Salt Lake City: Church of Jesus Christ of Latter-day Saints, 1985), 30.
33. Denial of statehood was due to a number of contributing factors such as the following: the question of slavery in the Western territories and a Congress hesitant to make any new states, extreme anti-Mormon sentiment not only in popular culture but in the political arena, and the vast amount of land requested in the initial bid.
34. Nelson Winch Green, *Fifteen Years Among the Mormons: Being the Narrative of Mrs. Mary Ettie V. Smith, Late of Great Salt Lake City: Sister of One of the Mormon High Priests, She Having Been Personally Acquainted with Most of the Mormon Leaders, and Long in the Confidence of the Prophet, Brigham Young* (New York: H. Dayton, Publisher, 1860), viii.
35. Ibid., v.
36. Ibid., vi.
37. Ibid., vi.
38. Conflicts didn't magically end upon statehood, however. One of the most notable later battles was over the seating of Reed Smoot, a Mormon monogamist who had been elected to the United States Senate. Senator Smoot's appointment was in jeopardy for over three years while the Senate Committee on Privilege and Elections investigated claims that polygamy was still being practiced in the Church. When no violations were discovered, Senator Smoot was allowed to take his seat.
39. Grant Wacker, *Religion in Nineteenth Century America* (New York: Oxford University Press, 2000), 24–25.
40. George Brown Tindall, *America: A Narrative History* (New York: W. W. Norton and Co., Inc., 1997), 585.
41. Ibid., 596.
42. Richard Slotkin, *The Fatal Environment: The Myth of the Frontier in the Age of Industrialization, 1800–1890* (New York: Atheneum, 1985), 11.
43. Ibid., 19.
44. Qtd. in Curtis D. Johnson, *Redeeming America: Evangelicals and the Road to Civil War*, (Chicago: Ivan R. Dee, 1993), 116.
45. For a detailed discussion of American and Mormon visions of America, see Richard Vetterli, *Mormonism, Americanism, and Politics* (Salt Lake City: Ensign Publishing Co., 1961). Of particular interest is his chapter on "An American Religion," in which he argues that "Americanism, Constitutionalism, and Mormonism are, to them, divinely inspired, epoch-making, direct dispensations for the hand of an all-seeing God for the temporal and spiritual salvation of a world in chaos," (Ibid., 9).
46. See Joseph Smith, ed. *The Book of Mormon* (Salt Lake City: The Church of Jesus-Christ of Latter-day Saints, 1981), 2 Nephi 1:20, 1 Nephi 2:20 and 2 Nephi 1:9.

47. Ibid., 1 Nephi 13:12.
48. James E. Talmage, "The American Nation in Prophecy," *Liahona the Elders' Journal* (22 June 1937), 28–29.
49. Qtd. in Herbert Howe Bancroft, *History of Utah 1540–1886*, (San Francisco: The History Company, 1889), 261–262.
50. Franklin Walker, *San Francisco's Literary Frontier* (New York: Alfred A. Knopf, 1939), 118.
    One such performance occurred on Saturday 8 September, 1860 at Tucker's Academy. Billed as a "lecture," tickets to the reading cost $1 per couple. "Lecture." *Daily Evening Bulletin*. Sept. 4, 1860, Issue 127.
51. "*Polygamy* Given with a Fine Cast." *New York Times*, Dec 2, 1914.
52. *New York Times*, November 29, 1914.
53. "Amusement Notices," *New York Times*, 26 October, 1914.
54. The manifesto proclaimed the end of any new plural marriages, but did not dissolve existing ones. National concern about the continuation of polygamy—both from those still practicing from before 1890 and secret new marriages despite the Manifesto—is evidenced in Congressional unwillingness to seat elected officials who were known to be polygamists. This came to a head with the Reed Smoot Hearings at Congress (1903–1907). In response, a second manifesto was issued in 1904 by Mormon President Joseph F. Smith, clarifying that any who performed or entered into polygamous marriages would be subject to excommunication from the Church. For more information on the history of polygamy after the 1890 Manifesto, see Keith L. Cannon II, "After the Manifesto: Mormon Polygamy 1890–1906," *Sunstone* 37 (January-March 1983): 27–35.
55. "Burton's Theatre—*The Mormons* and *The Happy Family*," *New York Herald*, March 24, 1858 (emphasis mine).
56. For more information about *The Danites*, see Roger A. Hall, *Performing the American Frontier, 1870–1906*, (Cambridge: Cambridge University Press, 2001), 23–103; David Beasley, *McKee Rankin and the Heyday of American Theatre* (Waterloo, Ontario: Wilfrid Laurier University Press, 2002), 149–172; and Levi Damon Phillips, "Arthur McKee Rankin's Touring Production of Joaquin Miller's *The Danites*," (PhD diss., University of California, Davis, 1981).
57. *New York Herald*, March 24, 1858.
58. Andrew Sofer, *The Stage Life of Props*, (Ann Arbor: University of Michigan Press, 2003), 5.
59. Judith Milhous and Robert D. Hume, *Producible Interpretations: Eight English Plays, 1675–1707* (Carbondale: Southern Illinois University Press, 1985), 10.
60. Andrew Sofer, *The Stage Life of Props*, (Ann Arbor: University of Michigan Press, 2003), 4.
61. Here I need to thank Andrew Sofer for his clear and articulate thinking on the reanimation of the stage event. He lends strength and validity to the methodology of production analysis when he compellingly argues that "despite its limitations, the contextual reanimation of material stage objects is a legitimate exercise for scholars as well as students—and surely no less conjectural then an analysis, say, of Hamlet's unconscious life or of Lady Macbeth's past ... For by making visible what has been invisible in our readings of drama, we gain a much firmer sense of how a particular play moves in performance, as well as a tightly focused lens through which to examine the dramatic energies of a specific theatrical period," (Ibid., 6).
62. Jeffrey D. Mason, *Melodrama and the Myth of America* (Bloomington: Indiana University Press, 1993), 1.

166   Notes

63. Ibid., 188.
64. Ibid., 191.
65. Writers such as William S. Dye, author of arguably the first book-length critical study of melodrama, "A Study of Melodrama in England from 1800–1840" (1919), Arthur Hobson Quinn, *A History of the American Drama: From the Beginning to the Civil War* (1923), Montrose J. Moses, *The American Dramatist* (1917), Maurice Willson Disher, *Blood and Thunder: Mid-Victorian Melodrama and its Origins* (1949), Richard Moody, *America Takes the Stage* (1955), Frank Rahill, *The World of Melodrama* (1967), and James L. Smith, *Melodrama* (1973) all wrote evolutionary histories of nineteenth-century theatre where they conclude that theatre moved from the lesser form of melodrama to the greater form of realism.
66. Rosemarie Bank's work *Theatre Culture in America, 1825–1860* (Cambridge: Cambridge University Press, 1997) treats antebellum theatre through the lens of spatial historiography. Grounding her analysis in three sites, spaces of representation, liminal spaces, and spaces of legitimation, Bank examines theatrical, historical, and performative moments as contested events rather than historical facts (5). In a similar way, Bruce McConachie reveals the relationship between audience and theatrical articulation in order to trace the transformation of melodrama in the mid-nineteenth century. While his Marxist methodology requires a deep specificity similar to that of Bank, he organizes his findings around "the regularities of production, genre, and audience" in a chronological fashion. Bruce McConachie, *Melodramatic Formations: American Theatre and Society, 1820–1870* (Iowa City: University of Iowa Press, 1992), xii. John W. Frick's detailed work on temperance drama, *Theatre, Culture, and Temperance Reform in Nineteenth-Century America* (Cambridge: Cambridge University Press, 2003) reveals productions marginalized both in theatre and in reform studies. It is also an outstanding analysis of the production of ideology and performance on the melodramatic stage.
67. Jeffrey D. Mason, *Melodrama and the Myth of America* (Bloomington: Indiana University Press, 1993), 127.
68. Gary A. Richardson, *American Drama from the Colonial Period Through World War I: A Critical History* (New York: Twayne Publisher, 1993), 143–148.
69. Ibid., 144.
70. Ibid., 146.
71. Roger A. Hall, *Performing the American Frontier, 1870–1906* (Cambridge: Cambridge University Press, 2001), 32.
72. Ibid., 93.
73. *The Daily Inter Ocean*, December 18, 1880.

NOTES TO CHAPTER 1

1. Owen Davis, "Why I Quit Writing Melodrama," *American Magazine* 128 (September 1914): 29.
2. The perception of the marginalized status of melodrama studies remains valid. John Frick traces what he calls the "complex causality of neglect" in his introduction. He suggests that the neglect is threefold: 1. Theatre generally is largely missing from American studies, 2. Theatre studies undervalue melodrama, 3. Even theatre historians who examine melodrama don't considered temperance drama. Frick's discussion continues to contextualize the neglect in all of these fields, with particular emphasis on the continued "blind spot" in theatre history in regards to nineteenth century popular drama and melodrama in particular. John Frick, *Theatre, Culture and Temperance Reform in Nineteenth-Century America,* (Cambridge: Cambridge University Press, 2003), 2–3.

3. William S Dye, *A Study of Melodrama in England from 1800–1840* (Pennsylvania State College: Nittany Printing, 1919), 3.
4. Moses argued that melodrama is a scripted opera, with heightened language and emotions, and he uses 10.20.30 plays as his examples. Disher focused on what he calls "blood and thunder" plays, with an emphasis on how all melodrama reveals "virtue triumphant." Booth contextualized his definition of melodrama in a history that goes back to morality plays. See Montrose J. Moses, *The American Dramatist* (Boston: Little, Brown and Co., 1917); Maurice Willson Disher, *Melodrama: Plots that Thrilled* (London: Rockcliff, 1954); Michael R. Booth, *English Melodrama* (London: Herbert Jenkins, 1965).
5. Frank Rahill, *The World of Melodrama* (University Park: The Pennsylvania State University Press, 1967), xiv.
6. David Grimstead, *Melodrama Unveiled: American Theater and Culture 1800–1850* (Berkeley: University of California Press, 1987), xvii, 204–248.
7. Michael Hays and Anastasia Nikolopoulou, eds., *Melodrama: The Cultural Emergence of a Genre* (London: MacMillan, 1996), xiv.
8. Elaine Hadley, *Melodramatic Tactics: Theatricalized Dissent in the English Marketplace, 1800–1885* (Stanford: Stanford University Press, 1995), 3.
9. Bruce A. McConachie, *Melodramatic Formations: American Theatre and Society, 1820–1870* (Iowa City: University of Iowa Press, 1992), 157–257.
10. Jo-Ann Morgan, *Uncle Tom's Cabin as Visual Culture* (Columbia: University of Missouri Press, 2007), 6, 8.
11. Robert H. Abzug, *Cosmos Crumbling: American Reform and the Religious Imagination* (New York: Oxford University Press, 1994), viii.
12. Ibid., 30.
13. Ibid., 30–31.
14. Ibid., 30.
15. Religious scholar William G. McLoughlin contends, "Every historian has agreed that the years 1830–1860 constituted the greatest age of reform enthusiasm the nation has ever seen." William G. McLoughlin, "Revivalism" in *The Rise of Adventism: Religion and Society in mid-Nineteenth Century America*, ed. Edwin S. Gaustad (New York: Harper and Row Publishers, 1974), 145. While his use of the superlative may be optimistic, the period in question did see religious growth unparalleled by any other period of religious reform in America.
16. The Cane Ridge Kentucky Revival was a seminal camp meeting co-sponsored by Methodist, Baptist, and Presbyterian ministers. Between 10,000 and 25,000 people attended and the success of the meeting established it as the primary method for conversion and retention in the Appalachian mountain region and onto the frontier in Ohio and Illinois. Ellen Eslinger, *Citizens of Zion: The Social Origins of Camp Meeting Revivalism* (Knoxville: The University of Tennessee Press, 1999), 206–212.
17. The influx of immigrants grew the national population from around 5 million at the turn of the century to more than 20 million by 1850. Even accounting for the population explosion, the growth in Church membership is remarkable. Edwin S. Gaustad, "Introduction" in *The Rise of Adventism: Religion and Society in mid-Nineteenth Century America*, ed. Edwin S. Gaustad (New York: Harper and Row Publishers, 1974), xiii.
18. Sarah Meer, *Uncle Tom Mania: Slavery, Minstrelsy, and Transatlantic Culture in the 1850s* (Athens: University of Georgia Press, 2005), 105.
19. Thomas F. Gossett, *Uncle Tom's Cabin and American Culture* (Dallas: Southern Methodist University Press, 1985), 260.
20. Jeffrey D. Mason, *Melodrama and the Myth of America* (Bloomington: Indiana University Press, 1993), 90.

168   Notes

21. For a detailed discussion of this transfer, see Thomas F. Gossett, *Uncle Tom's Cabin and American Culture* (Dallas: Southern Methodist University Press, 1985), 260–282; Jeffrey D. Mason, *Melodrama and the Myth of America* (Bloomington: Indiana University Press, 1993), 88–126; and Sarah Meer, *Uncle Tom Mania: Slavery, Minstrelsy, and Transatlantic Culture in the 1850s* (Athens: University of Georgia Press, 2005), 105–129.
22. Sarah Meer, *Uncle Tom Mania: Slavery, Minstrelsy, and Transatlantic Culture in the 1850s* (Athens: University of Georgia Press, 2005), 110.
23. Harriet Beecher Stowe, *Uncle Tom's Cabin Or, Life Among the Lowly* (Boston and New York: Houghton, Mifflin, and Co., 1899), xi.
24. Daniel Gerould, ed. *American Melodrama* (Baltimore: Performing Arts Journal Publications, 1983), 14.
25. John Frick, *Theatre, Culture, and Temperance Reform in Nineteenth-Century America* (Cambridge: Cambridge University Press, 2003), 10.
26. Harriet Beecher Stowe, *Uncle Tom's Cabin Or, Life Among the Lowly* (Boston and New York: Houghton, Mifflin, and Co., 1852), 314.
27. Jeffrey D. Mason, *Melodrama and the Myth of America* (Bloomington: Indiana University Press, 1993), 125.
28. Rosemarie K. Bank, "The Second Face of the Idol: Women in Melodrama," in *Women in American Theatre*, eds. Helen Krich Chinoy and Linda Walsh Jenkins, (New York: Theatre Communications Group, 1987), 244.
29. The most notable of these were the Methodist "circuit riders." These itinerant preachers were responsible for a number of different "stations" (or single church congregations) that made up a circuit. The riders would constantly travel the circuit to minister to the faithful, and stop along the way to preach and convert others with the hope of establishing additional stations.
30. William G. McLoughlin, "Revivalism," in *The Rise of Adventism: Religion and Society in mid-Nineteenth Century America*, ed. Edwin S. Gaustad (New York: Harper and Row Publishers, 1974), 129.
31. Mark Twain, *Contributions to the Galaxy* (Gainesville: Scholars' Facsimiles & Reprints, 1961), 128.
32. For a detailed discussion of moral reform melodrama generally and museum theatres specifically, see Bruce A. McConachie, *Melodramatic Formations: American Theatre and Society, 1820–1870* (Iowa City: University of Iowa Press, 1992), 161–197. Frick discusses city melodrama in John W. Frick, "The Wicked City Motif on the American Stage Before the Civil War," *New Theatre Quarterly* 20:1, (2004): 19–27. For an analysis of how domestic melodrama reaffirmed the societal gender constructs see Hartmut Ilsemann, "Radicalism in the Melodrama of the Early Nineteenth Century," and Leon Metayer, "What the Heroine Taught, 1830–1870," in *Melodrama: The Cultural Emergence of a Genre*, eds. Michael Hays and Anastasia Nicolopoulou. (New York: St. Martin's Press, 1999). Rosemarie K. Bank argues that women in melodrama have far more agency than has been accorded them in traditional scholarship. See Rosemarie K. Bank, "The Second Face of the Idol: Women in Melodrama," *Women in American Theatre*, eds. Helen Krich Chinoy and Linda Walsh Jenkins (New York: Theatre Communications Group, 1987), 240–245. For a detailed examination of temperance drama, see John W. Frick, *Theatre, Culture and Temperance Reform in Nineteenth-Century America* (Cambridge: Cambridge University Press, 2003).
33. Rosemarie Bank, *Theatre Culture in America, 1825–1860* (Cambridge: Cambridge University Press, 1997), 110.
34. William G. McLoughlin, "Revivalism" in *The Rise of Adventism: Religion and Society in mid-Nineteenth Century America*, ed. Edwin S. Gaustad (New York: Harper and Row Publishers, 1974), 127.

35. Bayard Taylor, *The Prophet* in *The Dramatic Works of Bayard Taylor*, Marie Hansen-Taylor, notes (Boston: Houghton, Mifflin, and Co., 1880), 327.
36. Taylor suggested in some of his writings that the model for David Starr was Rev. Edward Irving, a founder of a Scottish sect called the Catholic Apostolic Church, but there are too many specific references to Mormon doctrine and events in Joseph Smith's life to ignore its influence on the play.
37. "Bayard Taylor's New Tragedy," *Boston Daily Advertiser,* September 12, 1874.
38. "Bayard Taylor's New Poem, The Prophet—A Mormon Tragedy—Review of This Last and Greatest of The Author's Works," *Daily Inter Ocean,* September 16, 1874.
39. Bayard Taylor, *The Prophet* in *The Dramatic Works of Bayard Taylor,* Marie Hansen-Taylor, notes (Boston: Houghton, Mifflin, and Co., 1880), 151.
40. Ibid., 164.
41. Ibid., 156.
42. Ibid., 164.
43. Ibid., 162.
44. There was an enormous upheaval in Christian religious alignments during the Second Great Awakening that seems to fit into two categories: splinter groups of established religions and new religious formations. Generally, new religions either professed a totally new form of Christianity, or were three or more times removed from the original organization. For the purposes of this chapter, I focus on this second category since The Church of Jesus Christ of Latter-day Saints is a new religious formation. The other groups I consider are movements that had a significant impact on American Society before they faded, or are religions which still function today: The Quakers, Shakers, Oneida Perfectionist, Millerites, Christian Scientists, Seventh Day Adventists, and Jehovah's Witnesses.
45. Joseph Smith, ed. *Doctrine and Covenants* (Salt Lake City: The Church of Jesus Christ of Latter-day Saints, 1981), JS-History, 1:25.
46. Robert H. Abzug, *Cosmos Crumbling: American Reform and the Religious Imagination* (New York: Oxford University Press, 1994), 127.
47. While the Mormon system of polygamy is clearly an example of radically reevaluated marriage, the practice was never preached as a societal *reform*. Instead it was a particular commandment meant for certain members of the Church for a certain period of time.
48. Charles E. Hambrick-Stowe, *Charles G. Finney and the Spirit of American Evangelicalism* (Grand Rapids: William B. Eerdmans Publishing Co., 1996), 190.
49. Angelina Grimké Weld, *Letters to Catherine E. Beecher, in reply to An Essay on Slavery and Abolitionism, addressed to A. E. Grimke,* in *The Public Years of Sarah and Angelina Grimke: Selected Writings 1835—1839,* ed. Larry Ceplair (New York: Columbia University Press, 1989), 196.
50. John G. Cawelti, *Adventure, Mystery, and Romance: Formula Stories as Art and Popular Culture* (Chicago: University of Chicago Press, 1976), 34.
51. Ibid., 14.
52. Bruce A. McConachie, *Melodramatic Formations: American Theatre and Society, 1820–1870,* (Iowa City: University of Iowa Press, 1992), 42, 181.
53. Joseph Smith, ed. *The Book of Mormon* (Salt Lake City: The Church of Jesus-Christ of Latter-day Saints, 1981), Moroni 10:3-4 (emphasis mine).
54. For a detailed discussion on the similarities and differences between melodrama structure and the well-made play, see Bruce McConachie, *Melodramatic Formations: American Theatre and Society, 1820–1870* (Iowa City: University of Iowa Press, 1992), 225–228.

55. Jeffrey D. Mason, *Melodrama and the Myth of America* (Bloomington: Indiana University Press, 1993), 120–121.
56. Bayard Taylor, *The Prophet* in *The Dramatic Works of Bayard Taylor,* Marie Hansen-Taylor, notes (Boston: Houghton, Mifflin, and Co., 1880), 163–164.
57. David C. Le Shana, *Quakers in California; The Effects of 19th Century Revivalism on Western Quakers* (Newberg OR: Barclay Press, 1969), 97.
58. Daniel Gerould, ed., *American Melodrama* (Baltimore: Performing Arts Journal Publications, 1983), 133.
59. Grant Wacker, *Religion in Nineteenth Century America* (New York: Oxford University Press, 2000), 101.
60. Jackson's economic policies of tariffs on foreign goods, and his push to dismantle the Bank of the United States, were perceived by the nation as strong support for individual American growth, despite the damaging economic effect of both policies. George Brown Tindall, *America: A Narrative History* (New York: W. W. Norton and Co., Inc., 1997), 474.
61. Nathan Hatch, *The Democratization of American Christianity* (New Haven: Yale University Press, 1989), 5.
62. Winthrop S. Hudson, "A Time of Religious Ferment" in *The Rise of Adventism: Religion and Society in mid-Nineteenth Century America,* ed. Edwin S. Gaustad (New York: Harper and Row Publishers, 1974), 8–9.
63. Smith records that he received a vision of God the Father and Jesus Christ: "I saw a pillar of light exactly over my head, above the brightness of the sun, which descended gradually until it fell upon me . . . When the light rested upon me I saw two Personages, whose brightness and glory defy all description, standing above me in the air. One of them spake unto me, calling me by name and said, pointing to the other—*This is My Beloved Son. Hear Him*!" Joseph Smith, ed. *Doctrine and Covenants* (Salt Lake City: The Church of Jesus Christ of Latter-day Saints, 1981), JS-History, 1:49. Smith was told that none of the churches available to him were correct and that he should not join any of them. Albanese refers to this occurrence as the "inaugural vision of a prophet" (218) and the Church of Jesus Christ of Latter-day Saints was organized on belief in Smith as a prophet ten years later, on 6 April 1830.
64. Joseph Smith, ed. *Doctrine and Covenants* (Salt Lake City: The Church of Jesus Christ of Latter-day Saints, 1981), Section 35:13–15.
65. Bruce McConachie, *Melodramatic Formations: American Theatre and Society, 1820–1870* (Iowa City: University of Iowa Press, 1992), 160.
66. Christine Leigh Heyrman, *Southern Cross: The Beginnings of the Bible Belt* (New York: Alfred A. Knopf, 1997), 5.
67. Ellen Gould Harmon White, *The Story of Prophets and Kings as Illustrated in the Captivity and Restoration of Israel* (Mountain View, CA: Pacific Press, 1943), 537.
68. Ellen Gould Harmon White, *That I May Know Him: The Morning Watch Texts with Appropriate Selections* (Washington: Review & Herald, 1964), 215.
69. Charles E. Hambrick-Stowe, *Charles G. Finney and the Spirit of American Evangelicalism* (Grand Rapids: William B. Eerdmans Publishing Co., 1996), 37–38.
70. Eliza R. Snow, *Biography and Family Record of Lorenzo Snow: One of the Twelve Apostles of the Church of Jesus Christ of Latter-day Saints, Written and Compiled by His Sister, Eliza R Snow Smith* (Salt Lake City: Deseret News Co., 1884), 11.
71. Dion Boucicault, "The Art of Acting" in *Laurel British Drama: The Nineteenth Century,* ed. Robert W. Corrigan (New York: Dell Publishing Co., 1967), 30.
72. Bayard Taylor, *The Prophet* in *The Dramatic Works of Bayard Taylor,* Marie Hansen-Taylor, notes (Boston: Houghton, Mifflin, and Co., 1880), 37–38.

NOTES TO CHAPTER 2

1. Mormon characters have appeared recently in television shows from *South Park* to *Frasier* to *House*. Jokes about Mormons remain in popular culture on these shows, in films, and with stand-up comics. The site www.ldsfilm.com keeps lists of Mormon characters in contemporary media.
2. Two different tracks for evaluating nineteenth-century sentimental fiction and its relationship to American culture were established in the work of Ann Douglas and Jane P. Tompkins in what is now referred to as the Douglas-Tompkins debate. Douglas' pioneering work reads sentimental fiction as a destructive view of womanhood wherein female authors rationalized a male-dominated discourse of Calvinist theology. See Ann Douglas, *The Feminization of American Culture* (New York: Knopf, 1977). Tompkins radically criticized this work by suggesting that sentimental fiction be viewed as a highly politicized vision of women's experience, social knowledge, and reform agendas. See Jane P. Tompkins, *Sensational Designs: The Cultural Work of American Fiction, 1790–1860* (New York: Oxford University Press, 1985). For an expanded discussion of the Douglas-Tompkins debate, see Laura Wexler, "Tender Violence: Literary Eavesdropping, Domestic Fiction, and Educational Reform" in *The Culture of Sentiment: Race, Gender, and Sentimentality in 19th Century America*, ed. Shirley Samuels (New York: Oxford University Press, 1992), 9–15. For a history of the use of "separate spheres" in nineteenth-century studies, see Linda K. Kerber, "Separate Spheres, Female World, Woman's Place: the Rhetoric of Women's History" in *No More Separate Spheres!*, eds. Cathy N. Davidson and Jessamyn Hatcher (Durham: Duke University Press, 2002), 29–65.
3. Barbara Welter, "The Cult of True Womanhood, 1820–1860," *American Quarterly* 18 (1966): 151–174. This work has been much cited and reprinted; the idea of a "cult of true womanhood" has become an embedded aspect of women's nineteenth-century history.
4. Barbara Welter, *Dimity Convictions: The American Woman in the Nineteenth Century* (Athens: Ohio University Press, 1976), 21
5. Carolyn Sorisio, *Fleshing Out America: Race, Gender, and the Politics of the Body in American Literature, 1833–1879* (Athens: University of Georgia Press, 2002), 47.
6. The play's plot is based largely on the real-life devotion of Young to his last wife Amelia, a romance that was widely published at the time. See Mrs. Catherine Van Valenburg Waite, *The Mormon Prophet and His Harem; or, An Authentic History of Brigham Young, His Numerous Wives and Children*. 5th ed. (Chicago: J. S. Goodman and Co., 1868), 191 for her exposé on Young's wives. Chapter 11 discusses all of his wives, listing Amelia as "the last love." See Eugene Traughber, "The Prophet's Courtship: President Young's Favorite Wife, Amelia, Talks," *Salt Lake Tribune*, March 11, 1894, for a celebrated interview with Amelia after Brigham's death.
7. Henry J. McKinley, *Brigham Young; or The Prophet's Last Love* (San Francisco: Excelsior Press, 1870), 4.
8. Ibid., 8.
9. Ibid., 9.
10. Ibid., 16.
11. Ibid., 4.
12. Ibid., 3, 4.
13. Ibid., 36.
14. Ibid., 37.

15. Linda K. Kerber, "Separate Spheres, Female World, Woman's Place: the Rhetoric of Women's History" in *No More Separate Spheres!*, eds. Cathy N. Davidson and Jessamyn Hatcher (Durham: Duke University Press, 2002), 37.
16. Amy Kaplan, "Manifest Domesticity" in *No More Separate Spheres!*, eds. Cathy N. Davidson and Jessamyn Hatcher Durham: Duke University Press, 2002), 184.
17. Foucault, Michel, "Of Other Spaces," trans. Jay Miskowiec, *Diacritics* 16 (1986), 25.
18. Henry J. McKinley, *Brigham Young; or The Prophet's Last Love* (San Francisco: Excelsior Press, 1870), 34.
19. Thomas Dunn English, *The Mormons, or Life at Salt Lake City* (New York: Samuel French, 1858), 33.
20. Elizabeth Reitz Mullinex, *Wearing the Breeches: Gender on the Antebellum Stage* (New York: Saint Martin's Press, 2000), 77–78.
21. Ibid., 78.
22. Joseph Smith, ed. *Doctrine and Covenants* (Salt Lake City: The Church of Jesus Christ of Latter-day Saints, 1981), 132: Introduction.
23. Emma Hale Smith, Joseph's first wife, allegedly burned the original of the revelation. While there are a number of conflicting accounts that question the validity of the tale, the only extant version of the revelation is a copy made by Joseph C. Kingsbury, at the request of Bishop Newel K. Whitney. See Richard S. Van Wagoner, *Mormon Polygamy: A History* (Salt Lake City: Signature Books, 1989), 58–61 for the various accounts. Emma Smith was a life-long opponent of polygamy and never publicly acknowledged that her husband ever took plural wives, or was unfaithful to her in any way. After Smith's death in 1844, she left the LDS Church and formed the Reorganized Church of Jesus Christ of Latter-day Saints, with her son at the head.
24. Eastern colonialists followed Reformation's ideas and generally established civil control over marriages. The Church of England was the established church in the South and allowed (in the absence of Ecclesiastic courts) both civil and religious ceremonies to be binding. With America's expansion into the West, and with the proliferation of new religions during the Great Awakenings, many marriages went back to the Catholic model of marriage as a religious ceremony rather than a civil contract.
25. Kathryn M. Daynes, *More Wives Than One: Transformation of the Mormon Marriage System, 1840–1910* (Urbana: University of Illinois Press, 2001), 59–60.
26. Homespun, "Lydia Knight's History," *The First Book of Noble Women's Stories* (Salt Lake City: Juvenile Instructor's Office, 1893), 31.
27. John Humphrey Noyes, founder of the community, "criticized monogamy and extolled the virtues of group marriage." William M. Kephart and William W. Zellner, eds. *Extraordinary Groups: An Examination of Unconventional Life-Styles* (New York: St Martin's Press, 1994), 75. Community members were therefore to consider themselves married to every member of the opposite sex in the group. While Noyes coined the term "free love," sexual relations in the complex marriage system were in actuality strictly regulated. No two members could cohabitate without the approval of a third-party community leader, and members were not allowed to form monogamous relationships.
28. Rosemary Radford Ruether, *Christianity and the Making of the Modern Family* (Boston: Beacon Press, 2000), 95. For more on alternative communities in the nineteenth century, see Flo Morse, *Yankee Communes: Another American Way* (New York: Harcourt Brace Jovanovich, 1971) and William M. Kephart and William W. Zellner, eds. *Extraordinary Groups: An Examination of Unconventional Life-Styles* (New York: St Martin's Press, 1994).
29. *Deseret News*, Extra, September 14, 1852.

30. Leonard J. Arrington and Davis Bitton, *The Mormon Experience: A History of the Latter-day Saints* (New York: Vintage Books, 1980), 199–201.
31. Horace Greeley, "Two Hours With Brigham Young," Salt Lake City, Utah, July 13, 1859.
32. Ibid.
33. Cassandra Johnson Pomeroy, "Sarah Melissa Holman," *Daughters of Utah Pioneers*, (Mesa AZ, 1930).
34. B. W. Hollenbeck, *Zion* (Clyde, OH: A.D. Ames, 1886), 15.
35. Examining the extreme records from the period has led historians over the past hundred years to take distinct sides on the issue. Any claim to objectivity from historians writing about polygamy is negated by the clearly pro- or anti-Mormon stance they invariably take. Even historians who take into account both versions of the history generally cannot avoid making judgments about the validity of the records on one side or the other. For perhaps the best resource of original research and analysis of polygamy from a socio-historical perspective, see Kathryn M. Daynes, *More Wives Than One: Transformation of the Mormon Marriage System, 1840–1910* (Urbana: University of Illinois Press, 2001).
36. B. W. Hollenbeck, *Zion* (Clyde, OH: A.D. Ames, 1886), 17.
37. Herman Isidore Stern, *Evelyn Gray, or the Victims of Our Western Turks: A Tragedy in Five Acts* (New York: John B. Alden, 1890), 189.
38. Richard F. Burton, *The City of the Saints and Across the Rocky Mountains to California*, 1861 (New York: Alfred A. Knopf, 1963), 215.
39. The so-called "Utah War" (1857–1858) between Mormon militia and the U.S. Army occurred when the Buchanan administration sent soldiers to quash a perceived Mormon uprising. Mormons, afraid that the army had been sent to massacre them, used guerilla tactics to keep the Army out of the Salt Lake Valley. While there were a few skirmishes and some destruction of property, the war never escalated to any actual battles. Once the Army realized that there was no real threat of rebellion from the Mormons, negotiations shifted the governorship of Utah Territory from Brigham Young to Alfred Cummings and the Army was allowed to peacefully enter Utah.
40. George Clinton Densmore Odell, *Annals of the Stage* (New York: Columbia University Press, 1927–49), Vol. 8, 13.
41. George Rupert MacMinn, *The Theatre of the Golden Era of California* (Caldwell, Idaho: The Caxton Printers, Ltd., 1941), 208.
42. Ibid.
43. Brigham Young, *Journal of Discourses* (Salt Lake City: Deseret Book, 1974), 266.
44. George Burnap, *The Sphere and Duties of Woman* (Baltimore, 1854), 47.
45. Barbara Welter, *Dimity Convictions: The American Woman in the Nineteenth Century* (Athens: Ohio University Press, 1976), 26.
46. Amy Kaplan, "Manifest Domesticity" in *No More Separate Spheres!* eds. Cathy N. Davidson and Jessamyn Hatcher (Durham: Duke University Press, 2002), 190–191.
47. Ibid., 191.
48. Herman Isidore Stern, *Evelyn Gray, or the Victims of Our Western Turks: A Tragedy in Five Acts* (New York: John B. Alden, 1890), 81.
49. B. W. Hollenbeck, *Zion* (Clyde, OH: A.D. Ames, 1886), 5.
50. Ibid., 10.
51. Ibid., 38.
52. Barbara Welter, *Dimity Convictions: The American Woman in the Nineteenth Century* (Athens: Ohio University Press, 1976), 38.
53. Amy Kaplan, "Manifest Domesticity" in *No More Separate Spheres!*, eds. Cathy N. Davidson and Jessamyn Hatcher (Durham: Duke University Press, 2002), 201.

54. Thomas Dunn English, *The Mormons, or Life at Salt Lake City* (New York: Samuel French, 1858), 3.
55. B. W. Hollenbeck, *Zion* (Clyde, OH: A.D. Ames, 1886), 5.
56. Ibid.
57. Ibid.
58. Ibid., 21.
59. Jeffrey Ogden Johnson, "Determining and Defining 'Wife': The Brigham Young Households," *Dialogue: A Journal of Mormon Thought* 20 (1987): 62.
60. Givens suggests that anti-Mormon literature of mesmerism and bondage established a "utopia" in which polygamy was the construction of "some indignant—but apparently envious—novelistic fantasizers." Terryl L. Givens, *The Viper at the Hearth: Mormons, Myths, and the Construction of Heresy* (New York: Oxford University Press, 1997), 144–145. In this utopian world, Givens argues, American men are (in relationship to the victims they save) "nineteenth-century knights-errant, dispensers and defenders of women's prerogatives" (150–151).
61. Herbert Sussman, *Victorian Masculinities: Manhood and Masculine Poetics in Early Victorian Literature and Art* (Cambridge: Cambridge University Press, 1995), 10.
62. Michael S. Kimmel, *Manhood in America: A Cultural History* (New York: Oxford University Press, 2006), 57–58.
63. Ibid., 65–66.
64. Henry J. McKinley, *Brigham Young; or The Prophet's Last Love* (San Francisco: Excelsior Press, 1870), 15.
65. Ibid., 16.
66. Ibid., 17 (emphasis mine).
67. Ralph Waldo Emerson, *Selected Works: Essays, Poems, and Dispatches with Introduction*, ed. John Carlos Rowe (Boston: Houghton Mifflin, 2003), 204–205.
68. Terryl L Givens, *The Viper at the Hearth: Mormons, Myths, and the Construction of Heresy* (New York: Oxford University Press, 1997), 145.
69. B. W. Hollenbeck, *Zion* (Clyde, OH: A.D. Ames, 1886), 24.
70. Ibid.
71. Ibid.
72. Ibid.
73. In her work on race, gender and the politics of the body, Sorisio demonstrates that there are clear historical ties between the advocates of human rights (anti-slavery) and advocates of women's rights. She reviews the work of Van Evrie, who observes that not only did the abolition movement aid in the birth of the American women's movement, but that both groups faced similar obstacles of scientific essentialism: "scientists considered women of all races and African Americans childlike, in a permanent stage of adolescence that would eventually be labeled 'arrested development.'" Carolyn Sorisio, *Fleshing Out America: Race, Gender, and the Politics of the Body in American Literature, 1833–1879* (Athens: University of Georgia Press, 2002), 29.
74. Lisa Z. Sigel, *Governing Pleasures: Pornography and Social Change in England, 1815–1914* (New Brunswick: Rutgers University Press, 2002), 2.
75. Rosemarie K. Bank, "The Second Face of the Idol: Women in Melodrama" in *Women in American Theatre*, eds. Helen Krich Chinoy and Linda Walsh Jenkins (New York: Theatre Communications Group, 1987), 240.
76. Ibid., 243.
77. Mrs. T. B. H. Stenhouse, *"Tell It All": The Story of a Life's Experience in Mormonism. An Autobiography . . . Including a Full Account of the Mountain Meadows Massacre, and of the Life, Confession, and Execution of Bishop John D. Lee* (Hartford, CT.: A.D. Worthington and Co., 1874).

78. The "twin relics of barbarism" and the representation of polygamist women as slaves in anti-Mormon melodramas in the larger context of national politics reveals a surprising lack of concern over the actual lives of Utah women. In the legislation that followed the Civil War, the rights of plural wives were systematically stripped. Women who did, in fact, want to leave their polygamists marriage were not allowed to testify against their husbands since their testimony was invalidated by the fact that they were in fact wives—a strange legal paradox in which a plural wife couldn't be recognized as a wife except in court, where she couldn't testify because she was married to the defendant. The milestone 1881 *Miles v. United States* decision legalized the rejection of testimony from plural wives. Miles wasn't convicted of bigamy because his plural wife's testimony was deemed invalid. This decision also legalized jury selection on the basis on religious bias—Mormons who believed that polygamy was a commandment were not allowed to serve on juries. Even more damaging was the Edmunds-Tucker Act of 1886 that, in addition to disincorporating the Church and seizing all Church property and assets over $50,000, disenfranchised women and declared that the children of all polygamous marriages were illegitimate. Women were not re-enfranchised until 1895, five years after the Church's official abandonment of polygamy, when the right to vote and hold office was written into the Utah State Constitution.
79. B. W. Hollenbeck, *Zion* (Clyde, OH: A.D. Ames, 1886), 20 (emphasis mine).
80. Gloria Steinem, "Erotica and Pornography: A Clear and Present Difference," in *Take Back the Night: Women on Pornography*, ed. Laura Lederer, (London: Bantam 1982), 23.
81. For a discussion of the definition of pornography, with citations from a variety of recent sources, see Laura Kipnis, *Bound and Gagged: Pornography and the Politics of Fantasy in America* (New York: Grove Press, 1996).
82. B. W. Hollenbeck, *Zion* (Clyde, OH: A.D. Ames, 1886), 22.
83. Thomas Dunn English, *The Mormons, or Life at Salt Lake City* (New York: Samuel French, 1858), 10.
84. Herman Isidore Stern, *Evelyn Gray, or the Victims of Our Western Turks: A Tragedy in Five Acts* (New York: John B. Alden, 1890), 130.
85. Rosemarie K. Bank, "The Second Face of the Idol: Women in Melodrama" in *Women in American Theatre*, eds. Helen Krich Chinoy and Linda Walsh Jenkins (New York: Theatre Communications Group, 1987), 242.
86. Henry J. McKinley, *Brigham Young; or The Prophet's Last Love* (San Francisco: Excelsior Press, 1870), 12.
87. Marcus Wood, *Slavery, Empathy, and Pornography* (Oxford: Oxford University Press, 2002), 133.
88. B. W. Hollenbeck, *Zion* (Clyde, OH: A.D. Ames, 1886), 11.
89. Ibid., 25.
90. Henry J. McKinley, *Brigham Young; or The Prophet's Last Love* (San Francisco: Excelsior Press, 1870), 27.
91. Ibid., 32.
92. Ibid., 34.
93. Ibid., 35.
94. Ibid., 21.
95. B. W. Hollenbeck, *Zion* (Clyde, OH: A.D. Ames, 1886), 35.
96. Herman Isidore Stern, *Evelyn Gray, or the Victims of Our Western Turks: A Tragedy in Five Acts* (New York: John B. Alden, 1890), 129–130.
97. Judith Rasmussen Dushku, "Feminists" in *Mormon Sisters: Women in the Early Church,"* ed. Claudia L. Bushman (Logan: Utah State University, 1997), 177–185.
98. Horace Greeley, "Two Hours With Brigham Young," Salt Lake City, Utah, July 13, 1859.

99. George Givens specifically explores the hostility towards the Church in Illinois from this perspective. For his complete argument, see George W. Givens, *In Old Nauvoo: Everyday Life in the City of Joseph* (Salt Lake City: Deseret Book, 1990).
100. Brigham Young, "Discourses," *Deseret News*, July 28, 1864, 294.
101. Mark Twain, *Roughing It* (New York: The American Publishing Co., 1872), 117–118.
102. Herman Isidore Stern, *Evelyn Gray, or the Victims of Our Western Turks: A Tragedy in Five Acts* (New York: John B. Alden, 1890), 27.
103. Eric A. Eliason, "Mark Twain, Polygamy and the Origin of an American Motif," *Mark Twain Journal* 38 (2002): 5.
104. Richard F. Burton, *The City of the Saints and Across the Rocky Mountains to California*, 1861 (New York: Alfred A. Knopf, 1963), 251–252.
105. Eric A. Eliason, "Mark Twain, Polygamy and the Origin of an American Motif," *Mark Twain Journal* 38 (2002): 6.
106. Thomas Dunn English, *The Mormons, or Life at Salt Lake City* (New York: Samuel French, 1858), 23.
107. Ibid., 25.
108. Henry J. McKinley, *Brigham Young; or The Prophet's Last Love* (San Francisco: Excelsior Press, 1870), 30.
109. Ibid., 2.
110. Thomas Dunn English, *The Mormons, or Life at Salt Lake City* (New York: Samuel French, 1858), 25.
111. B. W. Hollenbeck, *Zion* (Clyde, OH: A.D. Ames, 1886), 9.
112. Thomas Dunn English, *The Mormons, or Life at Salt Lake City* (New York: Samuel French, 1858), 6.
113. Henry J. McKinley, *Brigham Young; or The Prophet's Last Love* (San Francisco: Excelsior Press, 1870), 13.
114. Rev. Daniel Wise, *Bridal Greetings: A Marriage Gift in Which the Mutual Duties of Husband and Wife are Familiarly Illustrated and Enforced* (New York: Carlton and Phillips, 1854), 113.
115. Henry J. McKinley, *Brigham Young; or The Prophet's Last Love* (San Francisco: Excelsior Press, 1870), 31.
116. Ibid.
117. Lisa Tickner, "Sexuality and/in Representation: Five British Artists" in *The Art of Art History: A Critical Anthology*, ed. Donald Prezioni (Oxford: Oxford University Press, 1988), 359.
118. Henry J. McKinley, *Brigham Young; or The Prophet's Last Love* (San Francisco: Excelsior Press, 1870), 38.
119. Ibid.
120. Ibid.

NOTES TO CHAPTER 3

1. See William Burrows, "The Mormon Samson: Porter Rockwell," *Weber: The Contemporary West*, 21.3, (Spring/Summer 2004), http://weberjournal.weber.edu/archive/archive%20D%20Vol.%2021.2-24.1/Vol.%2021.3/Burrows%20Ess.htm#76 and David L. Bigler, "The Aiken Party Murders and The Utah War, 1857–1858," *The Western Historical Quarterly* 38.4 (2007): 457–476 for details on the Aiken Massacre and Porter's participation and indictment in it. See Hubert Howe Bancroft, *The History of Utah, 1540–1886* (San Francisco: The History Company, 1889), 562–563 for details of the trial and acquittal of Sylvanus Collet, Porter's partner.

2. William C. Culberson, *Vigilantism: Political History of Private Power in America* (New York: Greenwood Press, 1990), 9.
3. John G. Cawelti, "Myths of Violence in American Popular Culture," *Critical Inquiry* 1 (1975): 524–525.
4. William C. Culberson, *Vigilantism: Political History of Private Power in America* (New York: Greenwood Press, 1990), 9.
5. Ibid., 86.
6. Walter Benjamin, "A Critique of Violence" in *Reflections, Essays, Aphorisms, Autobiographical Writings,* trans. Edmund Jephcott (New York: Harcourt Brace Jovanovich, 1978), 277.
7. Ibid., 295.
8. Ibid.
9. Ibid.
10. Herman Isidore Stern, *Evelyn Gray, or the Victims of Our Western Turks: A Tragedy in Five Acts* (New York: John B. Alden, 1890), 6–7.
11. John Morton Blum et al., *The National Experience: A History of the United States* (New York: Harcourt Brace Jovanovich, 1985), 277.
12. Roger A. Hall, *Performing the American Frontier, 1870–1906* (Cambridge: Cambridge University Press, 2001), 9. See also Gary A. Richardson, *American Drama from the Colonial Period though World War I: A Critical History* (New York: Twayne Publishers, 1993), 146–147.
13. Herman Isidore Stern, *Evelyn Gray, or the Victims of Our Western Turks: A Tragedy in Five Acts* (New York: John B. Alden, 1890), 6–7.
14. John Morton Blum et al., *The National Experience: A History of the United States* (New York: Harcourt Brace Jovanovich, 1985), 277.
15. The removal of Native Americans can also be read through the doctrines of Manifest Destiny and Popular Sovereignty—I have the right to live here, so you can't, but you should be grateful because I will establish a political system that gives everyone a voice in the processes of government. It did not seem to occur to Americans that the removal, discrimination, and extermination of Native Americans meant that they weren't able to use the freedoms brought to them by civilization.
16. Herman Isidore Stern, *Evelyn Gray, or the Victims of Our Western Turks: A Tragedy in Five Acts* (New York: John B. Alden, 1890), 235.
17. This foundational religious belief is one of the unique features that sets Mormon-Indian policies apart from negotiations between Indians and other white settlers. In other ways, Mormon interactions ranging from friendly and supportive to manipulative and hostile, mirrored other interactions between Indians and Americans.
18. Daniel H. Wells to William H. Dame, 13 August 1857, file 8, box 47, William R. Palmer Collection, Sherrat Library, Southern Utah University, Cedar City. Quoted in David L. Bigler, "The Aiken Party Murders and The Utah War, 1857–1858," *The Western Historical Quarterly* 38.4 (2007): 459.
19. Lawrence George Coates, "A History of Indian Education by the Mormons, 1830–1900" (PhD diss., Ball State University, 1969), 55–56.
20. Leonard J. Arrington and Davis Bitton, *The Mormon Experience: A History of the Latter-day Saints* (New York: Vintage Books, 1980), 146–148.
21. For a detailed analysis of Mormon-Indian relations, see Sondra Jones, "Saints or Sinners?: The Evolving Perception of Mormon-Indian Relations in Utah Historiography," *Utah Historical Quarterly* 72.1, (2004): 19–46.
22. W. Paul Reeve, *Making Space on the Western Frontier: Mormons, Miners, and Southern Paiutes* (Urbana: University of Illinois Press, 2006), 101, 106.

23. Ibid., 148.
24. Joaquin Miller, *The Danites in the Sierras* in *American Plays: Selected and Edited with Critical Introductions and Bibliographies ,1876*, ed. Allan Gates Halline (New York: American Book Co., 1935), 384.
25. Jack W. Crawford, *Fonda; or The Trapper's Dream* in *Three Plays by J. W. (Capt. Jack) Crawford: An Experiment in Myth-Making*, ed. Paul T. Nolan (London: Mouton and Co., 1966), 103.
26. Ibid., 134.
27. Herman Isidore Stern, *Evelyn Gray, or the Victims of Our Western Turks: A Tragedy in Five Acts* (New York: John B. Alden, 1890), 145.
28. Ibid., 112.
29. Memorial & Resolutions to the President of the United States, 1856–58, General Assembly, Utah Territory, 1852–59, MIC 3150, reel 3, Utah State Archives, Salt Lake City. Quoted in David L. Bigler, "The Aiken Party Murders and The Utah War, 1857–1858," *The Western Historical Quarterly*, 38.4 (2007): 459.
30. John M. Bernhisel to Brigham Young, 2 April 1857, folder 1, box 61 (reel 71), LDSA. Quoted in David L. Bigler, "The Aiken Party Murders and The Utah War, 1857–1858," *The Western Historical Quarterly* 38.4 (2007): 459.
31. David L. Bigler, *Forgotten Kingdom: The Mormon Theocracy in the American West, 1847–1896* (Spokane, WA: The Arthur H. Clark Co., 1998), 15. Bigler concludes that an independent political system could not function within the United States, and with statehood, the efforts towards a theocracy were abandoned. Other sources that explore politics in this period in Utah history are Bitton and Arrington's chapter "The Kingdom and the Nation" in *The Mormon Experience* (New York: Vintage Books, 1980), and Richard Vetterli, *Mormonism, Americanism, and Politics* (Salt Lake City: Ensign Publishing Co., 1961).
32. Davis Bitton and Leonard J. Arrington, *Mormons and Their Historians* (Salt Lake City: University of Utah Press, 1988), 161.
33. A study of Utah elections from 1852–1870 reports that 97.4 percent of the Mormon votes in the period supported the Mormon ticket. From 1847–1874, not one Church-endorsed candidate failed to win an election. See Ronald Collett Jack, "Utah Territorial Politics: 1847–1876" (PhD. diss., University of Utah, 1970) further discussion of the specifics of Utah governmental practices.
34. David L. Bigler, *Forgotten Kingdom: The Mormon Theocracy in the American West, 1847–1896* (Spokane, WA: The Arthur H. Clark Co., 1998), 51.
35. Herman Isidore Stern, *Evelyn Gray, or the Victims of Our Western Turks: A Tragedy in Five Acts* (New York: John B. Alden, 1890), 145–146.
36. The official stance of the Church of Jesus Christ of Latter-day Saints on the doctrine of Blood Atonement was given under the direction of Church President Wilford Woodruff in the Manifesto of the Presidency and Apostles on December 12, 1889. It states, in part, "We denounce as entirely untrue the allegation which has been made, that our church favors or believes in the killing of persons who leave the church or apostatize from its doctrines. We would view a punishment of this character for such an act with the utmost horror; it is abhorrent to us and is in direct opposition to the fundamental principles of our creed. The revelations of God to this church make death the penalty of capital crime, and require that offenders against life and property shall be delivered up and tried by the laws of the land. We declare that no bishops or other courts in this church claims or exercises civil or judicial functions, or the right to supercede, annul, or modify a judgment of any civil court. Such a course, while established to regulate Christian conduct, are purely ecclesiastical, and their punitive powers go no further than the suspension or excommunication of members from church fellowship." B.H.

Roberts, *A Comprehensive History of the Church of Jesus Christ of Latter Day Saints* (Provo: Brigham Young University Press, 1965), vol. 4, 136.
37. William Lysander Adams, "Melodrama entitled *Treason, Strategems, and Spoils* in Five Acts," *Oregonian*, 1852.
38. Herman Isidore Stern, *Evelyn Gray, or the Victims of Our Western Turks: A Tragedy in Five Acts* (New York: John B. Alden, 1890), 58.
39. "Fresh Literature: *Evelyn Gray*," *The Los Angeles Times*, October 13, 1890.
40. Thomas Dunn English, *The Mormons, or Life at Salt Lake City* (New York: Samuel French, 1858), 8–9.
41. Ibid., 41.
42. Ibid., 17.
43. Durwood Ball, *Army Regulars on the Western Frontier: 1848–1861* (Norman: University of Oklahoma Press: 2001), xiii.
44. Herman Isidore Stern, *Evelyn Gray, or the Victims of Our Western Turks: A Tragedy in Five Acts* (New York: John B. Alden, 1890), 23.
45. Jack W. Crawford, *Fonda; or The Trapper's Dream* in *Three Plays by J. W. (Capt. Jack) Crawford: An Experiment in Myth-Making*, ed. Paul T. Nolan (London: Mouton and Co., 1966), xiii.
46. Herman Isidore Stern, *Evelyn Gray, or the Victims of Our Western Turks: A Tragedy in Five Acts* (New York: John B. Alden, 1890), 59.
47. Thomas Dunn English, *The Mormons, or Life at Salt Lake City* (New York: Samuel French, 1858), 49.
48. The play originally toured under the title *California Through Death Valley*, a title copyrighted by Crawford in 1879, but for which no script exists. As with the work of Joaquin Miller, Crawford's plays were in fact written by (or at least co-authored) by a working playwright. Samuel W. Smith claimed credit for the original script of *California* that played successfully across the country from 1879–1881. This incited what one reported called "an interesting war of words" over ownership of the piece. See Will L. Visscher, "A Poet-Hermit," *The Atchison Daily Globe*, February 8, 1889. The result was Crawford's rewrite under the title *Fonda; or, The Trapper's Daughter*, which was copyrighted by John Wallace Crawford in 1888. This manuscript is now held in the Rare Book and Manuscript Collection of the Library of Congress. As *Fonda* is the title of the extant script, I will use it throughout to refer both to the original touring production of *California* for which there are extensive production archives and for the script itself.
49. Paul T. Nolan, ed., *Provincial Drama in America, 1870–1916—A Casebook of Primary Materials* (Metuchen, NJ: The Scarecrow Press, Inc., 1967), 55.
50. Jack W. Crawford, *Fonda; or The Trapper's Dream* in *Three Plays by J. W. (Capt. Jack) Crawford: An Experiment in Myth-Making*, ed. Paul T. Nolan (London: Mouton and Co., 1966), 93.
51. Ibid., 94.
52. Most notable was the "Fourth of July Oration" given by Rigdon: "We have proved the world with kindness; we have suffered their abuse without cause, with patience, and have endured without resentment, until this day, and still their persecutions and violence does not cease. But from this day and this hour, we will suffer it no more; . . . our rights shall no more be trampled on with impunity. The man or the set of men, who attempts it, does it at the expense of their lives. And that mob that comes on us to disturb us; it shall be between us and them a war of extermination, for we will follow them, till the last drop of their blood is spilled, or else they will have to exterminate us: for we will carry the seal of war to their own houses, and their own families, and one party or the other shall be utterly destroyed . . . We will never be the

aggressors, we will infringe on the rights of no people; but shall stand for our own until death." Sidney Rigdon, *Oration delivered by Mr. S. Rigdon on the 4th of July, 1838: At Far West, Caldwell County, Missouri* (Martin Mormon Pamphlet Reprint Series: Provo, UT, 1974), 12.

53. In October of 1838, between 200–250 members the Missouri militia attacked a settlement of about 35 Mormon families at Jacob Haun's mill, located on Shoal Creek in eastern Caldwell County, Missouri. The brutal attack eventually accounted for seventeen deaths and twelve serious injuries, four of which were fatal. The Haun's Mill Massacre, as it came to be known, was the culminating event in what some historians refer to as the "Mormon War"—a series of conflicts between Mormon settlers and their Missouri neighbors. The Haun's Mill Massacre is an important point in the history of the Church of Jesus Christ of Latter-day Saints as it has come to stand as the penultimate event of many other persecutions suffered by early Mormons before their exodus to Utah.

54. Although sympathetic witnesses denied the involvement of the Church's presidency in the Danite band, Avard and other witnesses convinced the court that he had only been following the orders of Joseph Smith. Avard avoided conviction, and Joseph Smith and his two counselors spent the winter in jail awaiting trials that never materialized. Joseph Smith, writing from jail, was adamant that Church leadership was unaware of the activities of the Danites and "had they known such things, they would have spurned them and their authors as they would the gates of hell." Smith reiterated that "the Presidency were ignorant as well as innocent of those things." Joseph Smith, *History of the Church*. Vol. 3. (Salt Lake City, UT: Deseret Book Co., 1980), 3:231.

55. European authors were also interested in the Mormon menace. Both Robert Louis Stevenson and Sir Arthur Conan Doyle, for example, wrote novels in which the villain was a Danite (*The Dynamiter* and *A Study in Scarlet* respectively).

56. The next year another exposé was published that revealed the secrets of the Danites by focusing on Porter Rockwell.

57. John Doyle Lee, *Mormonism Unveiled; Including the Remarkable Life and Confessions of the Late Mormon Bishop, John D. Lee; And Complete Life of Brigham Young Embracing A History of Mormonism From Its Inception Down to the Present Time, With An Exposition of the Secret History, Signs, Symbols, and Crimes of The Mormon Church. Also The True History of the Horrible Butchery Known as the Mountain Meadows Massacre*, 1877 (Albuquerque: Fierra Blanca Publications, 2001), 59.

58. These plot points are taken from the printed version of the script that was included in Joaquin Miller's collected works in 1882. The first stage version was presented by the McKee Rankin company and was written by P. A. Fitzgerald, based on the story *First Fam'lies of the Sierras* by Miller. Rankin bought the rights to Miller's story and his name, then paid Fitzgerald $25 per act ($125) total to draft the script. The staged version of *The Danites* had a number of differences to Miller's copyrighted version. The main differences are in characters rather than plot. Nancy Williams has a young brother who is supposedly killed by the Danites early in the play, but survives to contact his sister in a letter at the end of the play. 'The Widder," has a name—Huldah Brown, and "The Parson" has a much more significant role as her spurned suitor. There were also two other woman characters, Captain Tommy and Bunker Hill, who are omitted from Miller's version, but who did not figure largely in the plot. The only significant plot change is that Huldah was not

killed by the Danites in the stage version, but remains happily wedded to Sandy until the end.
59. *Spirit of the Times,* September 1, 1877.
60. "Review of *The Danites,*" *New York Mirror,* February 1, 1879.

    The reviews for the opening were generally mixed. Most critics found the plot too improbable and the play too long (the final curtain was at 11:30 pm). The most highly praised aspect of the show was its "fine spirit of poetry" that made the dialogue "lofty and eloquent" (*New York Times,* January 29, 1879). The sets were found to be more than adequate, and the acting solid, if uninventive. The popular success of the play was marked by years of play in New York City, a remount sponsored by Thomas Maguire in San Francisco, and the first completely American production tour to England. For the most detailed production history of *The Danites,* see Levi Damon Philips "Arthur McKee Rankin's Touring Production of Joaquin Miller's *The Danites*" (PhD diss.: University of California, Davis, 1981).
61. *Spirit of the Times,* August 23, 1877.
62. Roger A. Hall, *Performing the American Frontier, 1870–1906* (Cambridge: Cambridge University Press, 2001), 94.
63. "Review of *The Danites,*" *New York Mirror,* February 1, 1879.
64. Herman Isidore Stern, *Evelyn Gray, or the Victims of Our Western Turks: A Tragedy in Five Acts* (New York: John B. Alden, 1890), 86.
65. Ibid., 48.
66. It is ironic to note that both Lee and Hickman, the alleged leaders of the Danite Band (and therefore those most privy to its secrets) were never punished for their published revelations of all of the signs, oaths, and rituals of the band. Lee was executed for his part in the Mountain Meadows Massacre, but Hickman lived to see second and third publications of his memoirs.
67. Thomas Dunn English, *The Mormons, or Life at Salt Lake City* (New York: Samuel French, 1858), 28.
68. Ibid., 29.
69. Ibid., 30.
70. Joaquin Miller, *The Danites in the Sierras* in *American Plays: Selected and Edited with Critical Introductions and Bibliographies,* 1876, ed. Allan Gates Halline (New York: American Book Co., 1935), 383.

    In 1844 the months of conflict between Mormons in Nauvoo and their Illinois neighbors came to a head. A group of disaffected Mormons brought a printing press to Nauvoo, and in the one and only issue of the *Expositor,* the articles called for a repeal of the Nauvoo charter based on the "gross immoralities" and "illegal authority" of the Prophet Joseph Smith. George W. Harris, as president of the City Council saw destruction of the press as the best course of action, citing the charter law allowing the council to "remove all nuisances" in the city, and the press was destroyed. Governor Ford issued a warrant for Joseph Smith's arrest, but Joseph and his brother Hyrum met the Governor's militia on their way to Carthage to give themselves up. They were held in Carthage jail, under the guard of the Carthage Greys, a militia group that had sworn to kill President Smith. On June 27, 1844, a mob of men with blackened faces charged the jail, killing the Prophet Joseph Smith and his brother Hyrum, and wounding two other church leaders, Willard Richards and John Taylor.
71. "The Danites," *Spirit of the Times,* September 1, 1877.
72. Mark C. Carnes, *Secret Ritual and Manhood in Victorian America* (New Haven: Yale University Press, 1989), 1.
73. Ibid., 2.

74. The two other recorded Copperhead societies were the Order of American Knights and the Sons of Liberty. For a comprehensive examination of these four groups, see Frank L. Klement, *Dark Lanterns: Secret Political Societies, Conspiracies, and Treason Trials in the Civil War* (Baton Rouge: Louisiana State University Press, 1984).
75. Perhaps the best-known exception to this rule is the Ku Klux Klan, founded in 1866. In its nineteenth-century incarnation, the Klan worked to resist reconstruction. Due to its increasingly violent tactics, it came under federal notice and was disbanded by a series of "anti-Klan" laws passed in 1870. The modern Klan didn't resurface until 1915, and as such, is out of the scope of this study.
76. Jack W. Crawford, *Fonda; or The Trapper's Dream* in *Three Plays by J. W. (Capt. Jack) Crawford: An Experiment in Myth-Making,* ed. Paul T. Nolan (London: Mouton and Co., 1966), 107.
77. John G. Cawelti, "Myths of Violence in American Popular Culture," *Critical Inquiry* 1 (1975): 536.
78. Jack W. Crawford, *Fonda; or The Trapper's Dream* in *Three Plays by J. W. (Capt. Jack) Crawford: An Experiment in Myth-Making,* ed. Paul T. Nolan (London: Mouton and Co., 1966), 134.
79. Steven Mintz, "Regulating the American Family" in *Family and Society in American History,* eds. Joseph M. Hawes and Elizabeth I. Nybakken (Urbana: University of Illinois Press, 2001), 17.
80. Cathy Luchetti, *Children of the West: Family Life on the Frontier* (New York: W. W. Norton and Co., 2001), 71.
81. Most of the trouble between the Fancher party and the Mormons and Indians seems to stem from a small contingent calling themselves the "Missouri Wildcats." No complaint was made against the party until they arrived in Fillmore, Utah. In a letter to Brigham Young, George A. Smith says that the party "threatened the destruction of the town and boasted of their participation in the murders and other outrages that were inflicted upon the 'Mormons' in Missouri and Illinois," which included the murder of Joseph Smith. In Corn Creek, Smith reported that the party "poisoned the springs and the body of an ox which had died . . . ten Indians died from this poisoned meat, and a considerable number of cattle also died from the poisoning of the water." B.H. Roberts, *A Comprehensive History of the Church* (Provo: Brigham Young University Press, 1965), 142–3.
82. John Doyle Lee, *Mormonism Unveiled; Including the Remarkable Life and Confessions of the Late Mormon Bishop, John D. Lee; And Complete Life of Brigham Young Embracing A History of Mormonism From Its Inception Down to the Present Time, With An Exposition of the Secret History, Signs, Symbols, and Crimes of The Mormon Church. Also The True History of the Horrible Butchery Known as the Mountain Meadows Massacre,* 1877 (Albuquerque: Fierra Blanca Publications, 2001), 223.
83. See Ronald W. Walker, Richard E. Turley, Jr., and Glen M. Leonard, *Massacre at Mountain Meadows* (Oxford: Oxford University Press, 2008) for the most comprehensive study of the massacre. It covers the period from the organization of the Mormon Church to the massacre in 1857. It must be noted that Walker, Turley, and Leonard are active members of the LDS Church and that their research was funded in large part by the Church. Their conclusions have been read by some as just a further work of Mormon apologetics, but most reviewers agree that the meticulous research and exhaustive source work suggests that their conclusions are valid insofar as the existing records will allow them to be.
84. Juanita Brooks, *The Mountain Meadows Massacre* (Norman: University of Oklahoma Press, 1950), 63.

85. John Doyle Lee, *Mormonism Unveiled; Including the Remarkable Life and Confessions of the Late Mormon Bishop, John D. Lee; And Complete Life of Brigham Young Embracing A History of Mormonism From Its Inception Down to the Present Time, With An Exposition of the Secret History, Signs, Symbols, and Crimes of The Mormon Church. Also The True History of the Horrible Butchery Known as the Mountain Meadows Massacre*, 1877 (Albuquerque: Fierra Blanca Publications, 2001), ii.
86. Bill Hickman, Porter Rockwell, Ike Hatch, Eph. Hanks and Robert T. Burton were all actual historical figures connected to the Mountain Meadows Massacre. Bill Hickman was an early renegade of ill repute in Mormon history and guilty of various murders, said to be a "Danite Chief." Rockwell is almost legendary in Church history, serving for a time as a bodyguard to both Joseph Smith and Brigham Young. Ike Hatch is said to have been one of those murdered by Bill Hickman, a victim of Blood Atonement. Robert T. Burton was captain of the Nauvoo Legion, serving to guard mail and freight routes during the Civil War. It was under his direction that some of the Legion members took part in the Mountain Meadows Massacre. Ephraim (Eph) Hanks is often referred to in Church history as the "fearless Mormon scout;" he was headed east with the mail on the day of the Mountain Meadows Massacre, and was peripherally involved in that conflict.
87. Herman Isidore Stern, *Evelyn Gray, or the Victims of Our Western Turks: A Tragedy in Five Acts* (New York: John B. Alden, 1890), 176.
88. Ibid., 177, 181.
89. Thomas Dunn English, *The Mormons, or Life at Salt Lake City* (New York: Samuel French, 1858), 27.
90. Ibid., 37.
91. In anti-Mormon melodramas, not only do Mormons seek out women and children for violence, they are even cruel to animals. In *The Mormons*, for example, Elder Pratt's plans for a massacre start when he drives thorns into the hoofs of the settler's horses. He uncaringly points out, "The beasts will not feel them, for a while; but, in the course of a few hours' travel, they will penetrate to the quick. By noon the horses will be lame and our men on foot." Thomas Dunn English, *The Mormons, or Life at Salt Lake City* (New York: Samuel French, 1858), 11.
92. Ibid., 27.
93. Herman Isidore Stern, *Evelyn Gray, or the Victims of Our Western Turks: A Tragedy in Five Acts* (New York: John B. Alden, 1890), 179–180.
94. Ibid., 108.
95. Jack W. Crawford, *Fonda; or The Trapper's Dream* in *Three Plays by J. W. (Capt. Jack) Crawford: An Experiment in Myth-Making*, ed. Paul T. Nolan (London: Mouton and Co., 1966), 108.
96. "Western Poet-Scout Was a Picturesque Character," *Deadwood Magazine* (Sep/Oct 1998), http://www.deadwoodmagazine.com/archivedsite/Archives/CaptJack.htm.
97. Jack W. Crawford, *Fonda; or The Trapper's Dream* in *Three Plays by J. W. (Capt. Jack) Crawford: An Experiment in Myth-Making*, ed. Paul T. Nolan (London: Mouton and Co., 1966), 95.
98. "Western Poet-Scout Was a Picturesque Character," *Deadwood Magazine* (Sep/Oct 1998), http://www.deadwoodmagazine.com/archivedsite/Archives/CaptJack.htm.
99. Jack W. Crawford, *Fonda; or The Trapper's Dream* in *Three Plays by J. W. (Capt. Jack) Crawford: An Experiment in Myth-Making*, ed. Paul T. Nolan (London: Mouton and Co., 1966), 102.

100. Thomas Dunn English, *The Mormons, or Life at Salt Lake City* (New York: Samuel French, 1858), 49.

NOTES TO CHAPTER 4

1. Nineteenth-century authors were inconsistent in their spelling of the name Muhammad. It appears phonetically as Mahomet, Mohammad, Mohammed, Mohamed, Muhamed. I use the now-accepted spelling of Muhammad throughout, but quote earlier sources in their varieties of spelling.
2. Moon Club, *Deseret Deserted; or, The Last Days of Brigham Young. Being a Strictly Business Transaction in Four Acts and Several Deeds, Involving Both Prophet and Loss* (New York: Samuel French, 1858), 12.
3. Ibid., 13.
4. Ibid., 14.
5. Sometimes called The Year of Revolution, or the Spring of Nations, 1848 saw major uprising in the Italian States, France, the German States, the Hapsburg Empire, Hungary, Poland, Wallachia, and Brazil.
6. See U.S. Bureau of the Census, *Historical Statistics of the United States: Colonial Times to 1970* (New York: Basic Books, 1976).
7. "News of the Church," *Ensign*, October 2006, 74–76.
    Mormon conversion abroad had a number of effects on the Church and the perception of the Mormons in America. First, it supported the doctrinal imperative that the word of God as revealed to his prophets in the latter days be spread to the entire earth. It also served the practical purpose of increasing the Mormon population with international laborers, craftsmen, educators, and businessmen. Most important, however, was the growth of the church in membership numbers that made the Mormons a community of significant political power.
8. The cost of living in nonagricultural areas went up as much as 40% between 1853–1857. A terrible northeast winter in 1854–1855 overwhelmed charitable attempts to feed and house displaced workers, which led to a social service crisis. Between 1851 and 1853, property taxes in New York City increased 33%, and the city almshouse budget tripled between 1853 and 1856. Dale T. Knobel, *America for the Americans: The Nativist Movement in the United States* (New York: Twayne Publishers, 1996), 100–101.
9. John Higham, *Strangers in the Land: Patterns of American Nativism, 1860–1925* (New Brunswick: Rutgers University Press, 1988), 5.
10. In 1849, a secret nativist society called *The Order of the Star Spangled Banner* was formed in New York. Members of the society were called the Know-Nothings, as no one would admit to knowing anything about the order. By the mid-1850s, the Know-Nothings had grown in such numbers to form the American Party, which won six governorships and controlled legislatures in California, Connecticut, Delaware, Kentucky, Massachusetts, New Hampshire, Pennsylvania, and Rhode Island. They enacted a number of laws that penalized immigrants, including literacy tests for voting, state legislature restrictions of residency requirements, lobbies to abolish parochial schools, and campaigns to restrict public activities (such as baseball—a favorite sport of immigrants) on Sundays. Dale T. Knobel, *America for the Americans: The Nativist Movement in the United States* (New York: Twaye Publishers, 1996), 88–115.
11. See Dale T. Knobel, *America for the Americans: The Nativist Movement in the United States* (New York: Twaye Publishers, 1996); Susan M. Griffin, *Anti-Catholicism and Nineteenth-Century Fiction* (Cambridge: Cambridge

University Press, 2004); and Ali Behdad, *A Forgetful Nation: On Immigration and Cultural Identity in the United States* (Durham: Duke University Press, 2005).
12. Ali Behdad, *A Forgetful Nation: On Immigration and Cultural Identity in the United States* (Durham: Duke University Press, 2005), 122.
13. *Startling Facts for Native Americans called "Know-nothings," or a Vivid Presentation of the Dangers to American Liberty, to be Apprehended from Foreign Influence* (New York: "Published at Nassau Street," 1855), 74. Qtd. in Susan M. Griffin, *Anti-Catholicism and Nineteenth-Century Fiction* (Cambridge: Cambridge University Press, 2004), 4.
14. "The Mormon Kingdom; How It Is Pushing Its Way West Of The Rocky Mountains," *New York Times*, January 6, 1885.
15. John Higham, *Strangers in the Land: Patterns of American Nativism, 1860–1925* (New Brunswick: Rutgers University Press, 1988), 8–9.
16. Throughout this chapter, I use the terms Oriental and Eastern interchangeably. While today each has a specific geographical and theoretical connotation, in the nineteenth century these two terms were used broadly and identically. The only distinction made was between the Islamic Orient of the Ottoman Empire and North Africa (Turks) and the Asiatic Orient (Chinese). The title Turk therefore signified a wide number of countries, peoples, and practices. The representation of Turks in literature, travelogues, and theatre, however, was uniform and uniformly Islamic.
17. Alfred Henry Lewis, "The Viper on the Hearth," *Cosmopolitan*, March 1911, 439.
18. Homi Bhaba, *The Location of Culture* (London: Routledge, 1994), 85, 89.
19. Ibid., 86.
20. Ibid., 91.
21. Terryl L. Givens, *The Viper at the Hearth: Mormons, Myths, and the Construction of Heresy* (New York: Oxford University Press, 1997), 133.
22. Ali Behdad, *A Forgetful Nation: On Immigration and Cultural Identity in the United States* (Durham: Duke University Press, 2005), 115.
23. Bayard Taylor, *The Lands of the Saracen* (New York: G. P. Putnam, 1862), vi.
24. Ibid., 357.
25. Larzer Ziff, *Return Passages: Great American Travel Writing 1780–1910* (New Haven: Yale University Press, 2000), 139.
26. Thomas Jefferson first proposed this idea in 1787, and the hopeful discovery of such a route helped to fuel the explorations of Lewis and Clarke (1804–1806). Senator Thomas Hart Benton (1782–1858) was one of the greatest proponents of Manifest Destiny and imperial expansion. He lobbied for an overland railroad connecting the two coasts of America, a dream that he did not see completed. The joining of the transcontinental railroad at Promontory Summit in Utah Territory would not occur until 1869, about ten years after his death.
27. Malini Johar Schueller, *US Orientalisms: Race, Nation and Gender in Literature, 1790–1890* (Ann Arbor: University of Michigan Press, 2001), 28.
28. Ibid., 81.
29. Ibid., 32.
30. Frederick N. Bohrer, *Orientalism and Visual Culture: Imagining Mesopotamia in Nineteenth-Century Europe* (Cambridge: Cambridge University Press, 2003), 11.
31. Bayard Taylor, *The Prophet* in *The Dramatic Works of Bayard Taylor,* Marie Hansen-Taylor, notes (Boston: Houghton, Mifflin, and Co., 1880), 70–71.
32. Bayard Taylor, *The Lands of the Saracen* (New York: G. P. Putnam, 1862), 191.

33. Moon Club, *Deseret Deserted; or, The Last Days of Brigham Young. Being a Strictly Business Transaction in Four Acts and Several Deeds, Involving Both Prophet and Loss* (New York: Samuel French, 1858), 13.
34. Malini Johar Schueller, *US Orientalisms: Race, Nation and Gender in Literature, 1790–1890* (Ann Arbor: University of Michigan Press, 2001), 3.
35. Ibid., 24–25.
36. Raymond Schwab, *The Oriental Renaissance: Europe's Rediscovery of India and the East, 1680–1880,* trans. Gene Patterson-Black and Victor Reinking (New York: Columbia University Press, 1984), 9.
37. Jane Temple Peterson has documented further titles and details in her unpublished research. Jane Temple Peterson, "Deys, Beys, and Bashaws: Early American Drama's Response to a Muslim Threat," unpublished essay, presented at the Comparative Drama Conference (April 2004).
38. Richard Penn Smith was a Philadelphia playwright who wrote 20 plays, 13 of which were performed. *The Bombardment at Algiers* was based on a French play of the same title. The "indefatigable Dr. Jones" was a medical doctor with a degree from Harvard who also acted and wrote plays. He was popular and prolific; most of his 150 plays were staged during his lifetime and some played into the twentieth century. While *Bombardment* was never performed, *The Usurper* played at the National Theatre in the 1840–1841 season. It was one of at least four other plays about the Tripolitan Wars that saw performance during the decade. Richard Penn Smith, *The Bombardment of Algiers* in *America's Lost Plays* Vol. 13, eds. Ralphs H. Ware and H. W. Schoenberger (Bloomington: Indiana University Press, 1965), v-viii. Joseph Stephens Jones, *The Usuper; or, Americans in Tripoli*. In *America's Lost Plays* Vol. 14. Eds. Ralphs H. Ware and H. W. Schoenberger (Bloomington: Indiana University Press, 1965), 145–147.
39. Joseph Stephens Jones, *The Usuper; or, Americans in Tripoli* in *America's Lost Plays* Vol. 14, eds. Ralphs H. Ware and H. W. Schoenberger (Bloomington: Indiana University Press, 1965), 160.
40. Ibid.
41. Ibid., 156.
42. Elaine Hadley, "Home as Abroad: Orientalism and Occidentalism in Early English Stage Melodrama," *Texas Studies in Literature and Language* 41.4 (1999), 335.
43. John M. MacKenzie, *Orientalism: History, Theory, and the Arts* (Manchester: Manchester University Press, 1995), 176.
44. Ibid., 185, 205.
45. "Amusements: 'Sardanapalus' at Booth's," *New York Times,* August 15, 1876.
46. Ibid.
47. Ibid.
48. Herman Isidore Stern, *Evelyn Gray, or the Victims of Our Western Turks: A Tragedy in Five Acts* (New York: John B. Alden, 1890), 10.
49. "The Mormons; or Life in Salt Lake City," *New York Herald,* March 14, 1858.
50. Herman Isidore Stern, *Evelyn Gray, or the Victims of Our Western Turks: A Tragedy in Five Acts* (New York: John B. Alden, 1890), 55.
51. Max Adeler is the pen name for Charles Heber Clark, who along with satirists Samuel Clemens (Mark Twain) and Charles Farrar Browne (Artemus Ward), used a pseudonym for his satirical writings and wrote in specific about Mormons in Utah.
52. Max Adeler, *The Tragedy of Thompson Dunbar, A Tale of Salt Lake City* (Philadelphia: Stoddard, 1879), 10.

53. Ibid., 11.
54. In 1870, Salt Lake City had a population of nearly 13,000 people and Denver, the next closest Western city, had only 4,700. This had shifted by 1890 when the gold rush and the completion of railway lines exploded Denver's population to 107,000 while Salt Lake City grew more modestly to 45,000.
55. Herman Isidore Stern, *Evelyn Gray, or the Victims of Our Western Turks: A Tragedy in Five Acts* (New York: John B. Alden, 1890), 21.
56. Ibid., 27, 40.
57. Thomas Dunn English, *The Mormons, or Life at Salt Lake City* (New York: Samuel French, 1858), 1.
58. Ibid., 2.
59. Ibid., 3.
60. Ibid., 4–5.
61. Ibid., 5.
62. Jack W. Crawford, *Fonda; or The Trapper's Dream* in *Three Plays by J. W. (Capt. Jack) Crawford: An Experiment in Myth-Making*, ed. Paul T. Nolan (London: Mouton and Co., 1966), 95.
63. Ibid., 93.
64. Ibid., 95, 101, 106.
65. Moon Club, *Deseret Deserted; or, The Last Days of Brigham Young. Being a Strictly Business Transaction in Four Acts and Several Deeds, Involving Both Prophet and Loss* (New York: Samuel French, 1858), 3.
66. Benjamin G. Ferris, *Utah and the Mormons; History, Government, Doctrines, Customs, and Prospects of the Latter-day Saints from Personal Observation During a Six Month's Residence at Great Salt Lake City* (New York: Harper and Brothers, 1854), vii.
67. Ibid.
68. Ibid., 247.
69. "Drama," *Frank's Illustrated Newspaper*, April 10, 1858.
70. Henry J. McKinley, *Brigham Young; or The Prophet's Last Love* (San Francisco: Excelsior Press, 1870), 1–2.
71. Ibid., 27.
72. Herman Isidore Stern, *Evelyn Gray, or the Victims of Our Western Turks: A Tragedy in Five Acts* (New York: John B. Alden, 1890), 113–114.
73. Ibid., 122.
74. Henry J. McKinley, *Brigham Young; or The Prophet's Last Love* (San Francisco: Excelsior Press, 1870), 33.
75. Ibid., 11–12.
76. Jack W. Crawford, *Fonda; or The Trapper's Dream* in *Three Plays by J. W. (Capt. Jack) Crawford: An Experiment in Myth-Making*, ed. Paul T. Nolan (London: Mouton and Co., 1966), 99.
77. Moon Club, *Deseret Deserted; or, The Last Days of Brigham Young. Being a Strictly Business Transaction in Four Acts and Several Deeds, Involving Both Prophet and Loss* (New York: Samuel French, 1858), 17.
78. Ibid.
79. "Mme. Audouard's Lectures," *New York Times*, November 21, 1868.
80. Timothy Marr, *The Cultural Roots of American Islamicism* (Cambridge: Cambridge University Press, 2006), 218.
81. I infer this by Stern's choice in publishers. John B. Alden was the founder of the American Book Exchange that traded in used books and printed cheap books direct to customers rather than to bookstores. He had a reputation for low quality binding, but high volume sales. After expanding his business to include books of "quality *superior to our average* in the past, and, consequently, *at higher prices,*" he renamed the company the Alden Publishing

Company. "Great Success," *The Publishers' Weekly American Book Trade Journal* 40 (1891): 543.
82. Surgeon General's Office, *Statistical Report on the Sickness and Mortality in the Army of the United States, from January 1855-January 1860* (Washington D.C.: George W. Bowman, 1860), 301–302.
83. Tyler Anbinder, *Nativism and Slavery: The Northern Know Nothings and the Politics of the 1850's* (New York: Oxford University Press, 1992), 3–4, 8.
84. Herman Isidore Stern, *Evelyn Gray, or the Victims of Our Western Turks: A Tragedy in Five Acts* (New York: John B. Alden, 1890), 7.
85. Ibid., 7–8.
86. Leonard J. Arrington and Davis Bitton, *The Mormon Experience: A History of the Latter-day Saints* (New York: Vintage Books, 1980), 136.
87. Susan M. Griffin, *Anti-Catholicism and Nineteenth-Century Fiction* (Cambridge: Cambridge University Press, 2004), 9–10.
88. Herman Isidore Stern, *Evelyn Gray, or the Victims of Our Western Turks: A Tragedy in Five Acts* (New York: John B. Alden, 1890), 56.
89. Thomas Dunn English, *The Mormons, or Life at Salt Lake City* (New York: Samuel French, 1858), 25.
90. Ibid., 39.
91. Ibid., 24–25.
92. Ibid., 38.
93. Herman Isidore Stern, *Evelyn Gray, or the Victims of Our Western Turks: A Tragedy in Five Acts* (New York: John B. Alden, 1890), 130–131.
94. For analyses of the nineteenth century Mormon-Islam connection, see J. Spencer Fluhman, "An 'American Mahomet': Joseph Smith, Muhammad, and the Problem of Prophets in Antebellum America," *Journal of Mormon History* 34.3 (2008), 23–45; Timothy Marr, *The Cultural Roots of American Islamicism* (Cambridge: Cambridge University Press, 2006), 185–218; Terryl L. Givens, *The Viper on the Hearth: Mormons, Myths, and the Construction of Heresy* (New York: Oxford University Press, 1997), 130–137; Marianne Perciaccante, "The Mormon-Muslim Comparison," *Muslim World* 82.3–4 (1992): 296–314; Arnold Green, "The Muhammad-Joseph Smith Comparison: Subjective Metaphor or a Sociology of Prophethood" in *Mormons and Muslims: Spiritual Foundations and Modern Manifestations*, ed. Spencer J. Palmer (Salt Lake City: Bookcraft, 1983); Arnold Green, "Joseph Smith, an American Muhummad? An Essay on the Perils of Historical Analogy," *Dialogue: A Journal of Mormon Thought* 6.1 (Spring 1971): 46–58.
95. Timothy Marr, *The Cultural Roots of American Islamicism* (Cambridge: Cambridge University Press, 2006), 199.
96. Herman Isidore Stern, *Evelyn Gray, or the Victims of Our Western Turks: A Tragedy in Five Acts* (New York: John B. Alden, 1890), 54–55.
97. Jack W. Crawford, *Fonda; or The Trapper's Dream* in *Three Plays by J. W. (Capt. Jack) Crawford: An Experiment in Myth-Making*, ed. Paul T. Nolan, (London: Mouton and Co., 1966), 102.
98. Henry J. McKinley, *Brigham Young; or The Prophet's Last Love* (San Francisco: Excelsior Press, 1870), 12.
99. In calling this production a melodramatic burlesque, I am recognizing the intersection between these two distinct forms. Both burlesque and melodrama challenged cultural assumptions using music and spectacle—they differed in their techniques. Burlesque shows generally referred to any plays that made fun of, or "burlesqued" the social mores, artistic interests, or notable events of the upper class. The shows used comedy, music, star actors, and most importantly, sex appeal, to challenge the status quo. By the mid-century, British burlesque had begun to feature female performers' legs, a

scandalous practice that American audiences fully embraced in *The Black Crook* (1866), with its corps de ballet in flesh-colored tights. Companies such as Lydia Thompson's Blondes capitalized on the trend by marrying the form of early burlesque with the style of the leg show, with some of the structural elements of melodrama.

100. Kurt Ganzl, *Lydia Thompson, Queen of Burlesque* (New York: Routledge, 2002), 148.
101. Moon Club, *Deseret Deserted; or, The Last Days of Brigham Young. Being a Strictly Business Transaction in Four Acts and Several Deeds, Involving Both Prophet and Loss* (New York: Samuel French, 1858), 15.
102. Andrew Sofer, *The Stage Life of Props* (Ann Arbor: University of Michigan Press, 2003), 17.

NOTES TO THE CONCLUSION

1. Qtd. in "One Hundred Wives," *The Daily Inter Ocean*, October 21, 1880.
2. Thomas Dunn English, *The Mormons, or Life at Salt Lake City* (New York: Samuel French, 1858), 36.
3. Ibid., 9.
4. Ibid., 17.
5. Susan Bennett, *Theatre Audiences: A Theory of Production and Reception* (London: Routledge, 1997), 2.
6. Thomas Dunn English, *The Mormons, or Life at Salt Lake City* (New York: Samuel French, 1858), 9.
7. Moon Club, *Deseret Deserted; or, The Last Days of Brigham Young. Being a Strictly Business Transaction in Four Acts and Several Deeds, Involving Both Prophet and Loss* (New York: Samuel French, 1858), 25.
8. Ibid.
9. Ibid., 28. Luny O'Flab and Tom Scott are also killed, leaving Sparks the only survivor of the battle. They are both resurrected, however, when Sparks realized that the scene change cannot occur unless all the bodies are somehow transported offstage. The heroes have to get up and walk off. The actor playing Brigham Young, Mr. Blake, won't leave and a policeman has to be called to lure him offstage with the promise of a drink.
10. John Evans, *History of All Christian Sects and Denominations; Their Origin, Peculiar Tenets, and Present Condition*, 2nd ed. (New York: James Mowatt, 1844). Qtd. in Terryl L. Givens, *The Viper at the Hearth: Mormons, Myths, and the Construction of Heresy* (New York: Oxford University Press, 1997), 63.
11. C. G. Finney, "Holiness Essential to Salvation," Oberlin Collegiate Institute, http://www.gospeltruth.net/1849–51Penny_Pulpit/500607pp_holiness_essentia.htm.
12. Moon Club, *Deseret Deserted; or, The Last Days of Brigham Young. Being a Strictly Business Transaction in Four Acts and Several Deeds, Involving Both Prophet and Loss* (New York: Samuel French, 1858), 28.
13. Judith Butler, *Gender Trouble: Feminism and the Subversion of Identity* (New York: Routledge 1990), 141.
14. Butler is specifically analyzing drag: "As much as drag creates a unified picture of 'woman' . . . it also reveals the distinctness of those aspects of gendered experience which are falsely naturalized as a unity through the regulatory fiction of heterosexual coherence. *In imitating gender, drag implicitly reveals the imitative structure of gender itself—as well as its contingency*,"

(Ibid., 137). The performance of manly women such as Marian in melodramas, however, functions in a similar way: by putting on certain aspects of masculinity, these inherently demonstrate the way in which being a man is constructed and performed.
15. Ibid., 141.
16. Moon Club, *Deseret Deserted; or, The Last Days of Brigham Young. Being a Strictly Business Transaction in Four Acts and Several Deeds, Involving Both Prophet and Loss* (New York: Samuel French, 1858), 23.
17. B. W. Hollenbeck, *Zion* (Clyde, OH: A.D. Ames, 1886), 17.
18. Ibid., 28–29.
19. Moon Club, *Deseret Deserted; or, The Last Days of Brigham Young. Being a Strictly Business Transaction in Four Acts and Several Deeds, Involving Both Prophet and Loss* (New York: Samuel French, 1858), 21.
20. Ibid., 27.
21. Benedict Anderson, *Imagined Communities: Reflections on the Origin and Spread of Nationalism* (London: Verso, 1991), 6.

Bibliography

PLAYS AND ANTHOLOGIES

Adams, William Lysander. "Melodrama entitled *Treason, Strategems, and Spoils* in Five Acts." *Oregonian*, 1852.
Crawford, Jack W. *Fonda; or The Trapper's Dream*. In *Three Plays by J. W. (Capt. Jack) Crawford: An Experiment in Myth-Making*. Edited by Paul T. Nolan. London: Mouton and Co., 1966.
English, Thomas Dunn. *The Mormons, or Life at Salt Lake City*. New York: Samuel French, 1858.
Hollenbeck, B. W. *Zion*. Clyde, OH: A.D. Ames, 1886.
Jones, Joseph Stephens. *The Usuper; or, Americans in Tripoli*. In *America's Lost Plays* Vol. 14. Edited by Ralphs H. Ware and H. W. Schoenberger. Bloomington: Indiana University Press, 1965.
McKinley, Henry J. *Brigham Young; or The Prophet's Last Love*. San Francisco: Excelsior Press, 1870.
Miller, Joaquin. *The Danites in the Sierras*. In *American Plays: Selected and Edited with Critical Introductions and Bibliographies*. 1876. Edited by Allan Gates Halline. New York: American Book Co., 1935.
Moon Club. *Deseret Deserted; or, The Last Days of Brigham Young. Being a Strictly Business Transaction in Four Acts and Several Deeds, Involving Both Prophet and Loss*. New York: Samuel French, 1858.
Smith, Richard Penn. *The Bombardment of Algiers*. In *America's Lost Plays* Vol. 13. Edited by Ralphs H. Ware and H. W. Schoenberger. Bloomington: Indiana University Press, 1965.
Taylor, Bayard. *The Prophet*. In *The Dramatic Works of Bayard Taylor*. Marie Hansen-Taylor, notes. Boston: Houghton, Mifflin, and Co., 1880.

NEWSPAPERS AND PERIODICALS

The Atchison Daily Globe (Atchison, KS)
Boston Daily Advertiser
Daily Evening Bulletin (San Francisco, CA)
The Daily Inter Ocean (Chicago, IL)
Deseret News, (Salt Lake City, UT)
Frank Leslie's Illustrated Newspaper
New York Herald
New York Mirror
New York Times

The North American (Philadelphia, PA)
Nick Nax
Salt Lake Tribune
The Spirit of the Times (New York, NY)

BOOKS

Abzug, Robert H. *Cosmos Crumbling: American Reform and the Religious Imagination.* New York: Oxford University Press, 1994.
Adeler, Max. *The Tragedy of Thompson Dunbar, A Tale of Salt Lake City.* Philadelphia: Stoddard, 1879.
Albanese, Catherine L. *America: Religions and Religion.* Wadsworth Publishing Co.: New York, 1999.
Anbinder, Tyler. *Nativism and Slavery: The Northern Know Nothings and the Politics of the 1850's.* New York: Oxford University Press, 1992.
Anderson, Benedict. *Imagined Communities: Reflections on the Origin and Spread of Nationalism.* London: Verso, 1991.
Anti-Mormon Almanac, for 1842 : containing, besides the usual astronomical calculations, a variety of interesting and important facts, showing the treasonable tendency and the wicked imposture of that great delusion, advocated by a sect, lately risen up, in the United States, calling themselves Mormons, or Latter Day Saints. With quotations from their writings and from public document no. 189, published by order of Congress, February 15, 1841, showing that Mormonism authorizes the crimes of theft, robbery, high treason, and murder; together with the number of the sect, their views, character of their leaders &c., &c. New York: Sold wholesale and retail at the Health Book Store, 126 Fulton Street, 1841.
Aristotle. *The Poetics of Aristotle Translation and Commentary.* Translated by Stephen Halliwell. London: Duckworth, 1987.
Arrington, Leonard J. and Davis Bitton. *The Mormon Experience: A History of the Latter-day Saints.* New York: Vintage Books, 1980.
Ball, Durwood. *Army Regulars on the Western Frontier: 1848–1861.* Norman: University of Oklahoma Press, 2001.
Ballou, Maturin Murray. *The Turkish Slave; or, The Mohametan and His Harem, a Story of the East.* Boston: F. Gleason, 1850.
Bank, Rosemarie K. *Theatre Culture in America, 1825–1860.* Cambridge: Cambridge University Press, 1997.
———. "The Second Face of the Idol: Women in Meoldrama." In *Women in American Theatre.* Edited by Helen Krich Chinoy and Linda Walsh Jenkins. New York: Theatre Communications Group, 1987.
Beasley, David. *McKee Rankin and the Heyday of American Theatre.* Waterloo, ON: Wilfrid Laurier University Press, 2002.
Behdad, Ali. *A Forgetful Nation: On Immigration and Cultural Identity in the United States.* Durham: Duke University Press, 2005.
Benjamin, Walter. "A Critique of Violence." In *Reflections, Essays, Aphorisms, Autobiographical Writings.* Translated by Edmund Jephcott. New York: Harcourt Brace Jovanovich, 1978.
Bennett, Susan. *Theatre Audiences: A Theory of Production and Reception.* London: Routledge, 1997.
Bhabha, Homi K. *The Location of Culture.* London: Routledge, 1994.
———. *Nation and Narration.* New York: Routledge, 1990.
Bigler, David L. *Forgotten Kingdom: The Mormon Theocracy in the American West, 1847–1896.* Spokane, WA: The Arthur H. Clark Co., 1998.

Blum, John Morton, William S. McFeely, Edmund S. Morgan, and Arthur M. Schlesinger Jr. *The National Experience: A History of the United States.* New York: Harcourt Brace Jovanovich, 1985.
Bohrer, Frederick N. *Orientalism and Visual Culture: Imagining Mesopotamia in Nineteenth-Century Europe.* Cambridge: Cambridge University Press, 2003.
Booth, Michael R. *English Melodrama.* London: Herbert Jenkins, 1965.
Boucicault, Dion. "The Art of Acting." In *Laurel British Drama: The Nineteenth Century.* Edited by Robert W. Corrigan. New York: Dell Publishing Co., 1967.
Bratton, Jacky, Jim Cook, and Christine Gledhill, eds. *Melodrama: Stage, Picture, Screen.* London: British Film Institute, 1994.
Brooks, Juanita. *The Mountain Meadows Massacre.* Norman: University of Oklahoma Press, 1950.
Brooks, Peter. *The Melodramatic Imagination.* New Haven: Yale University Press, 1976.
Bunker, Gary L., and Carol B. Bunker. "Woman Suffrage, Popular Art, and Utah." In *Battle for the Ballot: Essays on Woman Suffrage in Utah, 1970–1896.* Edited by Carol Cornwall Madsen. Logan: Utah State University Press, 1997.
Bunker, Gary L. and Davis Bitton. *The Mormon Graphic Image, 1834–1914: Cartoons, Caricatures and Illustrations.* Salt Lake City: University of Utah Press, 1983.
Burnap, George. *The Sphere and Duties of Woman.* Baltimore, 1854.
Burton, Richard F. *The City of the Saints and Across the Rocky Mountains to California.* 1861. New York: Alfred A. Knopf, 1963.
Butler, Judith. *Excitable Speech: A Politics of the Performative.* New York: Routledge, 1997.
———. *Gender Trouble: Feminism and the Subversion of Identity.* New York: Routledge, 1990.
Bushman, Richard. *Rough Stone Rolling: A Cultural Biography of Mormonism's Founder.* New York: Alfred A. Knopf, 2005.
Carnes, Mark C. *Secret Ritual and Manhood in Victorian America.* New Haven: Yale University Press, 1989.
Cawelti, John G. *Adventure, Mystery, and Romance: Formula Stories as Art and Popular Culture.* Chicago: University of Chicago Press, 1976.
Certeau, Michel de. *Heterologies: Discourse on the Other.* Translated by Brian Massumi. Minneapolis: University of Minnesota Press, 1986.
Culberson, William C. *Vigilantism: Political History of Private Power in America.* New York: Greenwood Press, 1990.
Daynes, Kathryn M. *More Wives Than One: Transformation of the Mormon Marriage System, 1840–1910.* Urbana: University of Illinois Press, 2001.
Disher, Maurice Willson. *Blood and Thunder: Mid-Victorian Melodrama and its Origins.* London: Frederick Muller Ltd., 1949.
———. *Melodrama: Plots that Thrilled.* London: Rockcliff, 1954.
Douglas, Ann. *The Feminization of American Culture.* New York: Knopf, 1977.
Dushku, Judith Rasmussen. "Feminists." In *Mormon Sisters: Women in the Early Church."* Edited by Claudia L. Bushman. Logan: Utah State University, 1997.
Emerson, Ralph Waldo. *Selected Works: Essays, Poems, and Dispatches with Introduction.* Editor John Carlos Rowe. Boston: Houghton Mifflin, 2003.
Eslinger, Ellen. *Citizens of Zion: The Social Origins of Camp Meeting Revivalism.* Knoxville: The University of Tennessee Press, 1999.
Evans, John. *History of All Christian Sects and Denominations; Their Origin, Peculiar Tenets, and Present Condition,* 2nd ed. New York: James Mowatt, 1844.
Ferris, Benjamin G. *Utah and the Mormons; History, Government, Doctrines, Customs, and Prospects of the Latter-day Saints from Personal Observation During a Six Month's Residence at Great Salt Lake City.* New York: Harper and Brothers, 1854.

Foucault, Michel. *The Archeology of Knowledge*, New York: Pantheon Books, 1972.
Franklin, J. Jeffrey. *Serious Play: The Cultural Form of the Nineteenth-Century Realist Novel.* Philadelphia: University of Pennsylvania Press, 1999.
Frick, John W. *Theatre, Culture, and Temperance Reform in Nineteenth-Century America.* Cambridge: Cambridge University Press, 2003.
Ganzl, Kurt. *Lydia Thompson, Queen of Burlesque.* New York: Routledge, 2002.
Gaustad, Edwin S. Introduction to *The Rise of Adventism: Religion and Society in mid-Nineteenth Century America.* Edited by Edwin S. Gaustad. New York: Harper and Row Publishers, 1974.
Gerould, Daniel, ed. *Melodrama.* New York: New York Literary Forum, 1980.
Gilmore, William J. *Reading Becomes a Necessity of Life: Material and Cultural Life in Rural New England, 1780–1835.* Knoxville: University of Tennessee Press, 1989.
Givens, George W. *In Old Nauvoo: Everyday Life in the City of Joseph.* Salt Lake City: Deseret Book, 1990.
Givens, Terryl L. *The Viper at the Hearth: Mormons, Myths, and the Construction of Heresy.* New York: Oxford University Press, 1997.
Gledhill, Christine, ed. *Home is Where the Hearth Is.* London: British Film Institute, 1987.
Gossett, Thomas F. *Uncle Tom's Cabin and American Culture.* Dallas: Southern Methodist University Press, 1985.
Green, Arnold. "The Muhammad-Joseph Smith Comparison: Subjective Metaphor or a Sociology of Prophethood." In *Mormons and Muslims: Spiritual Foundations and Modern Manifestations.* Edited by Spencer J. Palmer. Salt Lake City: Bookcraft, 1983.
Green, Nelson Winch. *Fifteen Years Among the Mormons: Being the Narrative of Mrs. Mary Ettie V. Smith, Late of Great Salt Lake City: Sister of One of the Mormon High Priests, She Having Been Personally Acquainted with Most of the Mormon Leaders, and Long in the Confidence of the Prophet, Brigham Young.* New York: H. Dayton, Publisher, 1860.
Griffin, Susan M. *Anti-Catholicism and Nineteenth-Century Fiction.* Cambridge: Cambridge University Press, 2004.
Grimstead, David. *Melodrama Unveiled: American Theater and Culture 1800–1850.* Berkeley: University of California Press, 1987.
Hadley, Elaine. *Melodramatic Tactics: Theatricalized Dissent in the English Marketplace, 1800–1885.* Stanford: Stanford University Press, 1995.
Hall, Roger A. *Performing the American Frontier, 1870–1906.* Cambridge: Cambridge University Press, 2001.
Hambrick-Stowe, Charles E. *Charles G. Finney and the Spirit of American Evangelicalism.* Grand Rapids: William B. Eerdmans Publishing Co., 1996.
Hankins, Barry. *The Second Great Awakening and the Transcendentalists.* Westport, CT: Greenwood Press, 2004.
Hansen, Klaus J. *Mormonism and the American Experience.* Chicago: University of Chicago Press, 1981.
Hatch, Nathan. *The Democratization of American Christianity.* New Haven: Yale University Press, 1989.
Hays, Michael and Anastasia Nikolopoulou, eds. *Melodrama: The Cultural Emergence of a Genre.* London: MacMillan, 1996.
Heilman, Robert Bechtold. *Tragedy and Melodrama: Versions of Experience.* Seattle: University of Washington Press, 1968.
Heyrman, Christine Leigh. *Southern Cross: The Beginnings of the Bible Belt.* New York: Alfred A. Knopf, 1997.
Higham, John. *Strangers in the Land: Patterns of American Nativism, 1860–1925.* New Brunswick: Rutgers University Press, 1988.

Homespun. "Lydia Knight's History." *The First Book of Noble Women's Stories.* Salt Lake City: Juvenile Instructor's Office, 1893.
Hudson, Winthrop S. "A Time of Religious Ferment." In *The Rise of Adventism: Religion and Society in mid-Nineteenth Century America.* Edited by Edwin S. Gaustad. New York: Harper and Row Publishers, 1974.
Hymns of the Church of Jesus Christ of Latter-day Saints. Salt Lake City: Deseret Book Co., 1985.
Johnson, Curtis D. *Redeeming America: Evangelicals and the Road to Civil War.* Chicago: Ivan R. Dee, 1993.
Kaplan, Amy. "Manifest Domesticity." In *No More Separate Spheres!* Edited by Cathy N. Davidson and Jessamyn Hatcher. Durham: Duke University Press, 2002.
Kaplan, E. Ann. *Motherhood and Representation: the Mother in Popular Culture and Melodrama.* New York: Routledge, 1992.
Kephart, William M. and William W. Zellner, eds. *Extraordinary Groups: An Examination of Unconventional Life-Styles.* New York: St Martin's Press, 1994.
Kerber, Linda K. "Separate Spheres, Female World, Woman's Place: the Rhetoric of Women's History." In *No More Separate Spheres!* Edited by Cathy N. Davidson and Jessamyn Hatcher. Durham: Duke University Press, 2002.
Kimmel, Michael S. *Manhood in America: A Cultural History.* New York: Oxford University Press, 2006.
Kipnis, Laura. *Bound and Gagged: Pornography and the Politics of Fantasy in America.* New York: Grove Press, 1996.
Klement, Frank L. *Dark Lanterns: Secret Political Societies, Conspiracies, and Treason Trials in the Civil War.* Baton Rouge: Louisiana State University Press, 1984.
Knobel, Dale T. *America for the Americans: The Nativist Movement in the United States.* New York: Twayne Publishers, 1996.
Launius, Roger D. and John E. Hallwas. *Kingdom on the Mississippi Revisited: Nauvoo in Mormon History.* Urbana: University of Illinois Press, 1996.
Lee, John Doyle. *The Mormon Menace: Being the Confession of John Doyle Lee, Danite, An Official Assassin of the Mormon Church, Under the Late Brigham Young.* Introduction by Alfred Henry Lewis. New York: Home Protection Publishing Co., 1905.
Le Shana, David C. *Quakers in California; the Effects of 19th Century Revivalism on Western Quakers.* Newberg OR: Barclay Press, 1969.
Levinas, Emmanuel. *Totality and Infinity.* Translated by Alphonso Lingis. The Hague: M. Nijhoff Publishers, 1979.
Logsdon, Guy William, ed. *"The Whorehouse Bells Were Ringing" and Other Songs Cowboys Sing.* Urbana: University of Illinois Press, 1989.
Luchetti, Cathy. *Children of the West: Family Life on the Frontier.* New York: W. W. Norton and Co., 2001.
MacMinn, George Rupert. *The Theater of the Golden Era in California.* Caldwell, Idaho: The Caxton Printers, Ltd., 1941.
MacKenzie, John M. *Orientalism: History, Theory, and the Arts.* Manchester: Manchester University Press, 1995.
Marr, Timothy. *The Cultural Roots of American Islamicism.* Cambridge: Cambridge University Press, 2006.
Mason, Jeffrey D. *Melodrama and the Myth of America.* Bloomington: Indiana University Press, 1993.
McConachie, Bruce. *Melodramatic Formations: American Theatre and Society, 1820–1870.* Iowa City: University of Iowa Press, 1992.
McLoughlin, William G. "Revivalism." In *The Rise of Adventism: Religion and Society in mid-Nineteenth Century America.* Edited by Edwin S. Gaustad. New York: Harper and Row Publishers, 1974.

Meer, Sarah. *Uncle Tom Mania: Slavery, Minstrelsy, and Transatlantic Culture in the 1850s*. Athens: University of Georgia Press, 2005.
Milhous, Judith and Robert D. Hume, *Producible Interpretations: Eight English Plays, 1675–1707*. Carbondale: Southern Illinois University Press, 1985.
Mintz, Steven. "Regulating the American Family." In *Family and Society in American History*. Edited by Joseph M. Hawes and Elizabeth I. Nybakken. Urbana: University of Illinois Press, 2001.
Moody, Richard. *America Takes the Stage*. Bloomington: University of Illinois Press, 1955.
Morgan, Jo-Ann. *Uncle Tom's Cabin as Visual Culture*. Columbia: University of Missouri Press, 2007.
Morse, Flo. *Yankee Communes: Another American Way*. New York: Harcourt Brace Jovanovich, 1971.
Moses, Montrose Jonas. *The American Dramatist*. Boston: Little, Brown, and Company, 1917.
Mullinex, Elizabeth Reitz. *Wearing the Breeches: Gender on the Antebellum Stage*. New York: Saint Martin's Press, 2000.
Nolan, Paul T., ed. *Provincial Drama in America, 1870–1916—A Casebook of Primary Materials*. Metuchen, NJ: The Scarecrow Press, Inc., 1967.
Odell, George Clinton Densmore. *Annals of the New York Stage*. New York: Columbia University Press, 1927–49.
Pinckney, Colesworth, ed. *The Lady's Token: or Gift of Friendship*. Nashua, NH: 1848.
Pomeroy, Cassandra Johnson. "Sarah Melissa Holman." In *Daughters of Utah Pioneers*. Mesa, AZ, December 2, 1930.
Quinn, Arthur Hobson. *A History of the American Drama: From the Beginning to the Civil War*. New York: HarperCollins Publishers, 1923.
Rahill, Frank. *The World of Melodrama*. University Park: Pennsylvania State University Press, 1967.
Reeve, Paul. *Making Space on the Western Frontier: Mormons, Miners, and Southern Paiutes*. Urbana: University of Illinois Press, 2006.
Richardson, Gary A. *American Drama from the Colonial Period Through World War I: A Critical History*. New York: Twayne Publisher, 1993.
Roberts, B.H. *A Comprehensive History of the Church of Jesus Christ of Latter Day Saints*. Provo: Brigham Young University Press, 1965.
Ruether, Rosemary Radford. *Christianity and the Making of the Modern Family*. Boston: Beacon Press, 2000.
Samuels, Shirley. *The Culture of Sentiment: Race, Gender, and Sentimentality in Nineteenth-Century America*. New York: Oxford University Press, 1992.
Schueller, Malini Johar. *US Orientalisms: Race, Nation and Gender in Literature, 1790–1890*. Ann Arbor: University of Michigan Press, 2001.
Schwab, Raymond. *The Oriental Renaissance: Europe's Rediscovery of India and the East, 1680–1880*. Translated Gene Patterson-Black and Victor Reinking. New York: Columbia University Press, 1984.
Sharp, William. "Structure of Melodrama." In *Melodrama (Themes in Drama)*. Edited by James Redmond. Cambridge: Cambridge University Press, 1992.
Shipps, Jan. *Mormonism: The Story of a New Religious Tradition*. Urbana: University of Illinois Press, 1987.
Sigel, Lisa Z. *Governing Pleasures: Pornography and Social Change in England, 1815–1914*. New Brunswick: Rutgers University Press, 2002.
Singer, Ben. *Melodrama and Modernity: Early Sensational Cinema and Its Contexts*. New York: Columbia University Press, 2001.
Slotkin, Richard. *The Fatal Environment: The Myth of the Frontier and the Road to Civil War*. Chicago: Ivan R. Dee, 1993.

Smith, James L. *Melodrama*. New York: Harper & Row, 1973.
Smith, Joseph, ed. *Doctrine and Covenants*. Salt Lake City: The Church of Jesus Christ of Latter-day Saints, 1981.
———, ed. *The Book of Mormon*. Salt Lake City: The Church of Jesus-Christ of Latter-day Saints, 1981.
———. *History of the Church*. Vol. 3. Salt Lake City: Deseret Book Co., 1980.
Snow, Eliza R. *Biography and Family Record of Lorenzo Snow: One of the Twelve Apostles of the Church of Jesus Christ of Latter-day Saints, Written and Compiled by His Sister, Eliza R Snow Smith*. Salt Lake City: Deseret News Co., 1884.
Sofer, Andrew. *The Stage Life of Props*. Ann Arbor: University of Michigan Press, 2003.
Sorisio, Carolyn. *Fleshing Out America: Race, Gender, and the Politics of the Body in American Literature, 1833–1879*. Athens: University of Georgia Press, 2002.
Startling Facts for Native Americans called "Know-nothings," or a Vivid Presentation of the Dangers to American Liberty, to be Apprehended from Foreign Influence. New York: Published at 128 Nassau Street, 1855.
Steinem, Gloria. "Erotica and Pornography: A Clear and Present Difference." In *Take Back the Night: Women on Pornography*. Edited by Laura Lederer. London: Bantam 1982.
Stenhouse, Mrs. T. B. H. *Exposé of Polygamy in Utah: A Lady's Life Among the Mormons: a Record of Personal Experience as One of the Wives of a Mormon Elder During A Period of More Than Twenty Years*. New York: American News Company, 1872.
———. *"Tell It All": The Story of a Life's Experience in Mormonism. An Autobiography . . . Including a Full Account of the Mountain Meadows Massacre, and of the Life, Confession, and Execution of Bishop John D. Lee*. Hartford, CT: A.D. Worthington and Co., 1874.
Surgeon General's Office. *Statistical Report on the Sickness and Mortality in the Army of the United States, from January 1855-January 1860*. Washington D.C.: George W. Bowman, 1860.
Sussman, Herbert. *Victorian Masculinities: Manhood and Masculine Poetics in Early Victorian Literature and Art*. Cambridge: Cambridge University Press, 1995.
Taylor, Bayard. *The Lands of the Saracen*. New York: G. P. Putnam, 1862.
Tickner, Lisa. "Sexuality and/in Representation: Five British Artists." In *The Art of Art History: A Critical Anthology*. Edited by Donald Prezioni. Oxford: Oxford University Press, 1988.
Tindall, George Brown. *America: A Narrative History*. New York: W. W. Norton and Co., Inc., 1997.
Tompkins, Jane P. *Sensational Designs: The Cultural Work of American Fiction, 1790–1860*. New York: Oxford University Press, 1985.
Turner, Frederick Jackson. *Beyond Geography: The Western Spirit Against the Wilderness*. New York: Viking Press, 1980.
Twain, Mark. *Contributions to the Galaxy*. Gainesville: Scholars' Facsimiles & Reprints, 1961.
———. *Roughing It*. New York: The American Publishing Co., 1872.
U.S. Bureau of the Census. *Historical Statistics of the United States: Colonial Times to 1970*. New York: Basic Books, 1976.
Van Wagoner, Richard S. *Mormon Polygamy: A History*. Salt Lake City: Signature Books, 1989.
Vetterli, Richard. *Mormonism, Americanism, and Politics*. Salt Lake City: Ensign Publishing Co., 1961.
Wacker, Grant. *Religion in Nineteenth Century America*. New York: Oxford University Press, 2000.

Waite, Mrs. Catherine Van Valenburg. *The Mormon Prophet and His Harem; or, An Authentic History of Brigham Young, His Numerous Wives and Children.* 5th ed. Chicago: J. S. Goodman and Co., 1868.

Walker, Franklin. *San Francisco's Literary Frontier.* New York: Alfred A. Knopf, 1939.

Walker, Ronald W., Richard E. Turley, Jr., and Glen M. Leonard. *Massacre at Mountain Meadows.* Oxford: Oxford University Press, 2008.

Weld, Angelina Grimké. *Letters to Catherine E. Beecher, in reply to An Essay on Slavery and Abolitionism, addressed to A. E. Grimke.* In *The Public Years of Sarah and Angelina Grimke: Selected Writings 1835—1839.* Edited by Larry Ceplair. New York: Columbia University Press, 1989.

Welter, Barbara. *Dimity Convictions: The American Woman in the Nineteenth Century.* Athens: Ohio University Press, 1976.

Wexler, Laura. "Tender Violence: Literary Eavesdropping, Domestic Fiction, and Educational Reform." In *The Culture of Sentiment: Race, Gender, and Sentimentality in 19th Century America.* Edited by Shirley Samuels. New York: Oxford University Press, 1992.

White, Ellen Gould Harmon. *The Story of Prophets and Kings as Illustrated in the Captivity and Restoration of Israel.* Mountain View, CA: Pacific Press, 1943.

———. *That I May Know Him: The Morning Watch Texts with Appropriate Selections.* Washington: Review & Herald, 1964.

Wise, Rev. Daniel. *Bridal Greetings: A Marriage Gift in Which the Mutual Duties of Husband and Wife are Familiarly Illustrated and Enforced.* New York: Carlton and Phillips, 1854.

Wood, Marcus. *Slavery, Empathy, and Pornography.* Oxford: Oxford University Press, 2002.

Yanow, Dvora. *Constructing "Race" and "Ethnicity" in America: Category-Making in Public Policy and Administration.* Armonk, NY: M. E. Sharpe, 2003.

Young, Brigham. *Journal of Discourses.* Salt Lake City: Deseret Book, 1974.

Ziff, Larzer. *Return Passages: Great American Travel Writing 1780–1910.* New Haven: Yale University Press, 2000.

ARTICLES

Bunker, Gary L. and Davis Bitton. "Illustrated Periodical Images of Mormons, 1850–1860." *Dialogue: A Journal of Mormon Thought* 10.3 (1977): 83–94.

Burrows, William. "The Mormon Samson: Porter Rockwell." *Weber: The Contemporary West,* 21.3, (Spring/Summer 2004), http://weberjournal.weber.edu/archive/archive%20D%20Vol.%2021.2-24.1/Vol.%2021.3/Burrows%20Ess.htm#76

Butler, Judith. "Performative Acts and Gender Constitution: An essay in Phenomenology and Feminist Theory." *Theatre Journal* 40 (1988): 519–531.

Cawelti, John G. "Myths of Violence in American Popular Culture." *Critical Inquiry* 1 (1975): 521–541.

Cannon, Keith L. II. "After the Manifesto: Mormon Polygamy 1890–1906." *Sunstone* 37 (January-March 1983): 27–35.

Bigler, David L. "The Aiken Party Murders and The Utah War, 1857–1858." *The Western Historical Quarterly* 38.4 (2007): 457–476.

Davis, Owen. "Why I Quit Writing Melodrama." *American Magazine* 128 (September 1914): 29–30.

Eliason, Eric. A. "Mark Twain, Polygamy and the Origin of an American Motif." *Mark Twain Journal* 38 (2002): 2–6.

Fluhman, J. Spencer. "An 'American Mahomet': Joseph Smith, Muhammad, and the Problem of Prophets in Antebellum America." *Journal of Mormon History* 34.3 (2008), 23–45.

Foucault, Michel. "Of Other Spaces." Translated by Jay Miskowiec. *Diacritics, 16* (1986), 25.
Frick, John W. "The Wicked City Motif on the American Stage Before the Civil War." *New Theatre Quarterly* 20:1, (2004): 19–27.
"Great Success." *The Publishers' Weekly American Book Trade Journal* 40 (1891): 543.
Green, Arnold. "Joseph Smith, an American Muhummad? An Essay on the Perils of Historical Analogy." *Dialogue: A Journal of Mormon Thought* 6.1 (Spring 1971): 46–58.
Hadley, Elaine. "Home as Abroad: Orientalism and Occidentalism in Early English Stage Melodrama." *Texas Studies in Literature and Language* 41.4 (1999), 330–351.
Johnson, Jeffrey Ogden. "Determining and Defining 'Wife': The Brigham Young Households." *Dialogue: A Journal of Mormon Thought* 20 (1987): 57–70.
Jones, Sondra. "Saints or Sinners?: The Evolving Perception of Mormon-Indian Relations in Utah Historiography." *Utah Historical Quarterly* 72.1 (2004): 19–46.
Lacayo, Richard. "Down on the Downtrodden." *Time,* December 19, 1994, 30–32.
Lewis, Alfred Henry. "The Viper on the Hearth." *Cosmopolitan,* March 1911: 439–50.
"News of the Church." *Ensign,* October 2006, 74–80.
Perciaccante, Marianne. "The Mormon-Muslim Comparison." *Muslim World* 82.3-4 (1992): 296–314.
Roberts, Mary Louise. "True Womanhood Revisited." *A Journal of Women's History* 14.1 (2002): 150–155.
Talmage, James E. "The American Nation in Prophecy." *Liahona the Elders' Journal* (June 22, 1937): 28–31.
Wells, Merle W. "The Idaho Anti-Mormon Test Oath, 1874–1892." *The Pacific Historical Review* 24:3 (August 1955).
Welter, Barbara. "The Cult of True Womanhood, 1820–1860." *American Quarterly* 18 (1966): 151–174.
"Western Poet-Scout Was a Picturesque Character." *Deadwood Magazine,* Sep/Oct 1998. http://www.deadwoodmagazine.com/archivedsite/Archives/Capt-Jack.htm (accessed November 1, 2008).

THESES AND DISSERTATIONS

Coates, Lawrence George. "A History of Indian Education by the Mormons, 1830–1900." PhD diss., Ball State University, 1969.
Cortez, Helen Magdalene. "The Rise of the Liberal Party in Utah." Masters thesis, University of California, Berkeley, 1929.
Dye, William S. "A Study of Melodrama in England from 1800–1840." PhD diss., University of Pennsylvania, 1919.
Jack, Ronald Collett. "Utah Territorial Politics: 1847–1876." Ph.D. diss., University of Utah, 1970
Phillips, Levi Damon. "Arthur McKee Rankin's Touring Production of Joaquin Miller's *The Danites.*" PhD diss., University of California, Davis, 1981.

OTHER SOURCES

Boggs, Gov. Lilburn W. *Executive Order.* Jefferson: 27 October, 1838.

Finney, C. G. "Holiness Essential to Salvation." Oberlin Collegiate Institute. http://www.gospeltruth.net/1849–51Penny_Pulpit/500607pp_holiness_essentia.htm (accessed October 29, 2008).

Peterson, Jane Temple. "Deys, Beys, and Bashaws: Early American Drama's Response to a Muslim Threat." Unpublished essay, presented at the Comparative Drama Conference, April 2004.

Rigdon, Sidney. *Oration delivered by Mr. S. Rigdon on the 4th of July, 1838: At Far West, Caldwell County, Missouri.* Martin Mormon Pamphlet Reprint Series: Provo, UT, 1974.

Index

A
Abzug, Robert H. 25–26, 35
Adams, Willaim Lysander 95
Adeler, Max 134, 186
Aiken massacre 20, 176n1
American Dream 119
American Party 120–121, 184n10. *See also* Know-Nothings
Americans 1, 8, 11–13, 22, 64, 83–85, 89, 97, 100, 112, 118–119, 122–125, 130, 133–134, 150–151, 155
   and Mormons 1, 8, 11–12, 100, 112, 124, 141, 146
   physically indistinguishable from Mormons 118, 151
Anderson, Benedict 159
animals 42–43
   cruelty to 183n91
anti-Catholicism 119–121, 145
Anti-Mormon Almanac, for 1842 162n.16
anti-Mormon melodrama 1–4, 15–16, 18–19, 21–22, 48–49, 52–53, 63–64, 66, 68–72, 79–82, 87–89, 92–93, 96–97, 113–116, 129–130, 140–141
   and Brigham Young 64, 66, 147
   and domesticity 74, 81, 157
   and heroes 61, 114–116
   and nativism 118
   and Orientalism 125, 127, 129–130, 134, 140
   in performance 15, 18
   and polygamy 21, 53, 61, 66, 80, 82, 175n78
   settings for 12, 99
   and violence 22, 87, 89, 93, 96, 109, 183n91
   and women 68, 70–72, 75, 77, 79, 113, 140, 159
anti-Mormonism 3–6, 20, 31, 49, 54, 121, 148–149, 163n27
army 8, 32–33, 93, 97, 99, 105, 110, 113, 131, 152–153, 157, 173n39
Arrington, Leonard J. 56, 91, 163
attractiveness, of Mormon women 78, 80

B
Bank, Rosemarie K. 19, 68, 166n66
Behdad, Ali 120
belief 3, 8–10, 12, 14, 29, 43, 59, 75, 78, 83, 86–87, 91, 119, 154–155, 163n25, 170n63
believers 33, 35–36, 38–39, 41, 43–44, 134, 155
Benjamin, Walter 85
Bennett, Susan 153
Bhabha, Homi 2–3, 122–123
Bigler, David L. 94
Bitton, Davis 4, 56
blood atonement 94–96, 178n36, 183n86
Blue Beard; or, the Mormon, the Maiden, and the Little Militaire 149–150
Boadicea, The Mormon Wife 136, 142–143
Boggs, Governer Lilburn W. 9–10, 83
Bombardment of Algiers, The 130, 186n38
bondage 21, 68–71, 79, 137, 174n60
Book of Mormon, The 9, 14, 37–38, 91, 147, 163n25
Booth's Theatre 103, 132
Boucicault, Dion 46

Index

Bowery Theatre 17, 42
Brigham Young; or, The Prophets Last Love 18, 20, 50–53, 62, 66, 71, 73, 79–80, 117–118, 133, 138–139, 148
Brooks, Juanita 111
Brooks, Peter 24
Bunker, Gary L. 4, 7
burlesque 6, 149–150, 188n99
Burton, Richard F. 59
Burton's Theatre 20, 59
Butler, Judith 156–157, 189n14
Byron, Lord George Gordon 132

C

Captain Jack. *See* Crawford, Jack W.
caricatures 4, 76, 140
Catholics 119–120, 123, 145
Cawelti, John G. 35–36, 83–84
Chicago 10, 31
children 8, 20, 50–51, 57, 60, 62, 64–65, 78, 87, 109–114, 116, 158, 175n78, 183n91
  of Brigham Young 64–65
  of Israel 8
  of polygamy 57, 60, 62, 78, 175n78
  violence against 110–114, 158, 183n91
Christ. *See* Jesus Christ
Christian Scientists 34, 169n44
church 9, 21, 27, 29, 31, 33–34, 36, 39, 41, 53, 67, 87, 105, 120–121, 146
Church of Christ 12
Church of England 172n24
Church of Jesus Christ of Latter-day Saints, The 3, 5, 8–12, 16, 34, 41, 55–56, 64, 94–95, 105, 119–120, 144–146, 161n15, 184n7. *See also* Mormon Church
  in anti-Mormon melodrama 31, 53, 87, 95, 105, 146
  establishment of 9, 12, 34, 41, 163n25
  and government 94, 164n38, 175n78
  membership 3, 8, 56, 75, 145–146, 162n15
  missionary program 119, 144, 163n25, 184n7
city 30, 87, 128, 130, 135
civilization 2, 11, 52, 84, 88–90, 92, 99, 177n15
Clark, Charles Heber. *See* Adeler, Max
Clemens, Samuel. *See* Twain, Mark

conversion 37–38, 43, 45, 91, 115, 127, 167n16
costumes 58, 123–124, 131–133, 142, 144, 149–150
Crawford, Jack W. 99–100, 115, 179n48
Crawford, Jack W., fictional character 93, 99–100, 108, 115, 152, 158
crime 94, 101–102, 105, 107–108, 111–12, 118–19
Culberson, William C. 84–85
culture 20, 36, 52, 128–129, 133, 140, 146, 150, 154, 159
  American 20, 154, 160
  international 146
  and literature 36
  Mormon 150
  Mormon and Turkish 140, 150
  Turkish 159
Custer, General George A. 13, 98
Custer City 99

D

Daily Inter Ocean 1, 31
dance 57, 117–118, 139–140
Danites 17–20, 59–60, 84, 86, 92, 97, 99–110, 112–113, 115–116, 152–153, 158
  in anti-Mormon melodrama 20, 59–60, 92, 99–101, 103, 105–8, 112–13, 116, 152–3, 158
Danites in the Sierras, The 17–20, 84, 92, 100, 102–104, 106, 108, 115–116, 178, 180–181n58
Daynes, Kathryn M. 55
death 9, 32–35, 43, 50, 59, 64, 75, 102, 108, 115, 153, 158, 161, 178n36, 180n52, 185n26
  martyrdom 32–34, 43
  violent 50, 59, 102–103, 108, 153
defense 31, 54, 85, 97, 108–109, 159
Denmark 146
Deseret Deserted; or, The Last Days of Brigham Young 18, 20, 105, 117–118, 128, 135–136, 148, 150, 154, 156, 158
design, theatrical 70, 77, 131–133, 149
devil 17, 59, 92, 113, 117, 139
Devil Among the Mormons, The. *See Utah; or The Devil Among the Mormons*
doctrine 3, 8–9, 14, 34–35, 37, 39, 55–56, 82, 88–89, 91–92, 94–95, 100, 137, 139, 163n25, 178n36

of celibacy 35
of complex marriage 56
of free agency 34
of original sin 163
of polygamy 3, 139, 148
of revival Christianity 37
of sacred America 9, 14, 91
of sanctification 35
Doctrine and Covenants, The 41, 163n25
domesticity 50, 52, 61–62, 77, 80
drink 30, 73, 113, 154, 189n9

E

East 22, 83, 108, 117, 123–31, 133–135, 138, 140, 151
Emerson, Ralph Waldo 66
emigrants 100, 108, 111, 115, 119
English, Thomas Dunn 59
escape 10, 31–33, 40, 59, 64, 67–68, 70–72, 74, 88, 135–136, 154–156, 158
Evelyn Gray; or, The History of Our Western Turks 90, 92, 94, 96, 98–99, 105, 109, 112–113, 115, 117–118, 133–135, 138, 142, 144, 146, 148
evil 29, 32–34, 36–40, 58, 66–67, 72, 78, 84, 87–88, 121, 136
exotic 16, 22, 121, 123–125, 127–128, 132–133, 151
exposition 38
extermination 177n15, 179n52
Extermination Order, The 9, 83

F

family 20, 25, 30, 41, 54, 57–59, 61–62, 67–68, 72–73, 81, 85–87, 108–110, 112, 156, 163n23, 179n52
  in anti-Mormon melodrama 58–59, 62, 72–73, 108–109
  in polygamy 57, 67
father 9, 51, 59, 61–62, 73, 108–109, 154
Finney, Charles Grandison 35, 37, 40–41, 45
Fonda; or, The Trappers Dream 18, 83–84, 92–93, 100, 108, 113, 115, 118, 135–136, 139, 148, 152, 158
Foucault, Michel 2
France 45, 119, 145, 184n5
Frank Leslie's Illustrated Newspaper 65, 98

French, Samuel 117
Frick, John 28, 166n2
frontier 6, 10, 14, 19, 27, 64, 83, 86–87, 89, 92, 97–98, 108, 110, 112, 133, 135–136
  as myth 13, 97
  in popular culture 6, 92
  setting 133, 135–136
frontier melodrama 19–20, 88–89, 114

G

Gannon, Mary 157
gender 4, 16, 19, 35, 49–50, 52, 63, 122, 140, 156–157, 174n73, 189n14
gendered behavior 54, 80–81, 156
Germany 119, 144–146
Gérôme, Jean-Leon 131
Gideon, brothers of 101. *See also* Danites
Givens, Terryl L. 4, 58, 66, 123, 163n26, 174n60
God 9–15, 26, 28–31, 33–35, 37–38, 40–41, 55–56, 88, 90–92, 102
  as director 26
  kingdom of 9, 88
  name of 102
  word of 163n25, 184n7
Gossett, Thomas F. 27
government 9–11, 41, 82, 89, 94–95, 97, 105, 120, 137, 158–159
  in California 95
  of Mormon Church 137
  in Utah 11, 94. *See also* Mormon theocracy
grace 30, 32, 34, 43, 51
Greeley, Horace 77
Griffin, Susan M. 145

H

Hadley, Elaine 24, 131
Hall, Roger A. 20, 89
happiness 50–51, 57, 62, 73, 136
harem 57, 126, 133, 137–140, 146–147, 150
Haun's Mill Massacre 9–10, 83, 101, 180n53
heart, manly 114–115
hell 38, 61, 63, 73, 134, 138, 180n54
hero 6, 24, 32, 34, 37, 39–40, 53–54, 61, 68, 70, 86–87, 97, 99–100, 114–116, 153–155, 157–158
heroine 2, 6, 24, 32–33, 39–40, 62, 70–73, 80–81, 113, 150

Hickman, Bill 102, 183n86
  fictional character 100, 112–14
Higham, John 119–121, 144
Hollenbeck, B. W. 57–58
home 7, 13, 50, 52, 58–59, 61–63, 67–68, 72–73, 78–81, 87, 99, 109–110, 112, 121, 132–133, 135–136
honorable violence 21, 83, 85, 87, 99, 114, 116, 122, 152–153, 157, 159
Hungary 146, 184n5
husband 30, 33, 39, 51, 53–54, 58, 60–63, 66, 70, 72–75, 78, 80–81, 103, 147, 157

I
identity 2–4, 21–22, 101, 117, 150, 152–153, 156, 159–160
  American 3, 17–18, 21–22, 49, 80, 85, 87, 115–116, 118, 122–123, 144, 152, 154–157, 159–60
  performance of American 1, 5, 15, 22, 144, 152
  unified American 2, 159–160
Illinois 10, 83, 167, 176n99, 182n81
immigrants 40, 43, 61, 64, 89, 99, 110, 118–19, 144–145, 147, 153, 167n17, 184n10
immigration 13, 121, 144–145
Indians 59, 64–65, 83, 90–93, 99, 110–111, 113–14, 130, 147–148, 177n17, 182n81. *See also* Native Americans
Ireland 119, 144, 146
Irish 88, 113–114, 117, 145–146, 152–153
Islam 131, 133–134, 137–138, 141–142, 147–149, 185n16
  and Mormonism. *See* Mormonism, and Islam
Italy 145

J
Jackson, Andrew 41, 170n60
Jesus Christ 9, 12, 14–15, 26, 30, 34–35, 38–39, 155, 162n15, 170n63
  church of 12
  gospel of 12, 14–15, 30, 39
justice 38, 46, 85–86, 94

K
Kaplan, Amy 52, 62
killing 94, 112–113, 116

Kimmel, Michael S. 64–65
kisses 7, 61, 71, 149
Know-Nothings 120, 184n10. *See also* American Party

L
laws 10, 12, 40, 65, 84–87, 90, 94, 97, 102, 108, 115–116, 120, 178n36, 184n10
Lee, John D. 102, 111, 149, 180n57, 182n82
Life of the Mormons 20
loss 50, 64, 80, 110, 117
love 12, 32, 39, 48, 50–51, 57, 59, 61, 63, 66, 71–74, 100, 103, 142, 146, 149
  making 71, 142, 149
  patriotic 12, 146
  romantic 32, 39, 51, 59, 63, 66, 71, 73, 100, 103

M
MacKenzie, John M. 131–2
madness 21, 50, 72–73, 75, 80
Mahomet 117–118, 139–140, 147, 184n1. *See also* Mohammad
manhood, American 49, 64, 66
Manifest Destiny 13, 41, 87–89, 92, 99, 110, 116, 185n26
Manifesto, The 1890 16, 151, 165
Marr, Timothy 148
marriage 7, 16, 28, 48, 51, 55–56, 61–63, 66, 68, 73, 138–140, 172n24
  in anti-Mormon melodrama 61–62, 66, 68, 73, 138–140
  polygamous 16, 55, 63, 165n54, 175n78
  religious ordinance 55–56
massacre 92, 100, 114, 173n39
McConachie, Bruce 43, 166n66
McKinley, Henry J. 50
media 6, 33, 120–121
Meer, Sarah 27
melodrama 6, 17–19, 21, 23–25, 27–43, 45–47, 50, 53, 58, 62, 68, 71, 135, 154–155, 166n65, 166n2
  definition of 23–24, 167n4
  audiences 41–42
  and burlesque 188–189n99
  domestic 30, 168n32
  genre 19, 23–25, 30, 32, 35–37, 47–48, 62, 154–155, 166n6

in performance 3, 17, 19, 21, 27, 32, 36, 38, 42–43, 45, 48, 58, 81, 154, 156–157, 159–160
and religion 21, 25, 27, 29–30, 33, 35–37, 41, 154
sensational 58, 69
structure 21, 23, 27, 29–30, 32–34, 38–40, 46, 115
temperance 166n66
melodramatic mode 24–25, 34–35, 46, 52, 154
Christian 23, 25, 27, 29, 31, 33, 35–37, 39, 41, 43, 45, 47, 155
Miller, Joaquin 20, 102–3, 179n48
mimicry 122
miners 5, 92, 103, 106, 108, 114
Missouri 9, 83, 86, 91, 101, 179–180n52, 182n81
Mohammed 134, 148, 184. *See also* Mahomet
monogamy 39, 81–82, 123, 172n27
Moon Club 117
moral polarity 25, 29, 36–40, 52
Mormon Battalion 8, 162
Mormon Church 8, 15, 48, 55, 63, 72, 76, 83, 93, 95, 105, 111, 119–120, 162–163, 180, 182–183. *See also* Church of Jesus Christ of Latter-day Saints, The
"Mormon Coon, The" 7, 162n20
"Mormon Love Song, The" 7, 162n20
Mormon Prophet, The 15
Mormon Question 11, 137, 141
Mormon theocracy 89, 158. *See also* government, in Utah
Mormon Turks 22, 121, 123, 129, 141, 145, 147, 149–151, 159
Mormonism 1, 4–5, 9, 22, 31, 37, 54, 60, 72, 75, 122–123, 137–138, 140–141, 146–148, 154–156, 162n15
in anti-Mormon melodrama 54, 72, 146, 150, 156
and Christianity 9
and Islam 137–138, 140–141, 147–149
Mormons 1–12, 14–18, 20–12, 48–49, 52–56, 58–63, 78–81, 83–84, 88–97, 99–101, 105–106, 109–119, 121–124, 133–142, 144–62
and Americans 1, 5–6, 11–12, 22, 52, 97, 112, 118, 141, 151–152, 156
and Catholics 119
and Christians 9, 12, 118, 144
fictional characters 2, 6, 90, 96, 100, 142, 147
and Indians 88, 91–93, 148
as indistinguishable from Americans 20, 22, 118, 122–123, 150–151
as polygamists 7, 21, 48–49, 53, 61, 140, 156, 175n78
in popular culture 3–5, 7–8, 16, 20, 49, 105, 151, 184n7
as Turks 123–124, 128–129, 137, 142, 144, 147–148, 150–151, 159
as villains 17, 20, 53, 59, 62, 65, 74, 86, 88, 90, 95–97, 100, 105–106, 109, 113–115, 158–159
violence against 83, 101, 181n70
violence by 83–84, 95, 111, 157, 173n39
Mormons; or Life in Salt Lake City, The 17–18, 20, 52–53, 59–60, 62, 70, 73, 78, 80, 105, 113, 115–116, 133, 135, 146–147, 152–154
Mormons; or, the Revolt of the Harem, The 138
mother 57–58, 61–62, 68–69, 72, 109, 111, 113
Mountain Meadows Massacre, The 83, 88, 102, 110–112, 135, 158, 181n66, 183n86
murder 10, 20, 33, 40, 60, 62, 83, 86–87, 95, 97, 103, 105–107, 112–114, 136, 158, 183n86
music 5–7, 11, 24, 43, 53, 103, 129, 131, 133, 162, 188n99
My Partner 19–20
myth 13, 19, 105, 123, 136, 147, 164

N

nation 6–7, 9, 12–14, 17, 22, 25–27, 61–62, 85, 87–89, 94–95, 99, 112, 121, 145, 154–155, 158–159
nationalism 145, 154, 159
nationalities 78, 145–146
Native Americans 22, 83, 89, 91, 110, 177n15. *See also* Indians
nativism 64, 118–121
Nauvoo 10, 75, 176n99, 181n70
Nephi 164–165
New York 1, 6, 9, 15–17, 20, 27, 30, 34–35, 37, 42, 56, 59, 78, 103–105, 132

New York City 6, 15, 17, 20, 30, 34, 42, 59, 78, 87, 103, 105, 126, 181n68, 184n8
New York Herald 17
New York Mirror 103–104
New York Times 1, 16, 103, 132, 152, 161n1

O

One Hundred Wives 1
Oneida Perfectionists 34–35, 55, 169n44
Orient 117, 123–133, 140, 147, 151, 159
Orientalism 117–118, 121, 123–124, 127, 129–132, 134, 137, 139–140, 149
outsiders 10, 19, 100, 102, 123, 154

P

paradise 26, 63, 117–118, 134–135, 147, 150
patterns 10, 20, 36–38, 63, 119–120, 127
performance 2, 15, 17–19, 21–22, 26, 30–31, 42, 64, 69, 125, 127–129, 131, 149–150, 153–155, 159–160, 166n66
Philadelphia 6, 149, 161n1
phrenology 50
piety 26, 50–51
pioneers 14–15, 135, 162–163n23
plural marriage. *See* polygamy
poetic justice 25, 29–30, 32, 34, 36–38, 52, 82, 155
policies 13, 41, 59, 89, 92, 121
politics 3, 25, 41, 49, 89, 154, 174n73, 178n31
polygamy 3–5, 10, 14–16, 20–22, 31, 33, 48–49, 51, 53–82, 121, 136–137, 139–140, 146–147, 151, 165n54, 173n35
    horrors of 21, 72, 113
    official abandonment of 16, 175n78
    rumors of 16, 63
    sexual fantasy of 48–49, 51, 53, 55, 57, 59, 61, 63, 65, 67, 69, 71, 73, 75, 77, 79
    Turkish 117, 139
Polygamy 15–16
pornography 48, 53, 68–69, 71
    genre 48
Portland 6, 95
Pratt, Orson 55

Pratt, Parley P. 56, 95, 97, 135
promised land 8, 14, 63
prophet 9–10, 16, 31, 33, 48, 51, 57, 66, 73, 81, 128, 138, 141
Prophet, The 16, 18, 25, 31–33, 36, 39, 42, 46, 48, 57, 73, 81, 95, 128, 141
purity 50–51, 54

R

race 4, 14, 16, 19, 22, 69, 92, 118, 120, 123–124, 137, 140–142, 144, 147–148, 159–160, 174n73
Rahill, Frank 19, 23–24
Rankin, McKee 20, 104, 180n58
Reeve, W. Paul 5, 91
Relief Society 75
religion 9, 12, 19, 21, 25–29, 31, 38–39, 41, 53, 55, 103, 112, 118, 120, 145–146, 169n44
    and melodrama. *See* melodrama, and religion
respectability 42–43
responsibility 32, 51, 80–81, 89, 109, 111, 163n25
revelations 9, 31, 43, 54–56, 102, 163n25, 172n23, 178n36, 181n66
revival
    churches 37–38
    of *Sardanapalus* 132
    worship 27, 29–30, 35, 45, 63
revival meetings 27, 29–30, 35, 37–38, 45, 63, 132
Rhodes, William H. 15
Richardson, Gary A. 19–20
Rigdon, Sidney 179–180
Rockwell, Orrin Porter 20, 112, 180n56, 183n86
Roosevelt, Theodore 14

S

saint 12–13, 48, 63, 66
Saints, Latter-day 11, 14–15, 115, 136, 152
Salt Lake City 10, 12, 59, 64, 70, 72, 77, 87, 90, 100, 105, 115, 117–118, 133–137, 141, 156
San Francisco 6, 60, 135, 181n60
saracen 124, 127
Sardanapalus 132–133
savages 12, 52, 87, 130
scalp 92–93, 116, 153
Schueller, Malini Johar 129

Second Great Awakening 9, 25–27, 29–31, 34–35, 37, 40, 43, 46–74, 154–155, 161n8, 169n44
secret brotherhoods 101–102, 105, 107, 109
self-control 42, 64, 80
self-defense 87
sentiment 44–45, 57, 122,
sentimental fiction 171n2
separate spheres 50, 52–53, 60, 171n2
sermon 26, 46, 58
settlers 11, 83, 100
Seventh Day Adventists 34–35, 39, 44, 169n44
sex 49–50, 61, 68, 70, 73
Shakers 34–35, 39, 55, 155, 169n44
shame 53, 72, 80
Shaw, Mary 16
sins 33, 35, 73, 90, 94, 137, 148, 155, 163n25
slavery 21, 28–29, 49, 67–72, 80, 89, 164n33
slaves 35, 62, 67, 73, 131, 175n78
Slotkin, Richard 13
Smith, Emma 75, 172n23
Smith, Joseph 4, 9–10, 20, 31, 34, 41, 54–55, 60, 75, 91, 147–148, 163nn25–26, 170n63, 180n54
Smith, Richard Penn 130, 186n38
Snow, Eliza R. 75
society 59, 77, 84–86, 89, 107, 110, 121, 133, 157, 159–160
   American 14, 26, 49, 60, 66, 101, 107, 116, 156
   secret 103, 107–108
Sofer, Andrew 18, 165n61
soldiers 41, 97, 99, 130–131, 157, 173n39
spectacle 24–25, 29, 40–41, 43–44, 52, 103, 188n99
Spirit of the Times 103
St. Louis 6, 135
Steinem, Gloria 69
Stenhouse, Mrs. T. B. H. 57, 69
Stowe, Harriet Beecher 28–29, 61, 67, 69
suffrage 3, 30, 35, 49, 76–77, 79, 156
sultana 137, 139–140, 147
Surgeon General 142
Sweden 146
symbols 53–54

T

Taylor, Bayard 25, 31, 124, 126–128

temple 9–10, 31, 74, 128, 133
theatre 15, 17, 26–27, 30, 42–43, 47, 70, 103, 121, 131, 134, 136, 150, 153, 166
   cosmic 26, 47
Thompson, Lydia 149–150
   and her Blondes 149, 188–189n99
threats 9, 11, 20, 65, 70, 73, 83, 89, 93, 97, 101, 110, 112, 118, 121, 151
Treason, Strategems, and Spoils 84, 95
Tripoli 130
Turkey 140
Turks 2, 22, 117, 123, 128, 142, 147–148, 150–151, 160, 185n16
Turner, Frederick Jackson 14
Twain, Mark 78

U

Uncle Tom's Cabin 23, 25, 27–29, 38, 40, 69
United States 5–6, 8–12, 14, 45, 55, 59, 77, 86, 89–91, 93, 96–97, 119–120, 124–125, 130, 134–136, 161n8, 162n16, 162–163n23
Usurper; or, Americans at Tripoli, The 130–131, 186n38
Utah 10–13, 16–17, 49, 55, 57, 62, 72, 74–75, 77, 82–84, 93–96, 118, 120–121, 133–137, 140–141, 147
   in anti-Mormon melodrama 62, 72, 96, 118, 133, 135–137
   and the East 134–135, 140
   statehood 12, 16, 82
   suffrage 77
   theocracy 10, 49, 93, 121, 178n33
Utah; or the Devil Among the Mormons 17
Utah territory 11, 59, 93–95, 136

V

villains 6, 17, 20–21, 23, 29, 32–33, 37, 39–40, 67, 70, 87, 103, 155, 180n55
violence 4, 10, 15–16, 19, 68–71, 80–81, 83–89, 92–93, 95–97, 99–102, 104–106, 108–110, 112–116, 122, 153, 157–160
   against Mormons 10, 83, 97, 115
   in anti-Mormon melodrama 87, 92, 113–115, 157–158
   ethics of 86–87, 89

208 *Index*

frontier 83, 85, 87
function of 84–85, 116
honorable 153, 158
and lawmaking 85–86
melodrama 88–89
by Mormons 83–84, 95, 112, 115, 157
vision 8–9, 14, 26, 29, 31–34, 40–41, 45–46, 48–49, 69–70, 74, 86, 91, 126–127, 129, 135, 151
Joseph Smith's first 9, 34, 41, 170n63
religious 31, 34, 45–46, 147
vote 21, 75, 77–78, 80, 90, 120, 135, 175n78

W
Wacker, Grant 40
war 11–12, 110, 130, 158, 179n52
Civil 6, 12, 21, 27, 49, 66, 84, 86–88, 99, 110, 114, 158, 161n10, 175n78, 183n86
Mexican-American 162–163n23
Tripolitan 130
Utah 83, 93, 135, 173n39, 176–8
wedding 55, 74
Weld, Ludovicus 25–26
Welter, Barbara 50
West 5, 7, 11, 13, 19, 22, 33, 55, 82–83, 88–90, 93, 97–100, 114, 127–129, 151
Western Turks 90, 142, 150
White, Ellen 34, 44
wife 20, 31–33, 43, 50–51, 54–55, 57, 59–61, 64–66, 69–75, 78–79, 82, 109, 138–139, 146–148, 152–153, 172n23
wives
international 146–147

plural 31–33, 51, 54–55, 57, 60–61, 64–67, 69–75, 78–79, 81–82, 96, 128, 133, 138–139, 146–148, 172nn23–24, 175n78
plural in anti-Mormon melodrama 61, 67, 69–75, 78–79, 81–82, 96, 128, 133, 138–139, 147–148
plural of Brigham Young 64–66, 171n6
plural of Joseph Smith 172n23
woman, true 50–51, 74, 80–81, 156
womanhood 49–50, 54, 57, 63, 67, 79, 171n2
women's rights 21, 35, 49, 75–77, 80, 174n73
Wyoming 77, 93

Y
Young, Amelia 82, 149, 171n6
fictional character 51, 53, 71, 73, 80–82, 139
Young, Ann Eliza 22, 57
Young, Brigham 10–11, 15, 18, 48–53, 56–57, 62–66, 71, 77, 79–82, 91–96, 111, 117–118, 137–140, 146–150, 154–155, 182n81, 183n86
fictional character 33, 48, 51, 53, 62–63, 65–66, 71, 79–82, 87, 92, 94–96, 105, 117–118, 138–140, 148–150, 154–155
Young, Seraph 77

Z
Zion 32, 59, 72, 76, 87, 136
Zion 18, 32, 52, 57, 59, 61–63, 69–72, 74, 76, 80, 87, 133, 136, 149, 157

For Product Safety Concerns and Information please contact our EU representative GPSR@taylorandfrancis.com
Taylor & Francis Verlag GmbH, Kaufingerstraße 24, 80331 München, Germany